COLLEGE FAITH 2

150 Christian Leaders and Educators
Share Faith Stories from Their Student Days

Edited by

Ronald Alan Knott

ANDREWS UNIVERSITY PRESS
BERRIEN SPRINGS, MICHIGAN

Andrews University Press
213 Information Services Building
Berrien Springs, MI 49104-1700
TEL: 269-471-6134; FAX: 269-471-6224
aupo@andrews.edu
www.andrews.edu/universitypress

ISBN 1-883925-45-2
Library of Congress Card Number: 2004105910

Scripture quotations marked "AMP" are taken from the Amplified® Bible, Copyright © 1954, 1958, 1962, 1964, 1965, 1987 by The Lockman Foundation. Used by permission. (www.Lockman.org)

Scripture quotations marked (ESV) are from The Holy Bible, English Standard Version, copyright © 2001 by Crossway Bibles, a division of Good News Publishers. Used by permission. All rights reserved.

Scripture quotations marked (GNT) are from the Good News Translation – Second Edition © 1992 by American Bible Society. Used by Permission.

Scripture quotations marked "KJV" are from the King James Version.

Scripture quotations marked (NASB) are taken from the New American Standard Bible®, Copyright © 1960, 1962, 1963, 1968, 1971, 1972, 1973, 1975, 1977, 1995 by The Lockman Foundation. Used by permission. (www.Lockman.org)

Scripture quotations marked (NIV) are taken from the HOLY BIBLE, NEW INTERNATIONAL VERSION®. NIV®. Copyright ©1973, 1978, 1984 by International Bible Society. Used by permission of Zondervan. All rights reserved.

Scripture quotations marked "NKJV" are taken from the New King James Version. Copyright © 1982 by Thomas Nelson, Inc. Used by permission. All rights reserved.

Scripture quotations marked (NLT) are taken from the Holy Bible, New Living Translation, copyright © 1996. Used by permission of Tyndale House Publishers, Inc., Wheaton, Illinois 60189. All rights reserved.

Scripture quotations marked "NRSV" are taken from the Holy Bible, New Revised Standard Version Bible, copyright 1989, Division of Christian Education of the National Council of the Churches of Christ in the United States of America. Used by permission. All rights reserved.

Scripture quotations marked "RSV" are taken from the Holy Bible, Revised Standard Version of the Bible, copyright 1952 [2nd edition, 1971] by the Division of Christian Education of the National Council of the Churches of Christ in the United States of America. Used by permission. All rights reserved.

Project Director and General Editor	Ronald Alan Knott
Assistant Project Directors	Thomas Toews, Deborah L. Everhart
Line Editors	Ronald Alan Knott, Deborah L. Everhart
Copy Editors	Madeline Johnston, Deborah L. Everhart
Distribution Coordinator	Ernő Gyéresi
Cover Designers	Robert N. Mason, Jon H. Kim
Typesetter	Thomas Toews

Typeset: 10.2/12.5 ITC Berkeley Old Style

COLLEGE
FAITH
2

TABLE OF CONTENTS

PUBLISHERS' PREFACE

Come and hear, all ye that fear God, and I will declare what he hath done for my soul. Psalm 66:16

The psalmist has set a good example, an example that has been followed admirably by the 150 contributors to this second volume in the *College Faith* series of personal testimonies. Each of the writers tells a simple story, the essence of which is, "This is what the Lord did for me."

It's not always fashionable these days to be so transparent, so vulnerable, so full of conviction, so *plain*—unless, of course, we are ranting about a sporting event, a political candidate, a favorite restaurant, or a cheap entertainment—anything or anyone but Jesus. All too often, this irony is especially and depressingly true in the academy—even the Christian academy. Cultural individualism, hoary convention, a yearning for sophisication, or a presumption of impersonal objective analysis all whisper winsomely that everything would be so much more socially *comfortable* if the messy details of God's work in our lives remained a private affair.

The history of the Christian faith, of course, teaches the opposite. The church is strongest when personal, experiential faith—not just doctrinal faith—is proclaimed in the clearest terms. The blind man hauled before the Pharisees didn't have the benefit of a complete Christology. But he did have a vivid experience with Jesus. So he said: "One thing I know, that, whereas I was blind, now I see."

Many great revivals of primitive godliness began on college campuses, fueled by personal testimonies to the moving of the Holy Spirit. Testimony meetings in other times and in various traditions also helped shape the faith as we know it today.

It is our loss that those valuable spiritual exercises have fallen out of fashion in much of institutional Christendom. In response, we feel called to host some testimony meetings in book form. Thus, *College Faith 2* presents fifteen "meetings" (chapters) of ten testimonies each.

These are simple "meetings" and simple stories. They modestly recount the work of God in the lives of the writers while they were students somewhere in the stream of higher education, from freshman to doctoral candidate. Few of the testimonies are of the dramatic, Damascus-Road variety. All of them do what the psalmist and the Spirit call us to do.

In organizing these meetings we have resisted the powerful temptation to group testimones for narrative or thematic effect. Life, and testimony meetings, don't necessarily order their events into tidy packages that exude literary charm or desk-reference logic. The Spirit works in ways that to us may sometimes seem random or disconnected. Thus one will not find the stories about financial struggles neatly strung together. A story about the heartbreak of breaking up is not followed, inevitably, by one about the joy of finding a spouse. Rather, each meeting has been organized to provide a meaningful variety of testimonies covering a wide range of issues faced by any Christian student in any age: academic struggles, financial crises, satisfying or frustrating personal relationships, opportunities to witness, and, ultimately, the call to follow Jesus.

We praise our Lord for calling us to this good work. And we thank the writers who have opened their hearts for the benefit of the family of God. What rich benefits await that family when every reader fulfills our God-given obligation to do the same.

The Publishers
Andrews University Press

THE
FIRST
MEETING

"Come and hear, all ye that fear God, and I will declare what he hath done for my soul."

Psalm 66:16

David L. Jeffrey
Provost and Vice President for Academic Affairs, Baylor University

Marie S. Morris
Undergraduate Academic Dean, Eastern Mennonite University

Milton R. Sewell
President, Freed-Hardeman University

Wendy Lawton
President, The Lawton Doll Company

George P. Babcock
President, Atlantic Union College

Joe B. Brockinton
Vice President for Student Development, Asbury College

Lanny Hall
President, Howard Payne University

Tyler Blake
Professor of English, College of the Ozarks

Kimberly C. Thornbury
Dean of Students, Union University

John C. Ortberg, Jr.
Teaching Pastor, Menlo Park Prebyterian Church

THE COACH
AND THE GOLDBRICK

David L. Jeffrey
Provost and Vice President
for Academic Affairs
Baylor University
Waco, Texas

RAISED IN A LOG HOUSE in the backwoods of Ontario, I was a lanky and shy 17-year-old when I headed off to Wheaton College in 1958. I was drawn south partly because I had met the track coach, Gill Dodds, at a summer camp in Schroon Lake, upstate New York. I enrolled and went out for the track team, intrigued by the man who, for eleven years, had held the world record for the indoor mile.

I was no distance runner. I could scarcely get my pulse rate below 60, even when in good condition. Nor was I powerful enough to be effective in shorter sprints. One afternoon as I was doing warm-up laps around the track, Coach Dodds suddenly was at my shoulder. Lap after lap, he engaged me in conversation as effortlessly as some men would over a cup of coffee. I was gasping for breath; he was as relaxed as if lounging in a pool.

The next day he told me I would be running quarter miles for him. He instructed me to do a timed run each workout, and gave me a regime of weight-room work, a diet supplement, and a high-protein regimen. Soon I was running much better than I ever had in high school.

One day I came to time trials set to run my 440 yards (now 400 meters). I felt good and too easily outpaced my running mates, leading so comfortably around the last bend that I hardly needed a strong kick to break the tape a couple of strides ahead of my friends.

Much to my shock, Coach Dodds said that, despite my good time, I wouldn't be running on Saturday. In fact, I and one other runner would not have the usual day off after time trials. We were to show up at the track at 4 o'clock.

When we arrived, he made it abundantly plain that he was not pleased. Muttering something about "goldbricks," he sent us to the starting line for the 220, making us run three of these "in under 22 seconds," with two minutes rest between. This was to be followed by three 110-yard sprints on the bend, "under 11 seconds," with a minute between. He held the stopwatch and fired the pistol.

I collapsed after the first of the 110s, lost my lunch, and lay groaning on my face in the grass of the infield. Two running shoes appeared in front of my face. I couldn't lift my head. His voice was slow, soft, even kindly: "When you have not run your very best, Davy, even if you seem to have won, in every way that matters you have lost." He paused to let the words sink in, salt in my wounds. "On the other hand, when you run your flat-out best and at the tape you still lose, in my books you are a winner." He paused again. "It's the same way with God . . . and He always knows."

The shoes disappeared, and I eventually made my way to the locker room, showered in silence with my likewise silent teammate, and then went home.

The next week I ran differently at time trials. I got to run in the track meet and had my personal best time—finishing second to one swifter than I would ever be.

Father of many children, overworked in the effort to feed them, Gill Dodds burst his big heart wide open and died at 44 years of age. But his "punishment" to a Canadian ranch kid one cold rainy day on an outdoor track in Illinois was profoundly a gift of love. I remember, and have been harvesting the good of it all my life.

Whatever your hand finds to do, do it with all your might. Ecclesiastes 9:10 NIV

· ·

MY SWEET POTATO MAN

Marie S. Morris
Undergraduate Academic Dean
Eastern Mennonite University
Harrisonburg, Virginia

Whoever you are, no matter how lonely,
the world offers itself to your imagination,
calls to you like the wild geese, harsh and exciting—
over and over announcing your place
in the family of things. —Mary Oliver

AS A 21-YEAR-OLD new Christian living a carefree life in Spain, I realized that it was time to "do something with my life." Perhaps this meant going to college, but I wondered how I would decide. My newfound faith suggested that God was a good resource for such a weighty decision. I believed that God knew me better than I knew myself and thus saw more of the purpose of my life than I could see. Therefore, I reasoned, God should guide me. I was ambivalent about going to college. So I made a deal.

"God, I'll go to college if you find me a small-town American Christian college. It needs to be in the Midwest and have a two-year nursing program." This last criterion was part of my ambivalence. I had played a lot in high school and wasn't sure I was college material, so beginning with a two-year commitment seemed like a safe bet. Believing there to be no school fitting my description, I figured that I was "off the hook." But as I flipped through *Campus Life* magazine one day, I noticed an advertisement for a school in Kansas that met all of my criteria. Everyone thought I was crazy for thinking about going so far away. But I had asked God to provide, and God did. So off I went.

One might assume that I made a confident transition into this new environment. Not exactly so. Those first few days I was probably as lonely and homesick as anyone can be. I was certainly questioning my wisdom in making such a deal with God, as well as God's wisdom in suggesting such a place.

As I tearfully pondered my circumstance one day while walking down the street near campus, I encountered a man in a red plaid shirt and a straw hat digging in his garden. He kindly asked if I were a student at the college, chatted with me about his sweet potatoes, and extended to me the human touch of hospitality.

In the opening chapel service the next day, the president of the college was introduced, and out walked my sweet potato man! Imagine my surprise and delight. If the president of the college could genuinely befriend a lonely first-year student like me, I knew I'd be all right.

We each have a purpose and a place in the family of things, and they are woven together over time into a beautiful theme and contribution to life. Listen to your heart and listen to those who love you, but listen most of all to that still, small voice.

"Whoever you are, no matter how lonely, [God] calls to you . . . over and over announcing your place."

Fear not, for I am with you; be not dismayed, for I am your God. I will strengthen you, yes, I will help you, I will uphold you with My righteous right hand. Isaiah 41:10 NKJV

WORTH WAKING UP FOR

Milton R. Sewell
President
Freed-Hardeman University
Henderson, Tennessee

FROM THE TIME I was born in rural Alabama, near Florence, my father and mother took me to church. They were determined that I would be given the gift of being reared in a religious, faith-abiding home. We never missed a service. We lived a quarter of a mile from the church building and most often walked to church. We were also one of those families who were the last to leave, since it was a great social occasion to visit with everyone after services.

Taking us to church was not enough for my parents. They sent me to Mars Hill Bible School, where the Bible was taught every day. Good, godly teachers who cared deeply about the students reinforced what my parents and Sunday-school teachers taught, not only by word, but also by example.

Later, my parents encouraged me to attend Freed-Hardeman College in Henderson, Tennessee. In theory, the choice was mine; however, I knew deep down that it was also my parents' choice.

While in college, away from my parents, my faith began to wane. I began to question several things: Is there really a God? Is the Bible factual? Do we have evidence that supports the claim that the Bible is true? Why are we here? Where did we come from, and where do we go after we die? These typical questions arose in my mind after getting away from my parents' influence.

One Sunday morning I was so tired that I didn't want to get up and go to Bible class. I had stayed up late playing Rook in the dorm until the early hours of the morning. Now, all I wanted to do was sleep, as did others up and down the hallway. However, some of my best friends came by, knocked on the door, and said, "Let's go." Within a few moments, I was dressed and in Bible class.

The class that morning was about Genesis and the flood. The teacher, on the basis of his own research and documentation, explained why he believed the biblical account of the flood was true. I began to read and reread the account of the flood and knew that what the teacher had to say made sense. He also said there were other passages of the Bible that were just as interesting and factual.

The teacher made several comments that connected with me strongly at that critical moment in my faith experience. He said: "I do believe the Bible is true. Only God could put something together on this earth that is so well functioning." He also said, "Order does not come out of chaos without some sort of help." From that moment, my own personal faith began to grow. That teacher had no idea that I would still be quoting his comments decades later, and that they would so greatly impact my life. Nor will those buddies who knocked on my door that morning fully comprehend the significance of their terse invitation.

Since that pivotal moment, I grew in faith. And, as the years passed, I was able to instill that faith in my own children, who have experienced and survived those same stages of doubt. They have developed their own faith, and I am hopeful their children will have similar experiences.

How grateful I am that the Lord sent someone to get me out of bed early on that Sunday morning so that a godly Bible class teacher could show me evidences of God's love and revive my wavering faith. It surely was worth waking up for.

Train up a child in the way he should go: and when he is old, he will not depart from it. Proverbs 22:6 KJV
· ·

THE WORK OF MY HANDS FOR THE GLORY OF GOD

Wendy Lawton
President
The Lawton Doll Company
Turlock, California

I STARTED COLLEGE in 1968. War raged in Vietnam. Assassins' bullets killed both Robert Kennedy and Martin Luther King, Jr. Campuses spawned fledgling groups such as the National Organization for Women. As a generation, we prided ourselves on our social awareness. Collectively, we wanted to change the world.

Personally, however, I felt satisfied to tailor soft woolens into double-breasted suits. I didn't seek liberation; I only longed to get through a session of human figure drawing without blushing. What was wrong with me?

How I dreaded discussions about majors and career plans.

"I'm changing my major to microbiology," someone would say. "It's a field that holds the promise of curing cancer." Every head nodded in unison.

"I'm perfectly happy preparing for a career in social work," the next student might add. "With the pain and suffering caused by global poverty, I want to make a difference in people's lives." That resonated with our budding social consciousness.

I skirted the question. "I spend a lot of time in the art department." Heads nodded. "I minor in Art." Art was respectable—a free-spirit sort of thing.

"So, what's your major?"

"Home Economics," I'd confess.

Silence.

"You mean cooking and sewing?"

I, too, longed to do something "important" with my life like the career paths being charted by my fellow students, but I loved working with my hands. At the bookstore, I blew my budget on a book about classical Greek sculpture. I wasted hours of precious time on that book. I memorized each plane of those marble faces. What was wrong with me? Whatever was I going to do after college?

If only I had known to seek the clues. When God created me, those passions—textiles, art, sculpture—were planted deep inside. My eventual vocation developed out of my passion—there was no such career field in college. My school years only allowed me to discover what I loved. As I moved into the world of work, I experimented with jobs—trying things on.

In my free time I bought beautiful fabrics and created clothing. I found a septuagenarian dollmaker to study under. I began to sculpt and design dolls. Slowly, a career emerged. As my business and artistic skill grew, I gained media attention, won awards, and encountered a wider circle of people.

In the process I discovered that the work of our hands is simply a tool for touching people's lives. At the end of the day, the microbiologist and the social worker have the same mandate as I do—to establish the work of our hands to honor God.

I could have saved untold hours of angst had I just known how to read the clues.

May the favor of the Lord our God rest upon us; establish the work of our hands for us—yes, establish the work of our hands. Psalm 90:17 NIV

. . . .

BORROWED FAITH

George P. Babcock
President
Atlantic Union College
South Lancaster, Massachusetts

THAT JOB PROSPECT in hospital x-ray looked attractive. As a senior education major at Columbia Union College, I knew the hospital job would pay considerably more than what I could expect to earn as a teacher. It was something to think about as I eagerly anticipated graduation.

Then I contracted hepatitis. The doctors despaired of my life. They explained that my only hope lay in massive doses of steroids—doses so massive, in fact, that while the last young man who'd received such treatment had lived, he had become totally blind. With death as my only alternative, I signed the forms allowing the treatment.

As my condition began to stabilize, the doctors told me that now an intestinal blockage and a staph infection complicated my condition. They predicted I'd be in the hospital at least another month. I lost all hope of completing my work and graduating on schedule, so I asked my wife to drop me from college classes.

She filled out the usual drop forms and took them to the academic dean for his signature. He refused to sign them. "Don't be in such a hurry," he said. "We're praying for George, and we'll work with him when he recovers. We want him to graduate."

My wife reported the dean's response, but I still felt hopeless. One of my classes was comprised entirely of lectures. How could I possibly handle that in my condition? But a classmate, Noel Shanko, solved the problem. He taped the lectures for me. In the evenings, my wife sat in my hospital room, typing out the lectures on an old manual Underwood. Yet, even with that help, I was too sick to do much serious studying.

One day, while still in the hospital, I received a call to become a school principal when I graduated. I thought about the lucrative job prospect in the hospital x-ray department; but while my life hung in the balance, I promised God that if He would spare me, I'd teach for Him regardless of salary.

Again, in the third week of my troubles, I asked my wife to turn in those drop forms for me. She tried, and again the dean refused to sign them. "George is a good student," he said. "Once he's on his feet, he can catch up. Tell him to put his faith in God. We're all praying for him." I knew that was so. Several college staff members had come to me in person and prayed for me.

I tried one more time to drop out, with the same results, so I quit trying to drop out and began studying in my hospital bed. At the end of the sixth week, I was released from the hospital, but my eyesight was failing. During the next few months, my eyeglass prescription had to be changed four times. How could I teach if I were blind? With my own weak faith, I clung to the dean's certainty. He was so sure that God would heal me and I would graduate. For the moment, I had to get along by borrowing his faith.

Finally I did make it back to classes; I studied hard, and with encouragement from all my teachers, I graduated in May. The dean beamed as he shook my hand at commencement. "Well, George, you made it with the Lord's help. I knew you would."

For more than 40 years now, I've served as a Christian educator all over the world. How often I thank God for sparing my life and for giving me a Christian administrator who shared his sure faith with an unsure student.

And the prayer of faith shall save the sick, and the Lord shall raise him up. James 5:15 KJV

· ·

HIS PROMISE
MY OBEDIENCE

Joe B. Brockinton
Vice President for
Student Development
Asbury College
Wilmore, Kentucky

AFTER SIX YEARS of high-school teaching, I felt led to return to graduate school as a full-time student. Although I was not certain how we would survive financially, my wife, our 22-month-old son, and I relocated 1,000 miles from our home to begin this adventure.

Since my wife was six-months pregnant with our second child, we decided that she would not work outside the home and we would live off of my graduate-assistant stipend of $400 per month. In an effort to make ends meet, we learned to live more simply. We even lived in government-subsidized housing.

Throughout our lives, my wife and I had been taught the importance of tithing, but in light of our meager income and very tight budget I rationalized that we could not afford to tithe at this time. For a couple of months, we did not tithe and we barely scraped by. I had convinced myself that I was responsible for meeting our needs through whatever means I could muster, but it wasn't working.

One Sunday, as our pastor spoke on tithing from Malachi 3, I was challenged by the prophet's question, "Will a man rob God?" (Malachi 3:8). As I squirmed in my seat and argued with God that we simply could not afford to tithe, it became very clear to me that, more importantly, I could not afford to live in disobedience. Although I didn't know how our needs would be met, I determined in my heart that I would obey this clear biblical mandate.

God had declared in Malachi 3:10, "Bring the whole tithe into the storehouse, so that there may be food in My house, and test me now in this . . . if I will not open for you the windows of heaven and pour out for you a blessing until it overflows." I claimed the promise and began to tithe immediately.

A few weeks later, our daughter was born and we incurred significant expenses for which we were not prepared. At the same time, a woman from our former church felt led to send us a check that more than met our need. We did not know this woman well, nor could she have known about our need. In that moment God confirmed what I should have known all along: When I trust God and obey Him, He will keep His promise and meet my needs from His boundless supply. Twenty years have passed, and I am more convinced than ever that God provides for those who trust and obey Him.

"Bring the whole tithe into the storehouse, so that there may be food in My house, and test Me now in this," says the LORD of hosts, "if I will not open for you the windows of heaven and pour out for you a blessing until it overflows." Malachi 3:10 NASB

. . . .

WORDS FITLY SPOKEN

Lanny Hall
President
Howard Payne University
Brownwood, Texas

MY UNIVERSITY YEARS represented a time of searching for identity and wrestling with the highs and lows of my sense of self-worth. I found myself competing with other students for grades, working to be noticed by professors, wondering, most of all, if I would ever be the "somebody" I desired to be.

Many times I felt as if I did not have what it would take to be successful. I experienced moments—even days—questioning whether I would ever master the subjects required in my degree. I dreamed of teaching government and history in a high school, but often questioned whether my dream would be fulfilled.

During my sophomore year at North Texas State University (now the University of North Texas), I took a demanding European history course under the leadership of a dignified and brilliant professor, Dr. Gordon Healey. One day as Dr. Healey was quietly returning our first exams, he came to my desk and held out my blue book in his hand. As I reached for it, my eyes immediately focused on the grade. It was the most beautiful B- I had ever seen, because I had expected to see a much lower grade. In the thrill of that moment I was not prepared for what Dr. Healey would say to me. As he released the booklet into my hand, he whispered, "Mr. Hall, I thought you would have done better on this."

I was stunned! Not only did he know me, but he thought that I was capable of doing better in his class. Did this mean that my professor actually thought that I might be an "A" student?

I cannot begin to express just how much that did for my sense of self-worth. "Perhaps I *am* capable of doing better. At least one faculty member has confidence in me," I thought to myself.

Later in my academic pilgrimage, my major education professor, Dr. Watt Black, and I walked together for a short distance down the hall of the building that housed the education department. In a brief conversation he asked me a question that changed my life: "Have you ever considered pursuing a doctorate?"

"Wow, another professor at the same university must have confidence in me," I thought.

Over the years, I have often reflected on the words of those two professors. Oh, the power of words in raising our spirits! What a significant impact a simple statement or question can have! In day-to-day small talk, the words of university personnel have great potential for positive and negative influences on students.

I believe that God puts people in our lives to say just the right words to us—just when we need those words the most. I thank God for Professors Healey and Black. I am thankful that they were encouragers. While their words may have been routine for them, their brief encounters with me had lifelong, and life-changing, value.

A word fitly spoken is like apples of gold in pictures of silver. Proverbs 25:11 KJV

THE PENDELUM
AND THE GIFT

Tyler Blake
Professor of English
College of the Ozarks
Point Lookout, Missouri

MY FIRST DATE, as a college freshman, was with my cousin. I had met a girl I liked, and was amazed that she agreed to go on a date, only to discover that she was "family." (And yes, our relatives live in Arkansas.) The next day my father called with the news that I actually had a cousin on campus and I should look her up. Dad's timing was always a little slow.

Next, I dated a senior. I was one proud freshman. Yet what I thought was a great trophy turned out to be a real downer. I now know the difference between seniors and freshman. Seniors have seen it all: the "special" speakers in chapel, the zany get-to-know-you activities (such as the rootbeer-fest, complete with belching contest), and they are tired of it. But freshmen are still impressed. So everywhere we went, the same conversation ensued:

Me: "Wow, this is cool!"

Her: "Oh, they do this every year. It's pretty cheesy, don't you think?"

After this second debacle, I put my superficialities aside and dated a girl who had great character but was in no danger of becoming a supermodel. It was truly noble of me.

My dating relations continued to follow a pendulum effect. I would date a girl based largely on her appearance, and then swing back to someone with solid values but with less, shall we say, aesthetic appeal. It seemed that God was asking me to choose between the two. But with my readily discernable lack of athletic prowess—not to mention rugged good looks—it was also beginning to look as if God were going to save me the trouble of making *any* decision as far as a mate was concerned.

The last girl I dated was a blond cheerleader. You guessed it: I was swinging toward the "looks only" side of the pendulum. I said a little prayer of forgiveness, and proceeded to ask her out.

Not only did Regina say yes, but she was a combination of everything I had hoped for in a mate. At dinner I was amazed that the stunning (a word I don't often use) cheerleader sitting across from me was anything *but* superficial. How could a woman this beautiful have so much depth? And with all those looks, where did she ever locate that natural humility?

Six months later we were engaged, and a year after that married. We now have three terrific kids, mostly because this beautiful, intelligent woman is also a perfect mother.

The chances of going off to college 700 miles away and having my first date turn out to be my cousin are about one in a billion. But honestly, the chances of having found *exactly* the wife for me were a billion times that. I can't explain why God gave *me* the perfect wife. Maybe He knew my weak character would require one. I don't deserve anything He has ever given me. As John 3:27 says, "A man can receive only what is given him from heaven." And, trite as it may sound, that's what I got: a gift from heaven.

A man can receive only what is given him from heaven. John 3:27 NIV
· ·

THE VALUE OF THE LONG VIEW

Kimberly C. Thornbury
Dean of Students
Union University
Jackson, Tennessee

IN MY FRESHMAN YEAR, no more than five weeks after my arrival at college, my parents received a phone call. I was on the line with an impetuous request. "Please, Mom and Dad," I implored, "let me come home." Unlike typical freshman, homesickness was not my problem. Rather, I tried to convince my parents that my real calling lay in working for an organization that aided homeless teenagers in New York City. "And I need to go there *now*," I contended. "I don't need to sweat out college for four years before doing what God has called me to do."

My parents, both of whom are college professors, sought resolutely to stall my plans. Higher education, they explained, possessed inherent value, and I would be foolish to abandon college at such an early juncture. I finally agreed to carry on with my education, and proved my parents right.

By staying in college and not giving in to my initial impulse, I learned the virtue of patience, the value of a long view, and the fact that a calling from God is a call to prepare for future service. As a freshman, I had little idea of precisely the path upon which Divine Providence would guide me. Twelve years after that crucial phone call with my parents, I am completing a Ph.D., and have the opportunity to serve as a Dean of Students. I daily minister to students on our campus, helping them to understand the importance of their preparation for their future vocations. I nurture, mentor, and counsel a new generation of college students beset by the same desires and uncertainties that I had. Because the same God guides my students, I trust that their present uncertainties will give way to future affirmation of the same Providence.

Call to me and I will answer you and tell you great and unsearchable things you do not know. Jeremiah 33:3 NIV
· ·

MEGAS RHODOS
AND THE JOY OF DOING

John C. Ortberg, Jr.
Teaching Pastor
Menlo Park Presbyterian Church
Menlo Park, California

MY FIRST CLASS in New Testament Greek was at 8:00 on a Monday morning during the fall semester of my sophomore year. I thought that just staying awake through it would be a moral victory.

The man who taught the course was a long-time Wheaton professor, around fifty years old with a distinctive head of red hair (later on, when we got to know him much better, we took to calling him *Megas Rhodos*, which is Greek for "Big Red"). He opened our very first class with a devotional centered around the question: "Why study Greek?"

He surveyed the usual responses to that question: that Greek would get us closer to the meaning of the New Testament authors, that it would enable us to handle the text with greater precision, that it would increase our biblical literacy, and so on. All of these answers, to our surprise, he dismissed as inadequate, as merely utilitarian.

The one really good reason for studying New Testament Greek, he said, is for the sheer joy of it. It was one way to fulfill the ancient command of loving God with all our minds. Learning was of value, he said, not simply because it can be a means to an end, but because it is an act of worship and devotion for its own sake. In wrapping our minds around the vocabulary and grammar of the New Testament world, it was possible for us to offer them more fully to God—to seek the delight that comes when the mind is filled with that which is noble and honorable and good.

What *Megas Rhodos* spoke of for five minutes, he incarnated throughout our years in college. He taught with a striking combination of humility (when anyone did particularly good work, he would say, "There's another example of the student going beyond the teacher") and precision. No one who struggled would fail to receive from him some kind of encouragement. No one who coasted would fail to receive from him some sort of challenge. There was something about his character that made anyone who sat in his class ashamed to do less than their best. ("His or her best," he would insist, if he were proofreading this.)

As time passed, his teaching began to extend beyond the classroom. His generosity of time marked every one of us in his circle. We began to meet regularly once a week for donuts and coffee, a time that became close to sacramental for us. He would tell horrible jokes, and tell them badly, laughing and blushing and fumbling the punch-line and jamming whoever sat next to him in the ribs—and something about his character and spirit created more joy than if he'd been a master comedian. He would challenge us about our life's direction: "Don't just aim for high salaries. Why don't you consider devoting yourself to church ministry?"

And so we did. In large measure due to him, I have been teaching— though in a different kind of classroom—for several decades. I'm getting close to 50 myself now. I teach for one reason—for the sheer joy of it. I learned from a master.

And you shall love the Lord your God with all your heart, and with all your soul, and with all your mind, and with all your strength. Mark 12:30 NASB

THE
SECOND
MEETING

"Come and
hear, all
ye that
fear God,
and I will
declare
what he
hath done
for my
soul."

Psalm 66:16

Ann Graber Hershberger
Professor of Nursing, Eastern Mennonite University

F. Gregory Campbell
President, Carthage College

Thomson K. Mathew
Dean, School of Theology and Missions, Oral Roberts University

Elizabeth B. Williford
Professor of Psychology, Belhaven College

Stephen Armstrong
Professor of Mathematics and Computer Science, LeTourneau University

Gordon Bietz
President, Southern Adventist University

John H. Aukerman
Professor of Christian Education, Anderson University

Andrew R. Jesson
Dean of Students, Simpson College and Graduate School

Gregg L. Frazer
Professor of Political Studies, The Master's College

Debra L. Sequeira
Professor of Communication, Seattle Pacific University

THE LEAVING

Ann Graber Hershberger
Professor of Nursing
Eastern Mennonite University
Harrisonburg, Virginia

HAVING BEEN A "GOOD" CHRISTIAN all my life, I was jarred when, in my sophomore year of college, I began to doubt parts and then the whole foundation of my previously strong faith. I was doing all the right things to nurture my faith. I was enrolled in a denominational Christian college pursuing a major that was easily linked with Christian service. I participated in Bible studies on my dorm floor, attended a small local church, and was active in outreach ministries on campus.

Still the questions came. Is my faith real? Is God real? How can I know? The questions built up emotions of anguish and even anger. I could not confide in my friends, for they would react in horror, fearing for my salvation, and assure me of their prayers—prayers I did not want. I could not talk to my parents for the same reasons. I was too embarrassed to disclose my thoughts to my teachers. I felt alone.

As my angst increased, I found I could not study, for the question of God overwhelmed everything. Life had no meaning. I often took walks around our small campus and particularly sought the wilder, uncultivated spaces. A particularly inviting space was a path though a field of tall grasses at the far edge of campus. Near the middle of the field stood a large oak tree that I had found to be a perfect place to study on Saturday afternoons. One evening, unable to concentrate on anatomy and physiology, I fled my pile of books in the library and walked that trail in the moonless night. When I reached the oak tree, I threw myself down on the ground.

"God, are you real?" I cried. "If you are real, let me alone." Perhaps I was asking God to reveal Himself to me, but the words were different—"let me alone."

There was no answer within or without. Then for one awful instant I was alone, utterly alone. The ground seemed to fall away from under me, and I felt a deep, dark, terrible nothingness.

It was enough. God had answered my prayer and had left me. There was no vision, no deep thoughts, no explanation, but I knew in the deepest parts of my being that God had truly been with me all those years. I also knew with certainty that I could not live without God. There would come myriads of questions about who God is, how God works, and how I relate to God. Thus, through joys and sorrows, through war and personal loss, through work in a profession that deals with pain and death, I rest on the inexpressible bedrock of God's presence. For "underneath are the everlasting arms" (Deuteronomy 33:27).

If I go up to the heavens, you are there; if I make my bed in the depths, you are there. If I rise on the wings of the dawn, if I settle on the far side of the sea, even there your hand will guide me, your right hand will hold me fast. Psalm 139:8-10 NIV

. . . .

A LONELY PRANKSTER AND A FERVENT PRAYER

F. Gregory Campbell
President
Carthage College
Kenosha, Wisconsin

THE AUTUMN OF 1956 was a tough time for the farmers of Central Texas. The growing season had produced yet another crop failure. The drought of several years still refused to abate. Not since the "dust bowl" of the 1930s had the land been so barren or the people so poor.

My dorm counselor at Baylor University was a ministerial student in his senior year. He served as pastor of an isolated and tiny Baptist church in the countryside outside Waco. The farmers could pay him practically nothing, but they did provide him an opportunity for his first pastorate. We students called him "Charley"; they called him "Reverend White."

In the dorm (actually a "temporary" army surplus barracks already twenty years old), Charley tried to keep order among fifty freshman men. He was a perfect foil. He never quite could catch up with the shaving cream fights or the water battles. I was immediately acclaimed "president" of the Garbage Can Rollers Club (a sport testing who could roll a can furthest down the hallway). The honorific title was ironic. I never had rolled a garbage can in my life. At age sixteen, 1,500 miles from home in a new and strange place, I was bitterly homesick. Charley could see I needed extra attention.

One day, he invited me to ride out with him to his country church for a Wednesday-evening prayer meeting. I realized he was trying to distract me from my loneliness. I said, "Sure, I'll go." Little did I expect an encounter that would remain etched in my memory almost half a century later.

In that small white-frame building, there were gathered perhaps twenty people whose weather-beaten faces betrayed the toil of their lives. Charley read a Scripture passage and gave a brief devotional. They sang a few hymns. I no longer know for sure, but my memory says they sang "Showers of Blessing," with its line: "Mercy drops round us are falling, but for the showers we plead."

Then came the prayer circle. For what seemed like an eternity—the emotion was so intense—individuals took turns praying aloud as their relatives and neighbors listened. Their vocabulary was basic, their grammar poor; the people were semi-literate, at best. Again and again, they prayed for rain, and lots of it.

There was one who carried a tragically heavy burden. Clasping her gnarled hands, with grime ground into the skin and dirt under the fingernails, she pleaded that God would send a miracle and save her son. He was a young man battling a deadly disease, no longer able to come to prayer meeting himself. For minutes on end, her voice rose and fell. Her tears flowed as she told God she had faith He could bring her son back to health again.

While driving back to campus that evening, Charley remarked that the woman really did believe God would perform a miracle even though the medical diagnosis was terminal. Were her prayers heard? Were they answered? Her son died a few weeks later. Did she lose faith? I never saw her again, but the transcendent fervor of her prayer convinces me she held true and strong. Her whole life had been one of coping, and her faith was the one great strength she had on her side.

Looking back, I think that trip to that country church was a turning point in my adjustment to college. I realized I was discovering new realities and moving into larger worlds. Some truths I was learning were unpleasant, even downright painful, but my own problems paled into insignificance, in comparison. I continued to torment Charley with dormitory pranks, but I think he was secretly pleased. He must have sensed I was going to make it now. He knew I was learning even about faith itself.

In the intervening years, I have studied and taught at major research universities. As a college president, I have insisted on the highest academic standards we can muster. I live by reason, continue to learn, and seek to think through any and all problems that arise. Yet, my strongest image of faith remains that farm woman praying for her son. Long ago, I realized that, when the embellishments of life are stripped away, when we are down to the basics, we all are like her—we can only live by faith. For that, we need the strength she had that comes from the grace of God.

The drought broke the following spring. Charley and I remain friends.

God is faithful, and he will not let you be tested beyond your strength, but with the testing he will also provide the way out so that you may be able to endure it. 1 Corinthians 10:13 NRSV

· ·

A SAMARITAN
IN THE CROWD

Thomson K. Mathew
Dean
School of Theology and Missions
Oral Roberts University
Tulsa, Oklahoma

IT WAS A SOUTH INDIAN SUNNY DAY. Thiruvalla, home of the famous Mar Thomas College in Kerala State, was preparing to greet India's lady prime minister, Indira Gandhi, who was scheduled to pass through the city to speak at a large political rally. I was an undergraduate at Mar Thoma College, where classes were dismissed early to allow students to catch a glimpse of Javaharlal Nehru's daughter.

I stood in the midst of a huge crowd that seemed to grow as the temperature rose. Hundreds of Hindus, Muslims, and others were filling the city center where Mrs. Gandhi was scheduled to make a brief stop. With the rising heat and the crowd pressing around me, I began to feel sick. Suddenly, I passed out.

I awoke on a table in a nearby teashop. Next to me stood the man who apparently had carried me into that place. He had my books in his hands. The stranger brought me something to drink and made sure that I was okay. Once he was certain that I was fine, he gave me my books and began to leave. I thanked him for his kindness and asked him who he was. He smiled and simply said, "I am a Christian." Then he was gone. I have never seen him since.

A Christian among a multitude of Hindus and Muslims cared for me! Were I not a Christian, I would have become one that day. I was so touched by this modern Good Samaritan that I wanted to be one. That desire led me to become a chaplain and eventually a professor of pastoral care.

Praise be to the God and Father of our Lord Jesus Christ, the Father of compassion and the God of all comfort, who comforts us in all our troubles, so that we can comfort those in any trouble with the comfort we ourselves have received from God. 2 Corinthians 1:3, 4 NIV

LOST AND FOUND IN A WASTELAND

Elizabeth B. Williford
Professor of Psychology
Belhaven College
Jackson, Mississippi

MY CHILDHOOD could have been the script for a movie about life in small-town America. I was raised in a loving Christian home, attended school with the same children from kindergarten through high school, and had the same best friend for most of that time. I went on to attend a small religiously affiliated college where I quickly made Christian friends and soon felt at home on the campus. A year or so after graduation, I married a fellow classmate from a lovely Christian family. Life seemed wonderful.

So why was I pursuing a graduate degree at one of the largest party schools in the nation? This was the question I often asked while in a state akin to shock. My husband had been transferred in his job, and I had applied and been accepted to the nearby university. It was overwhelming in many ways. Fortunately, the number of students in my graduate program was small, and my classmates and I bonded over the first round of qualifying examinations. However, I was amazed to discover that none of my peers or professors professed a faith in Christ.

Though the students took studying seriously, the same seriousness was applied to relaxation when the tests were over. Partying was the general way of life. Many classmates even started the day with beer as their breakfast beverage. I knew that I would find no Christian fellowship among my cohorts. Even more upsetting, the Protestant church near campus was offering Sunday-school classes with topics on politics, ecology, and self-esteem, a far cry from the intensive Bible study to which I had been accustomed.

At the same time, my husband began drifting away from God as he became close friends with two of my classmates—a drift that later became incompatible with Christianity and resulted in a divorce. He mocked my "small-town morality" and even helped plan a party with a Jim Jones Guyana theme glorifying suicide. Thus, while I strongly believed that God had brought me to this place at this time for a reason, I felt a deep need for other believers in my life to keep me focused on God and His will. My prayers intensified as I asked God to bring me the support I needed.

Several weeks later I was assigned to work on a statistical project with a new faculty member. In one of our meetings, the professor surprised me by asking if I knew of a good local Protestant church. Here was another believer who felt as lost as I did! In our subsequent conversations during the time I was a student, I found clear encouragement and renewed commitment to my belief. God had indeed answered my prayer for support, had shown me that I was not alone in a spiritual wasteland, and had strengthened my faith in the process.

Let us therefore come boldly to the throne of grace, that we may obtain mercy and find grace to help in time of need. Hebrews 4:16 NKJV

. . . .

FAITH VS. LOAN

Stephen Armstrong
Professor of Mathematics
and Computer Science
LeTourneau University
Longview, Texas

I WAS PREPARING to register for my second semester at St. Paul Bible College (now Crown College). The school allowed students to pledge to make tuition payments over time, but they were required to pay their room and board in full at registration time. I had barely paid for the first semester and had no funds for the second. Notices were posted of the availability of government loans, but taking out a loan did not seem to be an act of faith. I intended to "trust the Lord." The deadline for loan applications came and went, and I did not apply.

I met with Rev. Viron Miller, the treasurer, and asked to be exempted from the rules. I informed him that I wanted to demonstrate faith and trust God for my needs. To this day I can still hear his reply in my mind: "Son, faith is an admirable quality, but what that boils down to is that the college ends up trusting the Lord . . . for your bill." Even though the institution taught and practiced faith, its rules for school bills existed for good reason.

I believed that God would supply, but how? Would someone send me a check? I watched the mailbox faithfully—no checks. Would an anonymous donor deposit money in my school account? The monthly statement had no such entries. I went through the registration process in a daze, right up to the point where the last stop was the bursar's office where I was to make the required payment. I told the clerk that I had nothing. I really wasn't sure what to do at this point.

She informed me that the committee that granted the government loans was meeting right at that moment across the hall. If I filled out the application, she would walk the papers into the meeting. This was God's answer. The advantages for that loan included a low rate of interest and the delay of required payments. Furthermore, I was eventually to be forgiven part of the loan for years of teaching in a public school.

God's means of supplying my need was different from what I had envisioned. The loan which at first had seemed a cop-out was, indeed, a means of God's provision. The whole experience was a valuable lesson in faith. I felt like Abraham, learning that God provides in unexpected ways. I can praise God that, over the years, His resources have always been abundantly sufficient.

So Abraham called that place The Lord Will Provide. And to this day it is said, "On the mountain of the Lord it will be provided." Genesis 22:14 NIV

· ·

AFFIRMATION
UNDER THE STARS

Gordon Bietz
President
Southern Adventist University
Collegedale, Tennessee

I "CHOSE" MY CAREER when I was five years old. I wanted to be a minister like my father. I lacked the advantage of much career counseling. I had not taken any tests to discover my interests, nor had I done a summer internship program to try the career out. I simply idolized my father. When people asked me what I wanted to be when I grew up, I said, "A minister."

All went fine until I got to college. There I ran into a lot of questions: Is this really what I want to do? Do I really know what it means to be a minister? Was the decision made when I was five years old the right one? Those questions grew ever more serious as I embarked on the language preparation. Greek didn't come particularly easily for me. In fact, there were three of us who worked on our Greek translations together, and the teacher called it "pooled ignorance"–not exactly words to inspire hope.

Also less than encouraging was the conventional image of most of the theology majors. I enjoyed life a lot and participated in my share of practical jokes on campus, but many of the theology majors that I knew were pretty stuffy. They wore conservative clothes and didn't seem to be the kind of people with whom I could readily identify.

So how did I finalize my career choice? I found that I did enjoy the classes that were to prepare me for my career (other than Greek), and my gifts and interests moved me in the direction of preparing for the ministry. I talked to people who encouraged me in the ministerial career path. I worked at a church youth camp during the summer and experienced some success in doing things that a minister would do.

One evening during a break between summer camp sessions, when all of the campers and many of the staff were gone, I lay on a log looking at the stars in the night sky and feeling as close to God as one can feel. There I committed my life to following the career choice that I had made when I was five years old. There was no evangelistic call or schmaltzy music–I was alone on a log, looking up at the sky. I came to the realization that my gifts and interests were in line with a career in the ministry, and I was being affirmed by people I respected who gave me encouragement toward that career. In the end, when it comes to a major decision such as a career move, one needs to consider his or her own gifts and interests, along with the advice of others, while listening quietly to the Lord.

There are different kinds of service, but the same Lord. There are different kinds of working, but the same God works all of them in all men. Now to each one the manifestation of the Spirit is given for the common good. 1 Corinthians 12:5-7 NIV

RESURRECTION REVELATION

John H. Aukerman
Professor of Christian Education
Anderson University
Anderson, Indiana

MY FIRST REAL FAITH CRISIS came during my junior year in college. I had been a Christian for four years, and had never had any doubts about the Christian faith. But during that junior year, I began to question the concept of the resurrection.

Had Jesus really been raised from the dead? Why would such an unusual event even be necessary? Surely God could provide for the salvation of the world without such drama. After all, He was God—He could do anything!

Why would the all-loving God purposely plan the suffering and death of His only Son, followed by the unnatural and unheard-of occurrence of a resurrection? Why would the omnipotent God even allow such a course of events? It just didn't make sense to my college-age mind.

I was doing the right thing—I was asking questions. It's during the college years that our "baby faith" is put to the test. And we ought not to shrink from the test. We ought to ask those questions, deal with those doubts, struggle with the tough issues of our faith.

So I talked with my friends about it. I read the Bible passages about the resurrection of Jesus. I studied Bible commentaries and theological articles about the resurrection. And most importantly, I prayed about it. I asked God to guide my thinking. I wrestled with God over what I perceived as bad planning or poor logic on His part.

Today I am convinced that prayer was the most important thing I did during my faith crisis. Reading, talking, and thinking were important, to be sure. But it was in prayer that I asked God directly about my doubts. And it was through prayer that God provided the answer I so desperately needed.

Weeks turned into months, and Easter approached. As a student active in congregational ministry, I was invited to help plan and lead a church's

Easter Sunrise Service. Given my spiritual condition and deep doubts about the resurrection, I probably should have declined that invitation. But I wasn't wise (or courageous) enough to say "No."

So on that Saturday night before Easter, I went even deeper into reflection and prayer, striving mightily with God. I needed an answer if I was to have any integrity at all when the sun came up the next morning.

It was in that context that I read John 14:19, "Because I live, you also will live." The light came on! The curtain was pulled back! The doubts vanished! It all made sense to me! My young, logical mind had an answer—Jesus had indeed been raised from the dead. It was necessary for Him to be raised to newness of life, life everlasting, so that I could experience eternal life. Because Jesus lives, we too shall live!

Before long, the world will not see me anymore, but you will see me. Because I live, you also will live. John 14:19 NIV

· ·

HEAVY WEIGHT
FOR A NAVY MAN

Andrew R. Jesson
Dean of Students
Simpson College and Graduate School
Redding, California

I HAD GROWN UP in a Christian home and accepted Christ as my Savior at the age of twelve. My decision followed an evening meeting where I heard a speaker clearly portray the image of hell and point to Jesus as the way to escape. An easy decision! I excitedly told my family and enjoyed their delight and affirmation.

From that time on, I ordered my life according to the expectations of the Christian community, participating in youth group and church activities and avoiding those things that Christians did not do. I sincerely wanted to please God (and my family) and, without much difficulty, did live in a way approved by my family and the church.

At the end of high school, I was given an opportunity to attend the Naval Academy. As the first from our large family to go to college, this was a blessing. I went with every intention of continuing to make the same lifestyle choices, choosing to do what I believed was right and honoring to God and avoiding what I knew was wrong. However, I found myself unprepared for the change in environment. There were Christian influences there, of course. I even joined the Officers' Christian Fellowship the first year. But, by the end of that year, I had been exposed to powerful temptations and began to engage in behaviors, both private and public, that I knew were wrong.

Eight years later, as I approached the end of my initial commitment to the Navy, I was a desperate man. My life was out of control. No matter how much I wanted to do what was right, I was powerless to do so. In my desperation, I made a decision to go back to school to study the Scriptures. I concluded that what I knew about Christianity was somehow distorted because of my inability to follow the Bible's clear teachings. The administration of the Alliance Theological Seminary graciously allowed me to enroll, though I had no intention of pursuing full-time Christian ministry. I knew I had nothing to share with others.

God met me wonderfully in the first month of school during Spiritual Emphasis Week. A pastor shared with us that we were never meant to be able to live the Christian life on our own. Jesus had given us His life through the Holy Spirit and wanted to empower us with His life to walk in righteousness. What a weight lifted off my shoulders. I began learning new things about having a relationship with God and discovered His power at work in me. I was filled with hope for change.

I will be forever grateful for the opportunity to hear the truth embodied in this verse: Christ in you, the hope of glory.

To them God has chosen to make known among the Gentiles the glorious riches of this mystery, which is Christ in you, the hope of glory. Colossians 1:27 NIV

. . . .

THE TWO-YEAR REBEL AND A LESSON FROM THE DEAN

Gregg L. Frazer
Professor of Political Studies
The Master's College
Santa Clarita, California

I ENTERED COLLEGE as a relatively immature eighteen-year-old for whom academic challenges had always been easily overcome. The combination of intelligence and immaturity threatened to be very unhealthy for me, as it is for many young people "on their own" for the first time.

Since the college was considerably more conservative and, in a very mild sense, more repressive than the atmosphere to which I was accustomed, I spent the first two years of college trying to break or to skirt every rule in the handbook. The fact that many of the rules seemed arbitrary and irrational exacerbated the situation and made my efforts to challenge the system take on the nature of a quest.

Most importantly, this "quest" diverted my attention from matters of ultimate consequence and hindered my spiritual growth. Two very simple messages delivered in close proximity to one another reoriented my thinking and laid the groundwork for my spiritual growth.

The first of these lessons came in a chapel message by the Dean of Students, of all people. Only God's providence can explain why I was listening to him. He spoke on Romans 13 and its application to everyday life. For the first time, I connected God's emphasis on authority structure with the respect for authority that had been drilled into me by my parents but which had been dormant in me for two years.

I realized that God required me to be subject to those in authority at the college, whether or not their mandates seemed reasonable. God expected me to obey all those in positions of authority, whether or not their policies reflected standards I would set if I were in charge. The rules themselves were relatively insignificant in comparison to my responsibility to honor God through my obedience.

Shortly after the fateful chapel message, my attention was similarly grabbed by an incident in my Christian Theology class. A student asked the professor what question he would first ask Jesus upon meeting Him face-to-face in heaven. The professor fell silent for some time and then responded in a barely audible voice, "Why me?" and dismissed the class.

The simple chapel message has guided my response to church leaders, political authorities, and employers ever since. The humbling reality behind the simple two-word question helped to remove barriers to spiritual growth in a proud young man.

Everyone must submit himself to the governing authorities, for there is no authority except that which God has established. The authorities that exist have been established by God. Consequently, he who rebels against the authority is rebelling against what God has instituted, and those who do so will bring judgment on themselves. Romans 13:1, 2 NIV

. . . .

AIMLESS AT
THE ALTAR RAIL

Debra L. Sequeira
Professor of Communication
Seattle Pacific University
Seattle, Washington

AS AN UNDERGRADUATE at San Francisco State University, I attended large classes in large dull lecture halls. I no longer belonged to any organized religion; I felt completely free from family rules and expectations. But after a year as a nameless student in those cement-block halls, a profound sense of loneliness forced me to reconsider the meaning of my education and my life.

I decided to visit some of my professors during office hours and talk with them about the courses I was taking and their research interests. Amazingly, they made time to converse with me. I listened to their stories and began to see them as real people.

One professor, Dr. Pauline Nelson, asked me a question that changed my life's path. Why was I doggedly pursuing a pre-medical degree when I seemed to thrive in her communication courses? At that moment, I had no adequate answer. Stuttering and stammering, I left her office before humiliating myself any further.

I wandered around campus aimlessly for hours, wondering how I had come to choose my current path. Was medicine truly my calling? Or was I seeking a prestigious career in which my deceased father would have taken pride? I realized that he would have been proud of me no matter what career I entered. But would he be proud of the choices I was currently making? I was acutely aware that I had disappointed my mother by leaving the church. In my own mind, I had not left the faith, just organized religion. One point was certain, however: Dad would not have been proud of my lifestyle and relationship choices. I had freedom, yes, but took little responsibility for my free choices.

By this time, it had grown dark and I could barely see through my tears. I took a streetcar to the nearest church, where I found myself at the altar rail crying and having a true conversation with God. Not since childhood had I been so comfortable approaching God with my problems. Why had it taken me so long to return to that familiarity? Now I was not using any of the prayers I had memorized as a child. Instead, I talked to God as I would have talked to my own father. My prayers were heartfelt and deeply intimate; I voiced my need for direction, to be healed, to be whole.

My anguish that night was the beginning of a long journey back to the church, to regular fellowship with other imperfect Christians, and, eventually, to my true vocation in higher education. As I think back, I realize that the journey began with conversation—with my professors, with myself, and with my God.

Blessed is the Lord! for God has heard the voice of my prayer. The Lord is my strength and my shield; my heart trusts in God, and I have been helped. Psalm 28:7, 8 *Book of Common Prayer*

THE
THIRD
MEETING

Wayne Baker
President, York College

K. Fawn Knight
Professor of English, Kentucky Christian College

C. David Peters
Professor of Political Science, Biola University

Jonathan Gates
Professor of English, Nyack College

Katherine Glynn
Chair, Department of Business and Social Entrepreneurship, Sterling College

Darryl L. Tippens
Provost, Pepperdine University

Craig L. Blomberg
Distinguished Professor of New Testament, Denver Seminary

Heewon Chang
Associate Professor of Education, Eastern University

Patrick Allen
Provost and Chief Academic Officer, Point Loma Nazarene University

D. Merrill Ewert
President, Fresno Pacific University

THE PREACHER
AND THE ADVOCATE

Wayne Baker
President
York College
York, Nebraska

IT WAS OUR SENIOR YEAR. My wife was working six days a week, and I worked two jobs: at 4:00 in the morning I delivered mail, and in the evening after classes we both delivered fruit baskets. I also preached on the weekends at a little country church about 150 miles from campus.

One Sunday in a sermon, I got excited and told my listeners that Christianity is a "heartfelt" religion, and I put my hand over my heart. The good brothers and sisters, who had a far more rational approach to their Christianity than their young preacher did, were sure that "error" was being taught. During the week that followed, meetings and phone calls among the church members resulted in the decision to fire the young preacher the following Sunday. On Thursday night, one godly elderly sister mercifully called and told me what was happening. She said, "You need to be prepared for a difficult time next Sunday."

One of my religion professors, Dr. J. Ridley Stroop, whom I didn't know well and who certainly didn't know me, was teaching a very large and wonderful class on Paul's epistles. After class on Friday, I explained my predicament to him, asking if he could give me some advice and Scripture that I might share on Sunday to explain what I had meant the previous week. He offered a few scriptural verses and then, seeing the desperation in my eyes, asked me, "What time do you leave?" I replied, "Around 5:30 A.M." He wrote down his home address and said simply, "I'll be ready; come by and pick me up. I'll go with you."

A case of "the nerves" did not allow me to remember anything of our three-hour drive through the Tennessee and Kentucky countryside. Nor do I remember the Sunday-school lesson or the sermon I preached that day. But I do recall the defiant silence from the audience through both services.

There was a "called meeting" of the whole church that afternoon. It opened with two men making their accusation against me for my "doctrinal error." When it was my turn to answer, I started to leave my seat, but Dr. Stroop placed his hand on my shoulder and sat me down. He arose in my place and for nearly forty-five minutes opened the Scriptures and discussed how God has always wanted "the heart of man committed to Him"—that God wants our emotions as well as our intellect so that our actions will follow. The meeting ended with apologies from the congregation. The young college student preached for another year at that little church.

God bless the godly teachers in Christian education who daily take the time to validate their teaching with deeds done in humility.

Who is wise and understanding among you? Let him show it by his good life, by deeds done in the humility that comes from wisdom. James 3:13 NIV

· ·

BACK TO THE FUTURE

K. Fawn Knight
Professor of English
Kentucky Christian College
Grayson, Kentucky

"WHAT'S YOUR MAJOR?" It's the question college freshmen most despise. I had arrived at college as a premed major, but one week of chemistry convinced me that I was not meant for medicine. I then decided to major in sociology, mostly because I really liked the professor of my social problems course. The major required on-site internships, so I was assigned to the Juvenile Detention Center in Los Angeles. I took the hot, crowded L. A. buses downtown, and then walked half a mile to "Juvie."

I was hit with a sense of claustrophobia when I entered the girls' center, locked doors closing behind me. Staff members were present, but I still felt very uneasy, surrounded by more than thirty juvenile offenders. Latina girls, black girls, white girls, a girl from Jamaica—a regular tossed salad of teens who were already in serious trouble with the law. In a strange way, I was not so much frightened of the inmates as shy. I couldn't think of anything to say to "them." Gradually, however, I began to learn names. Faces began to seem familiar. It became easier to talk casually with the girls. As the months passed, I learned one of the most important lessons God had to teach me—that "they" were not so very different from me. I learned to see people, not prisoners.

As promising as that experience was, by the end of that semester I had switched majors yet again, this time to English, leaving sociology with no regrets except to wish that I hadn't "wasted my time" in classes I didn't need. The girls at Juvenile Hall grew faint in my memory. I certainly never thought God was going to use my brief flirtation with sociology to open doors into ministry.

Then one day, 35 years later, I read an article about a woman who was running a volunteer program for literacy in a men's prison. "What a great idea," I thought. "Audiotape prisoners reading children's books so their kids can listen to their daddies reading to them." I could do that, I thought, and a ministry was born.

I didn't see the connection until a friend questioned me. "Aren't you afraid to be locked up with all those criminals?" she asked. "Why, no," I thought. "Not really." Suddenly it dawned on me: The time I spent as a sociology major wasn't wasted at all. I wasn't afraid to begin this ministry because I had already been in a prison many times. God used an almost-forgotten experience to open doors of service.

"Take your time," I tell students today when they are in my office agonizing over a change in major. "Be patient. God has something in mind for you, and He never wastes time."

"For I know the plans I have for you," declares the LORD, "plans to prosper you and not to harm you, plans to give you hope and a future." Jeremiah 29:11 NIV

A FAR MORE EXCELLENT PLAN

C. David Peters
Professor of Political Science
Biola University
La Mirada, California

THE MOST MISERABLE YEAR of my life was the one spent in law school. When a sophomore in high school, I had resolved to become an attorney—just like the popular Perry Mason of television. My undergraduate college studies revealed my true love for politics. An Oklahoma wheat farmer's son, I had been immersed in political discussion from the moment I could remember adult conversation. It became my dream to enter politics one day myself.

At twenty-one, I embraced law school, expecting to delight in it as much as I had in my courses in political parties, public opinion, legislation, and the American presidency. Instead, I found myself reading and briefing cases that seemed to have been written by bored and boring judges. At the end of that first semester, my grades were the lowest of my academic career. I was sorely depressed but expected to redeem myself with redoubled effort, a tactic which had been my salvation in earlier "lean" academic semesters. To my deep chagrin, my grades at the end of that year clearly revealed that it would be both emotionally and academically unwise to continue in such abject misery.

I was devastated by self-doubt and panic about what I should tell my family and friends. I had talked for years about becoming an attorney. I had been taught that anything could be accomplished through hard work and self-discipline. My poor academic showing made it difficult to talk to my mother, and almost impossible to talk to my father.

Sober self-examination reminded me of a decision I had made at the age of thirteen. My Grandmother Peters had invited me to pray with her, and I had decided to commit my life to Jesus Christ. In retrospect, I could see that her questions about law school and my life's goals clearly indicated her doubt regarding the wisdom of my desire to become an attorney. I realized I had chosen my career path unilaterally without seeking God's leading.

Now, in a painful maturation process, it was evident that God had a vital interest in every nuance of my life and that He would most certainly offer wisdom and direction if I would seek His face. Never had I prayed as I did at that pivotal juncture.

With God's clear leading this time, I transferred to the graduate school of political science. In one of the most satisfying years of my life, I completed my master's degree and accepted the position of instructor at then Biola College in La Mirada, California.

God more than satisfies! Not only have I been blessed to teach what I love for thirty-five years at Biola University—government, political science, and history—but I have served for twenty-five of those years in my parallel passion as a La Mirada city councilman and mayor. Not only is God *able* to supply above what we can ask or think, but He *does* so! God revealed a far more excellent plan for my life than I had even imagined.

Now to Him who is able to do exceedingly abundantly above all that we ask or think, according to the power that works in us, to Him be glory in the church by Christ Jesus to all generations, forever and ever. Amen. Ephesians 3:20, 21 NKJV

· ·

OFTEN ALONE, BUT NO LONGER LONELY

Jonathan Gates
Professor of English
Nyack College
Nyack, New York

AFTER GRADUATING from a small Christian liberal-arts college in the country, I enrolled in a large suburban Midwestern university to begin graduate study. Disconnected from family, church, friends, and everything familiar, I encountered a deep loneliness for the first time in my life.

I knew only faces and a few names of the students in my classes, and I felt out of place at the church I visited. After years of enjoying long conversations in the cafeteria and many late-night talks with friends, dinner alone at my apartment or alone with everyone else in McDonald's was dissatisfying. I attended some mixer parties and talked with other graduate students, but we were on different wavelengths.

I began to adjust to graduate school routines and made many acquaintances, but the loneliness continued to build. One morning as I walked down Spring Street toward class, a crowd of more than 250 gorgeous coeds flooded past me. Dumbstruck, I wondered what could possibly bring all these young women out at 8:30 on a muggy August morning. They all seemed to know each other and be having a great time.

After class, I found myself waiting to cross the street with Ben, someone I recognized from class. After I described what I had seen that morning, he explained that sorority rush had begun. As we walked, I realized that something was different about Ben. When we parted, he asked if I would like to go to the mall on Friday evening to eat and buy some tapes.

That Friday evening as we rode to and from the mall, and later visited at his apartment, we talked about our college experiences. Before long we were talking about our faith in God. Though we came from different backgrounds, we both named Jesus as Lord.

From then on, we ate meals, talked, and prayed together—sharing our disappointments, daily struggles, and plans. We discussed our coursework, studied the Scriptures, and occasionally went uptown to one of the popular graduate-student hangouts to fellowship with our friends. While Ben and I both built friendships with others in our graduate program and at a local church, our bond as brothers in Christ surpassed these other friendships.

The words of the Teacher in Ecclesiastes capture the importance of our uniting with our brothers and sisters in Christ, for just as a rope with many strands is strong, so is the man or woman of God who labors with another Christian. Though I was often alone that year, I was no longer lonely.

Two are better than one, because they have a good return for their work: If one falls down, his friend can help him up. . . . A cord of three strands is not quickly broken. Ecclesiastes 4:9-12 NIV

. . . .

BLAISE PASCAL
AND A BROKEN VESSEL

Katherine Glynn
Chair, Department of Business
and Social Entrepreneurship
Sterling College
Sterling, Kansas

I SAT IN THE GLOOM of the basement lounge of my 21-story dorm surrounded by snack machines and fresh out of the quarters needed for a sugar fix. It had been a very bad day in a very bad semester, and I began to wonder if there was really any logical reason why a fall from the twenty-first floor would *not* kill you.

There was no one to call. I had chosen badly, so I was on my own. My parents had moved hours away to be close to my West Pointer brother, and I had not been asked to follow. I had no car and no money. My heart was broken and empty, and I searched desperately to fill it, trying to be full . . . hence, the snack machines. Twinkies (do you have any idea what their shelf-life is?), cream-filled cupcakes, miniature pies, ice-cream bars . . . then alcohol, then destructive and abusive relationships, then more alcohol to dull the pain of the degradation. It was all a vicious cycle. What wouldn't kill me would make me fatter, out of control, or near death. Nothing worked, and I was ready to call it a day.

I started college as a philosophy major. I hoped that reading about great folks like Socrates, Plato, and Confucius would guide and focus my thinking. In the end, it was Blaise Pascal, a French physicist and philosopher of the seventeenth century, who finally struck a chord within me: *There is a God-shaped vacuum in every heart.* There it was . . . right in front of me all the time. I needed God, yet I had been stuffing myself with substitutes—with everything *but* Him.

Most broken clay vessels expect to end up in a heap somewhere; I know I did. What God was thinking when He reached down and placed me gently in the Potter's field I'll never understand, but I will never doubt again.

But the pot he was shaping from the clay was marred in his hands; so the potter formed it into another pot, shaping it as seemed best to him. Jeremiah 18:4 NIV

. . . .

KNOCKING ON THE DOOR OF FAITH

Darryl L. Tippens
Provost
Pepperdine University
Malibu, California

GOD HAS A FINE SENSE OF HUMOR. I know, because He has enjoyed a joke or two at my expense. Consider my choice of college, for example. It was the '60s, and the big universities were roiled by massive protests and demonstrations. I chose a placid Christian college that seemed a continent away from these political storms. But I soon found myself facing my own storm.

If there had been a definition of "true believer" in the dictionary, my picture might have been inserted there as the perfect illustration. Soon after I entered college, however, cracks in my faith began to show. My literature classes were the most challenging. Somehow I had enjoyed twelve years of public school without ever contending with Jean-Paul Sartre, Albert Camus, or existentialism. Now, in a Christian college (of all places!), I was encountering some very unsettling notions.

I retreated to the library to read my way through my doubts. Yet the more I read, the more confused I became. What a strange turn of events! I had chosen a Christian college to confirm my faith, but my faith seemed to be evaporating. Anxiety and despair settled over me.

One day I did a very simple thing. I selected the kindest and wisest professor I had met. Summoning my courage, I knocked on his office door. He invited me in. There, for the first time, this awkward and humiliated true believer confessed his confusion.

My professor was neither shocked nor offended. On the contrary, he was the soul of hospitality, welcoming the story of my struggle. Though I didn't leave his office with all the answers, I felt much better. For one thing, I didn't feel alone. Surprisingly, my doubt began to lift.

Since that day I have learned that honest doubt is not fatal; rather, it is often a necessary stage to a more authentic faith. I have learned that great men and women of God often undergo trials of uncertainty. I have learned that maintaining a seeker's heart, even while you doubt—especially while you doubt—is important. I have learned that you should be honest about your doubt, being willing even to doubt your doubt. I have learned that God does not abandon me when I encounter doubt; indeed, He is often closest to me when I struggle (Psalm 34:18). And I have learned that my knock on the professor's door was itself an act of faith, for in facing my doubts in community I weakened doubt's power over me.

Seek and you will find; knock and the door will be opened to you. Matthew 7:7 NIV

. . . .

THIS FAITH IS MINE

Craig L. Blomberg
Distinguished Professor
of New Testament
Denver Seminary
Denver, Colorado

I WAS NOT RAISED in an evangelical Christian home. I was brought up, however, to be a church-goer. When I was in the eighth grade, I was confirmed in a liberal wing of a mainline Protestant denomination. Thus, I didn't hear about Jesus being Lord of my life, at least in the sense of cultivating a personal relationship with the living God. My understanding of Christianity extended only as far as the assumption that I should go to church, believe that Jesus somehow died to save me, and try to live a good life.

It was only through parachurch groups in my high school (Campus Life/Youth for Christ) and in my college (Campus Crusade for Christ) that I first saw young people my age whose faith really made a difference on a daily basis. During my sophomore year I accepted Christ, as the process had been explained to me, and I "hit the ground running." I actively participated in both organizations during my seven years of high school and college studies.

I had been exposed to skeptical biblical criticism as early as my eighth-grade confirmation classes. The pastor showed us the parallel accounts of the Lord's Supper in the four Gospels and stressed how contradictory they were. In my college years, at a school historically related to the mainline Protestant denomination in which I was raised, I got a full dose of skeptical scholarship. A quarter-long, freshman-level introduction to the Bible dismissed large portions of it as legendary or mythological. A class on the Gospels began with our reading apocryphal stories about Jesus, which the teacher likened to other miracles found within the canonical Scriptures. A course on Paul dismissed nearly half of the letters attributed to him in the Bible as from someone else.

My faith was challenged. I delved into the library (a quite good one, because a more conservative seminary had, until about ten years earlier, resided on the same campus) and found all kinds of scholarship that presented a quite different and more convincing approach than what we were being taught in class. In fact, it was in those years that God began tugging on me to become the biblical scholar that I now am.

Over and over, I found that there were intellectually responsible replies to the skepticism that was touted in class as the "only approach for the truly educated."

Thus when people see that I teach at an evangelical seminary with a high view of Scripture, they often write me off as simply believing what I have to, given the context in which I work. But unlike many of my colleagues, I came to those positions not because they were what I was taught growing up, or even in college. The positions I hold I owe to the finest of scholarship, which I have had to uncover—at least in the early years—largely on my own, *in spite of* what I was being taught in my church and in college. This faith is mine.

Always be prepared to give an answer to everyone who asks you to give the reason for the hope that you have. 1 Peter 3:15 NIV

. . . .

ACTING AND WAITING IN THE LOVE OF GOD

Heewon Chang
Associate Professor of Education
Eastern University
St. Davids, Pennsylvania

"WHAT IS GOD'S WILL for my life?" This question dominated my spiritual search during my college days. I was looking for definitive answers for my day-to-day operations. I was certain that hearing such answers in a clear voice would leave me no margin of error in interpreting them; they would keep me from going astray.

I do not regret this focused, seemingly narrow-minded, search for God's will, because it led me to a greater understanding of who God is. In my serious, yet futile, efforts to keep something so grand in the limited container of my mind, I came to an incredibly liberating revelation: God neither gives orders to my daily actions nor punishes me for my daily shortcomings in spite of my best intentions. God will honor my desire to follow Him even in the absence of my clear understanding of His will.

This revelation came toward the end of my senior year at Yonsei University in Korea. I had been a serious student with a set goal of furthering my studies in the United States. I had applied to three universities that offered graduate programs which would allow me to combine education with anthropology. Of course, my prayers for God's will were part of the whole application process. Two rejection letters arrived, followed by a notification from the third school that my file was incomplete as of the deadline. I had done everything in a timely manner! What happened? What about God's will? Didn't I pray enough? I spent many of the following days feeling confused about God's will and too "paralyzed" to act.

That's when God touched me with a great sense of freedom—not with a clear, commanding voice telling me of His will, but with the assurance that I was loved independently of my decision. It was like my parents' love for me. They don't expect me to do exactly what they will. They may not tell me what I should do at every step. As I conduct my own life, I may fall short of their expectations or wishes, yet they understand that I desire to continue my relationship with them and foster it to its fullest. In the same way, I was assured that God would not withdraw His love from me because of my misunderstanding of His will.

Learning from this experience has transformed my faith. Now I don't waste my days just waiting for God to command. I walk in my Christian faith boldly with the understanding that God is Love. This love has rescued me from a confining, stifling, and sometimes paralyzing faith, and has led me to discover one that is liberating, ever expanding, and energizing.

There is nothing in all creation that will ever be able to separate us from the love of God which is ours through Christ Jesus our Lord. Romans 8:39 GNT

· ·

GOD'S ORDINARY HEROES

Patrick Allen
Provost and Chief Academic Officer
Point Loma Nazarene University
San Diego, California

I DIDN'T WANT TO GO to college. I came from an honest, hard-working, blue-collar family, and I grew up in a small town where only a few went on to college. Most who finished high school went to work in a local factory or on a farm, or they joined the military. There were few role models of the benefits of higher education.

I didn't know if I would fit in at a college. I wasn't special. I wasn't slick. I was just a small-town kid with no car, no fancy clothes, no money, and little confidence.

Early my first semester, I was struggling with these doubts when one of my professors mentioned that the heroes in the Bible were not extraordinary people. They were just ordinary people with courage and faith who served an extraordinary God. He said that they were people just like you and me—full of doubts and fears. God does not call us to be extraordinary. God calls us to be faithful.

Wow! The lights came on for me. My job is to show up every day and faithfully do my best. God's call to me includes, and for now accepts, all my doubts about Him and about myself. Thirty years later, I'm still on task—still answering the call. I'm just an ordinary person faithfully doing my small part in the extraordinary work of the kingdom.

My parents taught me about right and wrong, that there were consequences for my actions, that there were dignity and value in hard work, and that your word was your bond. I learned in college that we honor God when we faithfully use our gifts—no matter how ordinary they may seem to be.

When they saw the courage of Peter and John and realized that they were unschooled, ordinary men, they were astonished and they took note that these men had been with Jesus. Acts 4:13 NIV

. . . .

FROM DEFEAT TO DEBATE

D. Merrill Ewert
President
Fresno Pacific University
Fresno, California

AFTER AN UNDISTINGUISHED FRESHMAN year at Tabor College, I had hoped my grades would improve as a sophomore. They didn't. After the first round of exams, things were going so badly in two courses that I went to see my advisor, an English professor who also coached the debate team. I was desperate as I approached his office; I could see my dreams of graduate school slipping away. Worse, I began to wonder if I would even make it through college.

I explained to Professor Kenneth Kornelsen that my current trajectory was leading to a "D" in one course and an "F" in another. He listened to my story, then confidently told me I had nothing to worry about. The two exams, he pointed out, were a relatively small percentage of the final grades in their respective courses. He also offered suggestions as to how I might better prepare for future tests. Besides, he concluded, I had great potential and should plan on graduate school and consider a career in higher education. Even if I earned a "D" or an "F," he chuckled, it would become a source of great amusement someday when I told my own students about it. I was dumbfounded!

Professor Kornelsen then invited me to join the debate team. Based on what he had seen of my work in English, he said I'd make a wonderful debater. As I went out the door he told me, "Don't worry, Merrill. We've got this figured out. We're going to have a great semester!"

We? That's not how I felt when I went into his office. Then I feared *I* was going to fail. Now I knew *we* were going to succeed. I had entered alone and considering leaving school. I left as the newest member of the debate team, fully expecting to make the dean's list. And succeed *we* did. Debate became the center of my college life. I learned to think critically, evaluate data, construct arguments, and defend my ideas. I also made the dean's list.

I've long forgotten Professor Kornelsen's specific study tips, and other details of our conversation have grown fuzzy. But his confidence—based on a belief in God that was also a belief in others—has stayed with me in remarkable clarity. I now can admire how he subtly diverted the energy I was wasting on self-pity into a defining life experience. Yet when he had brought up the debate team, I thought he was just changing the subject. Today I know better.

Over the years, when students have come to me with their struggles in my courses, I've been guided by the memory of my conversation with Professor Kornelsen. I've tried to listen, to understand their problems, to offer practical advice, and to communicate my belief in their ability. I've looked for the God-given potential that Professor Kornelsen saw in me.

Being confident of this, that he who began a good work in you will carry it on to completion until the day of Christ Jesus. Philippians 1:6 NIV

THE FOURTH MEETING

"Come and hear, all ye that fear God, and I will declare what he hath done for my soul."

Psalm 66:16

Reo E. Ganson
President, Canadian University College

Neil T. Anderson
Founder and President Emeritus, Freedom in Christ Ministries

John E. Neal
President, Ottawa University

Shirley A. Mullen
Provost, Westmont College

James R. King, Jr.
Dean, School of Business, University of Mary Hardin-Baylor

David S. Dockery
President, Union University

Sue E. Williams
Professor of English, Olivet Nazarene University

William Swanson
Professor of Physical Education, Houghton College

John R. Jones
Dean, School of Religion, La Sierra University

Lisa Brandom
Professor of English, John Brown University

DECISION IN A FARM TRUCK

Reo E. Ganson
President
Canadian University College
Lacombe, Alberta

CANADIAN UNION COLLEGE certainly had seen many young men and women with more mischievous energy than I had. But I had my share.

My parents raised my brothers and me on a small farm. When we were in high school, they sold the farm and moved the family close to Canadian Union College. This allowed us to walk to classes, and yet we still had the advantage of living at home.

Although my parents were well meaning in this decision, it had a downside. We had an abundance of spare time. During the first years of college, study hadn't yet become a priority for me. My behavior often turned to mischief instead of activities constructive to the college or to myself. After one particular escapade, the administration decided that the time had come for a little well-designed discipline. They felt it might provide my parents some assistance in achieving their worthy goals for their son.

They sent me over to the college farm for a stint of free labor.

The morning was still dark when I climbed into the farm manager's truck. We had to haul home several tons of feed from a supplier several hours' drive from the college.

Although the long drive was uneventful as far as the work was concerned, it did provide many hours for quiet, meaningful discussion. There in the cab of that truck, a major part of the direction of my life was determined—not in an obvious, surface way, but hidden down deep in my will. During that long ride, the farm manager, in his own humble way, invited me to a life of service to our Lord as a gospel minister.

Today, I've worked for nearly thirty years in the education system as an elementary-school teacher, principal, college teacher, and president. And through it all, I have considered myself a gospel minister in the best sense of what that farm manager meant. The quiet but firm decision I made in that old farm truck on the encouragement of a dedicated staff member has been a guiding principle in my life ever since.

He shall feed his flock like a shepherd: he shall gather the lambs with his arm, and carry them in his bosom, and shall gently lead those that are with young. Isaiah 40:11 KJV

EDUCATING MY HEART

Neil T. Anderson
Founder and President Emeritus
Freedom in Christ Ministries
Knoxville, Tennessee

I WAS THE LEAD SYSTEMS ENGINEER on an anti-submarine, rocket-launched torpedo system. When I started my first semester of seminary at Talbot School of Theology, I stayed on the job as a consultant. I was to help get the first production model of the torpedo system up to specifications. I took off from work during the day to attend classes and made up the hours at night. A production engineer was assigned to work with me during the day shift. To say that he was worthless as a coworker would be too kind.

I couldn't count on him to show up. With no warning, he'd often be out for a day or two. His wife would call in for him, trying to offer some lame excuse. When he did show up, he would sit around eating sunflower seeds, which just about drove me nuts when I was dead tired. One night, in a desperate attempt to maintain my civility, I asked him if he ever went to church. He said he didn't, but he and his wife were talking about it for the sake of their three children. I managed, through my frustration, to invite him to our church. To my surprise, he agreed to come.

I met him the next Sunday and directed his children to the appropriate Sunday-school classes. He and his wife joined my wife and me in our class. The following Tuesday morning I got a call from my pastor. "I thought you would like to know that I visited your colleague last night," the pastor said. "I led him to the Lord."

Of course, I was thrilled. Then the pastor said, "You probably should also know that he is an alcoholic."

Suddenly everything made sense. That was why he was missing work so often. Even the sunflower seeds made sense now. He was eating lots of them because he felt they helped him with his problem. God had worked through my irritation to get my attention. Three weeks later my coworker was baptized. I had the privilege to disciple him that last fall of work during my first semester of seminary.

I realized that school is not just about finishing a degree and gathering information. Education best takes place in the context of committed relationships. It is part of the sanctification process. I would have missed the most valuable part of my education if I had set aside family and church to accomplish some cognitive objective. God wasn't trying merely to educate my mind in my seminary classes; He was trying to educate my heart. I learned that knowledge can make one arrogant, but love edifies.

I thank God for the lessons of that first semester of seminary. I determined to be a good witness at work, and make family and church my first priority. I decided that who I am, in terms of my character, is more important than what I know.

We who are strong ought to bear with the failings of the weak and not to please ourselves. Each of us should please his neighbor for his good, to build him up. Romans 15:1, 2 NIV

· ·

STARTING WITH THE WRONG PRONOUN

John E. Neal
President
Ottawa University
Ottawa, Kansas

GROWING UP WITH A SISTER two years ahead of me in school always meant that I had to endure endless comparisons to her, particularly since she was a strong student and involved in a wide variety of activities. "Oh, so you're Angie's brother . . ." became the most dreaded phrase in my young existence. I promised myself that when I went to college I would break out on my own, become my own person.

One day the chair of the music department at my sister's college visited my church. (My sister was also a musician, but, because she chose choral and vocal music in high school, I chose instrumental.) As the professor discussed with me the strengths of the college program and my plans for a career in music, I said that I wanted to go anywhere God wanted me—*except* my sister's school. Patiently, that godly professor explained that my plans for pursuing God's will started with the wrong pronoun—my life, my aspirations, my limitations on His leadership.

Well, you know the end of the story. I attended my sister's college, actually changed my major to vocal music, and found God's place and direction for my life. Four years of college provided ample opportunities for me to discover my unique niche and opened up many ways for God to work through and in me. As I have grown older, I now find myself no longer identified as Angie's brother, but as Gwen's husband, or Abby's (or Grant's or Caroline's) father.

You are not your own; you were bought at a price. Therefore honor God with your body. 1 Corinthians 6:19, 20 NIV

· ·

A PRISONER OF CHRIST IN A BUREAUCRATIC MESS

Shirley A. Mullen
Provost
Westmont College
Santa Barbara, California

I WAS ABOUT TO START my third year in graduate school. As in the previous two years, I showed up to collect my stipend check for teaching. This was the money I was to live on for the next few weeks. When I gave my name, the counter assistant said, "Sorry, we have no record of you being a student." I was shocked and somewhat panicked.

Once I had established that I had, indeed, been a regular full-time student for the past two years, I was told that I had a hold on my registration. I was sent to another office, where I was told that my name had not been cleared because I had not paid for a course taken during the summer at a branch campus three hundred miles away. I told the clerk that I had never even been to that campus. She told me that my name could only be cleared from the record by someone at the branch campus, since that was where the record had been generated.

I called the branch campus and explained my situation. I asked that they delete my name from the record as someone who supposedly owed the university money for a course that I had never taken. The person on the other end of the line said that this would be impossible, for, since I had never been a student there, she would not be able to access my name on the computer record.

Eventually, after several more office visits, the mistake was cleared up. But it was a nightmare. I lost most of two days of work sorting out the problem. I had been helpless in a bureaucratic, faceless mess.

Right in the middle of this experience, I happened to read Paul's letter to Philemon. What struck me was the first line: "Paul, a prisoner of Christ Jesus." I thought to myself, "No, Paul, you were a prisoner of the Roman Empire." Then I realized that Paul had made a choice to define the context of his situation not by external appearances, but by eternal realities. He was, ultimately, in the hands of God, not in the hands of the Roman Empire. God would have the final word. And Paul was determined to live by reality, not by appearances.

Though I would not want to compare my own experience to Paul's in most important respects, what occurred to me that day was that I had been defining myself as a "prisoner of the university," as if that was where my fate rested. It was liberating to be reminded that, whatever our circumstances, we are invited to name them in terms of eternal realities rather than external appearances. The real context of our lives is God and His purposes for us, not our momentary situation.

Paul, a prisoner of Christ Jesus, . . . grace to you and peace from God our Father and the Lord Jesus Christ. Philemon 1, 3 NIV

. . . .

DELIVERED

James R. King, Jr.
Dean
School of Business
University of Mary Hardin-Baylor
Belton, Texas

I DIDN'T REALLY WANT to be a dentist. That was my father's idea. And I didn't want to go to a large state university. But that is where my girlfriend would be going the following year. I wanted to go to a small private university, play baseball, and study William Blake. But to please my father and my girlfriend, I went to the large state university and became a pre-dental major.

Like most university freshmen, I spent my first year learning. Among other things, I learned that no matter how badly I wanted to please my father, I did not want to be a dentist. I wanted to major in business. I was not sure why. I had never taken any business classes. I also learned that my girlfriend had decided to be someone else's girlfriend. So I transferred to a private university with a good business program—and which just happened to be in the same town as my new girlfriend.

After taking a few classes in the business school, I decided to double major in accounting and quantitative business analysis. A new area called "Management Information Systems" was emerging in the Quantitative Business Analysis major. I fell in love with computers. They saved me hours on my accounting and statistics homework. And I could create baseball simulations for fun.

The month before graduation, I was invited for an office visit with a large consulting firm because of my background in computers, statistics, and accounting. It was a tremendous opportunity. But by the time I left the last interview, I had learned one more thing. I did not want to be a computer consultant any more than I wanted to be a dentist. But I could not understand why I felt this way. I was about to graduate without a job!

I returned to campus to visit with my advisor. When I finished my story, he asked if I had ever considered graduate school. I admitted I had not. He told me that if I entered the graduate program in business, he would allow me to teach a couple of statistics classes. His offer was very intriguing. I put interviewing on hold and applied to graduate school.

I was twenty-one years old when I taught my first class. By the time I walked out of class that first day, I knew that I had finally learned what God had in store for my life. It wasn't just teaching. It was the opportunity to directly impact lives. And as the years have passed, the feeling I had on that first day has only intensified.

While I had to learn that my father, my girlfriend, money, worldly success, and even my own self could not make my life decisions, God was preparing His path for me. And when I obeyed His call, He blessed me with a career which has been rewarding in many ways.

The Lord is my rock, my fortress and my deliverer. 2 Samuel 22:2 NIV

C. S. LEWIS, FRANCIS SCHAEFFER, AND THE HAND OF GOD

David S. Dockery
President
Union University
Jackson, Tennessee

I WAS STRUGGLING with uncertainties about my major, my future, and important questions of life. While I was a sophomore in college, God began to work in my life in fresh and exciting ways. Though I had been raised in a Christian home and attended church all my life, the reality of a personal relationship with God through Jesus Christ seemed foreign to me.

Through the help of friends and the guidance gained from a campus Bible study, I recommitted my life to Jesus Christ. God gave me an insatiable appetite for spiritual things. I started to read and study the Bible on a daily basis. The writings of C. S. Lewis, Francis Schaeffer, and others began to shape my thinking.

That year a sense of purpose, direction, and calling started to become clear in my life. I claimed a promise from Psalm 37:4-5: "Delight yourself in the Lord; and He will give you the desires of your heart. Commit your way to the Lord, trust also in Him, and He will do it."

Though I was still a struggling 19-year-old sophomore, trying to make sense of the new things I was learning, I began to live life with a confidence and calmness that I was in the caring and sovereign hand of God. I needed this assurance because life was spinning rapidly all around me. It was the early 1970s, and college campuses across the country were characterized by social unrest, civil-rights protests, "sit-ins," and Vietnam War protests. As I searched for answers and direction in this context, I found hope in Jesus Christ and direction from the Word of God.

Three decades later, college students face similar challenges and struggle with the same questions. The twenty-first-century world is a pluralistic, postmodern one. Who are we? Why are we here? Where do we belong? I would never have imagined thirty years ago, while struggling with these questions, that I would have the privilege of leading a Christian college. But

God has been more than faithful. Not only has He given me the desires of my heart, but He has given me a true delight in His presence.

Delight yourself in the Lord; and He will give you the desires of your heart. Commit your way to the Lord, trust also in Him, and He will do it. Psalm 37:4, 5 NASB

· ·

CULTURE SHOCK

Sue E. Williams
Professor of English
Olivet Nazarene University
Bourbonnais, Illinois

AFTER MY SOPHOMORE YEAR in college, I had the opportunity to go to France for the summer to study the language and culture. Although I was growing as a new believer at the Christian college I attended, my faith was tested during my trip abroad. The food, language, and sights in France were so different from my American experience that I felt isolated and lonely, even though there were other American students at the school. I was experiencing culture shock and homesickness, and I soon became disheartened. As a way of defense, I resisted the language and culture and questioned God's leading in my life. In fact, I wondered if God even cared about personal needs. The seeds of spiritual doubt were planted, and I was watering them with my negative attitude.

While sitting in a church service in Paris a few weeks later, I opened the Bible and read Paul's words to the Philippians: "For I have learned in whatsoever state I am, therewith to be content. I know both how to be abased and I know how to abound. . . . I can do all things through Christ which strengtheneth me" (Philippians 4:11-13).

The words leaped out to me, and I caught their application to my situation. I can't say that I immediately got over my homesickness, but my focus changed from self-pity to the recognition that God had provided me with this opportunity to grow. His presence became just as real to me in that Paris sanctuary as it had been at home on my college campus. In claiming Paul's words as my own, I learned that God's Word is dynamic and trustworthy. As a result, by the time I returned home, I realized that my summer in France had been one of the best experiences of my life. I had learned to appreciate the French culture, their beautiful language, and, more importantly, God's omnipresence.

Now, many years later, I am writing this story while on sabbatical in Busingen, Switzerland, where I am teaching far from my family in the States. Just a week ago terrorists attacked the United States and left all of us shaken and anxious about world safety. The truth of that spiritual lesson I learned years ago, however, is still vivid and true. I am content in Christ, and He continues to give me strength. Circumstances may bring loneliness and uncertainty, but we are never alone if we trust in Him.

For I have learned, in whatsoever state I am, therewith to be content. Philippians 4:11 KJV

· ·

KEEPING GOD
IN THE MIDDLE

William Swanson
Professor of Physical Education
Houghton College
Houghton, New York

GOD'S WILL FOR MY LIFE was the furthest thing from my mind when I was an undergraduate college student. Though raised in a wonderful Christian home by loving parents, I had strayed from my spiritual roots. I was anticipating a good job with a big salary when I left Illinois State University with an accounting degree. But I soon discovered the folly of pursuing my own will.

From the start, the wisdom of my choice of careers was questionable. I didn't enjoy my work or my colleagues, and, in all honesty, I wasn't a good accountant. Although I had a professional position with a prestigious firm, doors of opportunity kept closing. I was unhappy.

I left my accounting position after one year, but still felt no direction for my life. I drifted through a few jobs, and something significant happened during this time. A college friend invited me to church, and a spiritual revival began within me. For the first time in my life, I had a personal relationship with Jesus and wanted to follow His will for my life.

I had always had a strong interest in sports and participated in baseball at the college level, so I decided to return to Illinois State University to pursue a degree in physical education. And it clicked. I felt a genuine peace about my studies. I enjoyed going to classes! And all of the right doors started to open.

I obtained my master's degree and worked in YMCAs for about five years. I then felt God's calling to return to Illinois State University to pursue a doctoral degree in Education. Once again, God repeatedly confirmed that I was doing what He wanted me to do. All of the doors opened at just the right time. I enjoyed my studies and the people with whom I worked. And at the end of my three years of full-time graduate studies, God opened one more door. I received an offer from South Carolina State College to teach in their physical education department. I couldn't have accepted the job offer even a month earlier because of "loose ends" to tie up with my graduate studies. God's timing wasn't just good—it was perfect.

I am now in my eighth year of teaching physical education at Houghton College. I love going to work every day, and, more importantly, I am confident that I am doing what God wants me to do based on the gifts He has given me.

I know your deeds. See, I have placed before you an open door that no one can shut. I know that you have little strength, yet you have kept my word and have not denied my name. Revelation 3:8 NIV

ULTIMATE CONCERN

John R. Jones
Dean
School of Religion
La Sierra University
Riverside, California

AS I DROVE the truckload of freshly harvested peas back to the processing plant, I wondered what my friend Les had been talking about. We had just begun summer jobs with a large harvesting operation. He often got acquainted with students from across the country who worked the summer harvest for the adventure and the good money. Sometimes the conversations dipped into philosophical issues.

Les had met fellows from the University of Chicago who had been students of Paul Tillich—a theologian of whom I'd heard, but knew almost nothing. "What's this business of 'ultimate concern' they keep talking about?" Les asked me.

"I don't know; something about the convictions you're willing to pay an ultimate price for, I guess." I was uncomfortable with my ignorance. Les had offered to introduce me to his acquaintances, but I didn't want to meet them. My ministerial training began to feel parochial.

"The following drivers please report to the dispatch office," barked the loudspeaker back at the plant. "McDougal, Baker, Jones, . . ." all names of my fellow Adventists.

"Jones, we're letting you go. The management decided you guys who can't be flexible about your day off are too much trouble."

"But . . . But we agreed on this when we signed on for the summer," I stammered.

"So guess what? They changed their mind. So get outta here. Your final paycheck will be in the mail." The dispatcher was belligerent and gruff.

"Are you proud of this?" I demanded.

"Sorry, man. I had nothing to do with it," he muttered as he turned his back.

How could my faithfulness lead me into this? The Lord knew I needed that money for my training to serve Him. I could have landed better work if I'd known this was to be the outcome. And all for the sake of Sabbath. Was it worth it? I knew that if I agreed to work on occasional Sabbaths, I could have my truck-driving job again. A couple of my classmates had done so.

The following school year was grueling. I worked long hours to compensate for the earnings I had missed the previous summer. Still, the debts built up. It was clear that the coming summer would have to be much more profitable if I was to recover.

When I picked up the ringing phone in April, it took me a moment to recognize the gruff voice of the dispatcher from the previous June.

"Jones, we're making up our crews for the coming season, and we'd like to hold a place for you." In my silence, he must have caught my puzzlement and resentment. "Hey, man," he went on, "we've been talking. You Advent guys were among our best drivers. You put in an honest shift, worked hard in the field, and didn't fool around on the road. We can work in a few of you guys without too much problem. What do you say?"

"I don't know . . . ," my voice trailed off. He read my thoughts: *Would I get my summer messed up again?*

"It'll be okay, Jones. Trust me on this."

I did and was retained through the various harvests of the summer and even after the seasonal work was over. I worked long, well-paid days right up to my wedding in early September. Newly married and headed for seminary studies that fall, I was thinking, "Now maybe I can learn what that 'ultimate concern' was the theologians talked about."

Then it hit me: The Lord had already taught me that lesson in His own way.

And the world is passing away, and the lust of it; but he who does the will of God abides forever. 1 John 2:17 NKJV

. . . .

HEAVEN SENT

Lisa Brandom
Professor of English
John Brown University
Siloam Springs, Arkansas

IT WAS JANUARY of 1968. My husband and I had just moved to Oxford, Mississippi, with plans for full-time study at the University of Mississippi. We were as poor as Della and Jim in O'Henry's "The Gift of the Magi." We lay on a mattress on the bedroom floor of the antebellum house, having been too tired to assemble the bed frame after unloading the U-Haul trailer.

I rose to glance out the upstairs window. Once again, it had snowed overnight. "Do you want to go out and play in the snow?" I teased. "We could make snow angels."

My husband, always the planner, immediately rejected the idea. "What I need to do first is to clean that refrigerator from top to bottom with baking soda to get rid of that moldy, mildew smell," was his nonromantic reply. While he went about his task, I lazed on the mattress and thought about the upcoming conversations with my grandmother and mother. As sickening smells came from the now-open refrigerator, I began to feel nauseated. I reached for the saltine crackers I had placed beside the mattress the night before. I had known instinctively that I was pregnant. I could already imagine the family's reactions.

"How can you even think about bringing a baby into this world?" my grandmother would wail. It had been her reaction when my sister Judy had announced each of her own pregnancies.

The world was turbulent with the assassination of John F. Kennedy, the bombings of Jewish synagogues in Mississippi, the civil and racial unrest in the South, the Vietnam War, Woodstock, and the whole idea of free love. Had Garlan and I been unwise in planning a baby at this time of our lives? We were living on a shoestring budget with the promise of two work-study positions awaiting us. We would also take out loans to make ends meet.

I dreaded a conversation with my mother. She would burst into tears upon hearing the news. "Why are you calling?" she'd say. We never talked long-distance unless it was important.

"For the same reason Judy always calls," I'd reply. After she recovered from her tears, she would say, "God's always taken care of us. He's not going to let you down now. He'll provide."

The phone rang, startling me out of my reverie. It was the Director of Financial Aid at the university, offering me a work-study position in his office. I told him about my pregnancy. It was not cool to be a married, pregnant college student at a university awash with sororities, fraternities, and parties. He said, "That's fine with us. It might be I'll need to look around and find you an extra grant or something to help you get by a little better financially."

"Thank you, Lord," I whispered as I hung up the phone.

I continued to be anxious, however. Where would we put a baby? As Garlan and I cleaned the two-room apartment, assembled our bed, and hung pictures on the walls, we noticed a locked door off of our bedroom. This phenomenon in itself was not atypical in houses of this era. Our response, however, was. We set about finding a way to get into the room. Garlan located a key, the old kind that would fit practically any wooden door from the past. The door swung open to reveal a room approximately eight by ten feet with glorious sunlight flooding into it. We could immediately see the future: a nursery with a crib, a rocking chair by the windows, curtains with cherubs on them, and a clothes chest loaned to me by my namesake, Aunt Elise.

Do not be anxious about anything, but in everything, by prayer and petition, with thanksgiving, present your requests to God. Philippians 4:6 NIV

· ·

THE
FIFTH
MEETING

"Come and
hear, all
ye that
fear God,
and I will
declare
what he
hath done
for my
soul."

Psalm 66:16

Hanne Larson
Co-founder, Straight Ahead Ministries

Max R. Terman
Professor of Biology, Tabor College

John R. Visser
Professor of Business Administration, Dordt College

Mark L. Sargent
Provost, Gordon College

Susan Alexander Yates
Author and Speaker, FamilyLife

Elliott J. Anderson
Vice President of Student Development, Judson College

Stephen M. Pusey
Vice President for Academic Affairs, Trevecca Nazarene University

Jeffrey K. Greenberg
Professor of Geology, Wheaton College

Keith P. Keeran
President, Kentucky Christian College

Steven W. Fitschen
President and Executive Director, National Legal Foundation

DESTINY WITH A BIG BLUE BUS

Hanne Larson
Co-founder
Straight Ahead Ministries
Westboro, Massachusetts

EACH SUMMER while I was in college in the United States, I would fly back home to Denmark to work and save up money for the following school year. The Lord had faithfully provided affordable airline tickets. But the summer between my sophomore and junior years, ticket prices had gone up so high that it was beginning to look as if it would be impossible for me to go back home.

Just in time, I learned that some very good friends of mine who were in a gospel band were planning to tour Europe for the summer. Denmark was to be their first stop. They had gotten an incredible deal as a group on a charter flight to Germany, so I could go in with them. I was elated and could only say, "Wow, God, your plans are great!"

When we arrived in Germany, the Christian organization that was going to provide the van for the trip to Denmark said there wasn't enough room for me in the van. I couldn't believe it. It had seemed as if this was God's perfect provision for me, and now this.

So I was left in a small German town, not knowing what to do next and with very little money in my pocket. Now what, Lord?! I had been given the telephone number of that local Christian organization and was told I could call them after 10:00 that evening.

At 10 P.M. I made my somewhat desperate phone call. I was told that there would be a ministry bus going up to Denmark the next day. If I could find it, they were sure I could ride along. They knew which town the bus was in but they didn't know where it would be parked. If I was interested, I would have to take a train to one town and then catch a regular bus to the other town where their big blue ministry bus would be parked.

"Okay, God, this sounds like our only option." I used up the rest of my money to buy a train ticket and started out on my journey. When I got to the town where I had to catch the regular bus, I only had two minutes to get off my train and find it. I dashed through the station, not knowing which direction to run. I asked God, "Left or right?" In my heart I sensed, "Left." Just as I came out of the station tunnel, the bus I needed was just closing its doors. I waved my hands, and they let me on. I breathed a sigh of relief as I sat down, "Thank you, Lord."

When I arrived in the town where the big blue ministry bus was to be parked, I found it was a much larger town than I had anticipated. How was I ever going to find this bus? I stopped the first man I saw and asked if he had seen a big blue bus. He said, "Follow me." We walked for a long time up and down little winding streets. He took me right to the bus.

When I got there, the first person I ran into was a girl from Norway who was so discouraged that she was on the verge of turning her back on her faith. She had needed to talk with someone but couldn't find anyone who could speak her language. Through the long night journey on the bus, she and I sat on the floor talking about the things of God. As our bus trip was ending she turned to me and said, "Now I know that God is real and that He loves me. He sent you here just for me!"

And God is able to make all grace abound to you, so that in all things at all times, having all that you need, you will abound in every good work. 2 Corinthians 9:8 NIV

· ·

WHEN THE CHEERING STOPPED

Max R. Terman
Professor of Biology
Tabor College
Hillsboro, Kansas

I HARDLY FELT the ball leave the bat. I was stunned with the thrill of seeing my towering drive clear the deep center-field fence at Central Michigan University—giving my underdog team from Spring Arbor College the victory. The cheer of the crowd powered the chills pulsing up and down my spine as I trotted around the bases.

It seemed as if the basketball flew to the hoop by itself—that I was a spectator rather than the number 32 levitating above the defenders, flicking my wrist, and adding two points to the scoreboard for the college basketball team. As every athlete knows, getting into the "zone" is an almost magical experience. Points are scored, balls are intercepted, and pinpoint passes are made almost effortlessly, bringing roar after roar from the fans. Athletics was rewarding my psyche at the deepest level, and I was only a freshman! That's why it was so traumatic when the door to my athletic career closed the following year.

I entered college as a biology major, but my soul vibrated with the sounds of bats, gymnasiums, and the gridiron. In high school, athletic competition had fueled my life and the athletic limelight eclipsed all other interests. For the most part, my athletic performance during my freshman year at college was bright and sunny and full of promise. Quite unexpectedly, however, the vales of night covered my sophomore year almost from the start. I was no longer in the limelight but on the bench. Whether it was a new coach or more competition from highly skilled recruits or a combination of both, the result was that the crowds cheered for others and not for me. My frustration grew and my performance faded. The athletic door was closing and then slammed shut when the coach suggested that I not come out for the team the following year. Why was this happening? Why was God taking away the joy of my life?

As my athletic stardom fell, my science career blossomed. After I was freed from the grueling schedule of practices and games, a project about algae and the chemical nature of streams captured my time and imagination. I actually began to enjoy reading books and articles and going to nearby lakes and streams to take water samples. I looked forward to what the microscope would reveal the next day. Would the clear lake have different kinds of algae from the more turbid, cloudy stream leaving its borders? This latent curiosity about how the world works awoke and propelled me to graduate school for my doctorate in ecology and eventually to a position as a college professor and author. Scientific curiosity lay within me from the beginning. But it took one door closing to open another that led to a life which, for me, was much more suitable and satisfying.

And we know that in all things God works for the good of those who love him, who have been called according to his purpose. Romans 8:28 NIV

. . . .

THE NON-NEUTRALITY OF EDUCATION

John R. Visser
Professor of Business Administration
Dordt College
Sioux Center, Iowa

AS AN UNDERGRADUATE aeronautical engineering student at a major Midwestern university, I had precious few opportunities to take electives, so I was looking forward to taking an anthropology class for which I had been able to pre-register. Things were going fairly well in the class, but it was becoming increasingly obvious to me as the semester progressed that the instructor assumed (without discussion) that we were all the products of a Darwinian evolutionary process.

One day, he made the comment that humans were direct descendents of a particular strain of apes, which, by swinging in trees, had become accustomed to being in a vertical position, eventually learned to walk, and evolved into humans. I looked around my class of several hundred students and saw that most of them were dutifully writing this down in their notebooks, most likely spurred in part by the assumption that it eventually would reappear on a test.

I was prompted by this experience to realize that there is often no clear line between facts and beliefs. My instructor was doing much more than teaching a class; he was communicating what he understood to be true, which was in turn based on a construct of knowledge that he had accumulated from his parents, teachers, and cultural moorings. He had a very strong belief system, even though he was teaching at a "secular" university.

At that point I chose a bold path for someone who had been raised always to respect authority figures. I began to skip class (and the upcoming test) and poured my energy into writing a paper on the non-neutrality of education, the ease with which assumptions can be transformed into facts over successive generations, and the high calling teachers have not to pretend that they know more than they actually do. I don't know if my professor was impressed with my argumentation, bowled over by my chutzpah, or neither, but he accepted my paper in lieu of the test and even gave me a decent grade for the course.

Although this incident didn't immediately affect my career choice, I believe it was a stepping stone to a career in Christian higher education. I eventually left the business world and joined the staff at Dordt College, an institution in the Reformed tradition, which has a long and deep understanding of the key role that worldview plays in one's knowledge, assumptions, goals, attitudes, values, and actions. With colleagues there and in other Christian institutions of higher education, I have since been blessed with the task of presenting a (more than) viable alternative to the dualism, individualism, materialism, positivism, and other isms that permeate education today. I have participated in the spread of Christian higher education across the globe, helping young people see that Christ's lordship extends to every square inch of creation, and sharing in the joy that comes to their faces when they realize that this understanding, in some way or another, changes everything.

How many are your works, O LORD! In wisdom you made them all; the earth is full of your creatures. Psalm 104:24 NIV

. . . .

FAILURE AND FLAMES

Mark L. Sargent
Provost
Gordon College
Wenham, Massachusetts

MY FIRST YEAR in college did not go well. I had enrolled at a private California institution with academic prowess but only fraying ties to its founding denomination. After only a few weeks I was lonely and given to haphazard discipline. A fierce test or two, and some icy professors, soon eroded my shallow reserve of self-confidence. By summer I was working as night custodian at an elementary school and preparing for courses at a community college.

That was not how things were supposed to go. A college career that began with a scholarship and high hopes had taken a sudden and embarrassing detour. But that next year helped me recover some of my footing. It also widened my gaze.

For that, I can largely thank a patient, good-humored, even bookish youth pastor. In quiet, often intuitive ways, he reaffirmed that ideas, even doubts and failures, mattered to a life of faith. But he also knew that, as students, we could be insular and concerned about achievement. We needed to learn more about our neighbors.

During Easter week he took a few of us to churches and service programs in inner-city Los Angeles. We visited a rescue mission, a children's center, and a vibrant Pentecostal service. I walked the vacant lot where, only months before, the F.B.I. and a small radical group called the Symbionese Liberation Army (SLA) had been locked in a fiery shootout. One year earlier the SLA had kidnapped Patty Hearst, heiress of the wealthy newspaper publisher William Randolph Hearst. The pursuit of the captors had long filled the nation's front pages, and the quest reached a crescendo when six SLA members perished in the flames that consumed a small, wood-framed Los Angeles bungalow where they had been hiding.

On television, the story of the kidnapped heiress, the sound of gunfire, and the sight of the horrific flames had seemed larger than life—an apocalypse ready-made for the media. But standing there on the vacant lot, we were all struck by the eerie stillness and ordinariness of the scene. Although the charred home had long been bulldozed, the soil was still colored with ashes, and the weeds had started to reclaim the yard. It was hard to imagine the adjacent homes—mostly poor, weathered, and overcrowded—enduring a night beside the inferno that had once, if just for a few hours, seized the nation's attention.

On the way home we talked about our own uneasy emotions, and the pastor hinted that we may have seen a glimpse of the Gospel. Long before He ventured into the streets of Jerusalem, Jesus had walked into scenes like this—stark, sun-drenched villages where people struggled with want, loss, and broken-heartedness. He found victims living among the ruins of others. He brought a message of love, forgiveness, and reconciliation to the vacant lots and ashen fields of His own time.

I sensed anew that day why education mattered. What did I really know about all the people that Christ loves? What did I know about their obstacles and trials as well as their capacity, in the midst of violence and decay, for hope and faith?

Though I am still easily tempted by hopes for success, I recall those early college years when I faltered. And I can still hear that young pastor, at the end of that Easter week, reading for us the words of Isaiah:

The Spirit of the Sovereign Lord is on me, because the Lord has anointed me to preach good news to the poor. He has sent me to bind up the brokenhearted . . . to comfort all who mourn, and provide for those who grieve in Zion—to bestow on them a crown of beauty instead of ashes, the oil of gladness instead of mourning, and a garment of praise instead of despair. Isaiah 61:1-3 NIV

· ·

HE CHEERS WHEN WE SAY "I CAN'T"

Susan Alexander Yates
Author and Speaker
FamilyLife
Falls Church, Virginia

I SHOULD HAVE BEEN HAPPY, but I was miserable, more miserable than I'd ever been before I'd become a Christian. "Following Christ is so much more difficult than I thought it would be," I sighed. "I'm trying so hard to be a good believer and it just isn't working. Maybe something is wrong with me. I can't do this!"

It was my junior year at the University of North Carolina. I'd just returned to campus from a glorious summer of traveling around Europe with three of my best friends. While on our trip I'd met Ander and Jim, two law students from the University of Florida. They had asked me if I was a Christian and I had responded, "I think so; at least, I hope I am."

"Susan," they said, "God doesn't want you to think so or hope so. He wants you to know for sure." They shared with me the promise which is a picture of Christ standing at the door of our hearts, knocking. "If anyone hears My voice and opens the door," He says, "I will come in to him and will dine with him, and he with Me" (Revelation 3:20).

I realized that although I'd been in church all my life, I'd never actually asked Christ to come into my heart. Instead, I'd been living on an inherited, cultural faith. I needed my own personal faith. Even though it seemed weird at the time, I prayed with the guys and asked Jesus to come into my heart. It wasn't an emotional experience for me. It was more of a coming together of my heritage and becoming sure that I knew Jesus for myself. It was clearly a defining moment in my life.

But now, two months later and back at school, I was miserable. To an outsider my life didn't look much different. I'd always been a "good kid." I'd been successful in almost everything I'd tried, and I was known as a leader on campus. I figured that I could also succeed at being a great believer, and I set out to do just that. But the harder I tried to be a good Christian, the more frustrated I became. Finally, I decided to write Ander to tell him that I respected his faith, but that it just wasn't working for me. It was too hard.

His response was not at all what I expected. He replied, "Susan, I know exactly how you feel. I too felt the same way. Being a Christian is not about working to do it yourself. It's about coming to the point when we say, 'I can't do this God; you have to do it in me.' It's about relaxing and letting His Holy Spirit do it within you. You need to stop trying so hard and let Him work His will in your life."

What a relief! How countercultural. Being a Christian was not one more thing I had to succeed at. Instead, it was the place in which I needed to say, "I can't live this life, but You, O God, can do it in me." I think God cheers when we say, "I can't!"

Even today, years later, I keep learning the same lesson—that God delights when I stop trying so hard and instead rest in Him, asking Him to work His will within me. Living the Christian life is not about success. It's about surrender.

Faithful is He who calls you, and He also will bring it to pass. 1 Thessalonians 5:24 NASB

· ·

DRUMS, MONO, AND SANCTIFICATION

Elliott J. Anderson
Vice President of
Student Development
Judson College
Elgin, Illinois

MY SIBLINGS AND I could have all attended the University of Cincinnati for free. Our father was a professor there and loved it, but it was not the atmosphere he wanted for his children. My parents wanted us to become leaders among our peers and to become effective ambassadors for Christ through our career fields that ultimately all followed theirs—education. So we went to a private Christian college in Elgin, Illinois. The difference this decision made financially for my parents was somewhere in the sacrificial neighborhood of $150,000.

The primary response I gave for why I was attending Judson College was that it was the only college at which the coaches and the music director assured me that I could actively participate in both programs without compromising my ability to achieve in either area. Although this is a true answer, the real reason I chose Judson is that I didn't have a clue what I was doing in my life and I needed some direction and guidance. I had always found that barometer through my parents and my older brother. So, despite my reluctance to go to a "religious" school, I packed my bags and my drums and followed him to Judson.

As a freshman, my anti-authority mentality quickly earned me discipline in the dormitory and several trips to the dean's office. My attitude in the classroom was pathetic, and I skipped nearly half of my classes that first year. I repeatedly told my family that I was leaving Judson and the stupid rules that were somehow supposed to help me.

Midway through that first semester, I returned to my hometown accompanied by a female student who was also a freshman and a Cincinnati native. She was engaged and confused, and I took advantage of her vulnerability. This led to a year and a half of chaos in an unhealthy relationship that was predicated on dishonesty and mistrust. By the middle of my sophomore year, I was depressed and ill. I had suffered through two bouts of mononucleosis and a severe case of food poisoning, and I had lost my normal frenetic energy and joy for life.

It was then that I truly gave my life—my will—to the Lord for the first time. Though a perpetual extrovert, I spent hours alone in my room praying, reading the Word, and shunning social situations and activities other than the commitments to my sports, my music, and my roommates. It was there, in the basement of Wilson Hall, Room 101, that the Spirit showed me what sanctification was and why I needed it. I begged for His mercy and His wisdom and committed myself to a new life of equitable priorities and effort in all areas. How ironic and rewarding that the Lord has seen fit, almost twenty years later, to place me in the position of shepherding students through similar journeys.

May God himself, the God of peace, sanctify you through and through. May your whole spirit, soul and body be kept blameless at the coming of our Lord Jesus Christ. The one who calls you is faithful and he will do it. 1 Thessalonians 5:23, 24 NIV

. . . .

NOT CALLED TO PREACH

Stephen M. Pusey
Vice President for Academic Affairs
Trevecca Nazarene University
Nashville, Tennessee

THOUGH I WANTED to be a history teacher, I felt that God had "called" me to preach. I sought to carry out God's "will" for my life, yet I struggled with the fact that I had no passion for that calling.

Raised as the son and grandson of preachers, I grew up in a church culture that allowed little latitude in interpreting the meaning of God's call. A Christian vocation was seen as the preaching ministry in one of three areas— the local parish, evangelism, and the foreign mission field. Anything else was viewed as being out of God's will. My retired grandfather's efforts to have me practice preaching in churches brought little satisfaction to me and probably even less to congregants.

Everything changed the day I started college. All new freshmen were directed into a large room where advisors sat around tables. I approached an older gentleman sitting by himself. He quickly helped me select the courses I would need to start toward my intended career—my calling. In choosing one last class, he suggested that I take a history course to meet general requirements, indicating that a European history section was still open. I agreed and left without even learning the advisor's name.

Walking into my history class the next day, I was surprised to see the advisor standing at the front of the class. At that point, I embarked upon an exciting educational experience that lasted throughout my college years. Eventually I took every course the professor taught. Not only did I gain knowledge of the facts and interpretations of the past, but I also learned to think critically about the present and to integrate my Christian faith into the learning process and life itself. I was impressed by the way a Christian teacher could shape the minds and lives of students. By the end of my first semester, I had changed my major to history, convinced that teaching was a worthwhile and relevant Christian calling.

The call of God may not be to a particular vocation or job assignment. It is a call to a relationship with God in which I am free to use the talents, abilities, skills, and passions that He has given to me for the work of His kingdom. It is aligning my desires and actions with the very nature of God. As Oswald Chambers has stated, "God gets me into a relationship with Himself whereby I understand His call, then I do things out of sheer love for Him on my own account." My call was to teach; however, He calls us as individuals to a variety of vocations and areas of service. God's grace allows us to be who He has created us to be.

Five years after my graduation from that college, I returned as a teacher to replace my mentor upon his retirement. Now, years later, I daily continue to answer God's call.

But seek first his kingdom and his righteousness, and all these things will be given to you as well. Matthew 6:33 NIV

CRISIS IN THE IVORY TOWER

Jeffrey K. Greenberg
Professor of Geology
Wheaton College
Wheaton, Illinois

IN THE SPRING OF 1978 I was nearing completion of my doctoral work. I moved with my wife and newly adopted infant son from Chapel Hill, North Carolina, to Madison, Wisconsin, where I began my first real, post-education job. I was to be an Assistant Professor and

State Survey Geologist at the University of Wisconsin, with the expectation that my doctoral thesis would be completed in August.

My life goal was to make a name for myself as a researcher. In retrospect, I realize now that the Lord used at least three factors during the summer of 1978 to bring me to Him. First, the stress of writing a dissertation while moving my family was intense. Second, our new son was born premature and required significant care. Third, I was continually challenged in my new job by a very difficult coworker.

By August, I was overwhelmed with frustration. I alternated between periods of quiet inner turmoil and angry outbursts. My dear wife Diane offered me the salve of her gentle compassion. Her daily life was a struggle, too, but she was now drawing strength from a growing faith. I had observed her increasing involvement with charismatic prayer groups, first in North Carolina and then in Wisconsin. My initial understanding of these people made me quite skeptical of their activities. However, I knew Diane's intelligence and discernment would not allow any cult to grab her heart. Soon enough, because of what I saw in my wife, I was drawn to meet these Christians at a Monday-night meeting.

They were few, very humble and genuinely welcoming. I witnessed no bizarre behavior, only a strong certainty that God would hear their prayers. They spent significant time during their meetings offering simple songs and praise to Jesus.

I socialized with the prayer group once or twice after attending the first meeting. I returned to another prayer meeting in mid-August. The deadline for my final thesis draft was at hand, and I was furious about all the obstacles to my scholarly achievement at work. Never before had I been defeated in my quest for academic prominence. Now I was facing failure, and it was affecting everything. Physically, I was experiencing a tightness, with some pain, in my chest. Mentally, I was fearing death and was afraid of completely losing my temper at work. It seemed that the boiler was going to explode.

At just after midnight on August 22, my emotions did explode in weeping and shouting. For more than two hours, a young life's accumulation of demons flowed out in tears, angry words, and, finally, calls for help. Diane was at my side to cover me with prayer. When I was literally dehydrated from crying and sweating, she joined me at the side of our bed on our knees. She was already my wife, but truly she became my dear sister, too. We both knew that Jesus had allowed my stubborn pride and selfish ambition to take me down so that He could raise me up.

Thereafter, I still knew my calling was in academia, but the goal was to love the One who saved me and to seek His direction to enable my way.

Very truly, I tell you, unless a grain of wheat falls into the earth and dies, it remains just a single grain; but if it dies, it bears much fruit. Those

who love their life lose it, and those who hate their life in this world will keep it for eternal life. **John 12:24, 25 NRSV**

· ·

NOVEMBER RESOLVE

Keith P. Keeran
President
Kentucky Christian College
Grayson, Kentucky

IT WAS AN EXPERIENCE that burned itself into my memory and changed my life forever. Like most of the people who experienced the events of November 22, 1963, I remember exactly where I was and what I was doing the moment that I got the news.

I was a sophomore in college, and on that fateful afternoon another student and I were sitting in his yellow Volkswagen cramming information into our brains for an exam in Old Testament history. On the radio, the Eureka Brass Band of New Orleans distracted us for only a moment with its rendition of *When the Saints Go Marching In*. Completely unaware that at that very moment our world was being shaken by unbelievable tragedy, we barely heard the announcer break through with a special bulletin. "President Kennedy has been shot while traveling in a motorcade in Dallas, Texas!"

In a heartbeat everything had changed. We were riveted. The exam was forgotten—lost in the nightmarish haze of the unimaginable. Who could do such a thing, and why? Soon we were surrounded by dozens of stunned students and faculty straining in silence to catch every word. It was as though the moment was frozen in time. Everything seemed to stop as we waited for news of the President's condition. Then the announcement came that we had fearfully anticipated but emotionally rejected: "The President is dead!"

In the days that followed, the America I knew seemed a less friendly place. There was speculation of a government conspiracy to assassinate the President. Others said it was the Soviet Union or that the Mafia had ordered Kennedy's death. On campus, classes were temporarily suspended as students huddled with faculty in small groups trying to make sense of it all. "We live in a broken world," they said. "When men's hearts are full of evil, we all suffer from the consequences of their sinful deeds."

As thoughts were shared, one truth captivated my mind and heart: "Only Jesus has the power to mend a broken world." Science and technology are not enough. Medicine will not treat the kind of brokenness that kills a president or lets a child starve. I could be His voice and hands. The dark and bleak days of November had turned into a fresh resolve and a profound sense of divine purpose in my life. I now had compelling reasons to be vigilant in the pursuit of spiritual understanding and to apply myself to the tasks of learning and praying in preparation for service to the King of Glory.

There will be terrible times in the last days. People will be lovers of themselves . . . abusive, disobedient . . . ungrateful, unholy . . . brutal . . . treacherous . . . . But you, keep your head in all situations, endure hardship, do the work of an evangelist, discharge all the duties of your ministry. 2 Timothy 3:1-4; 4:5 NIV

• •

YELLOWSTONE OR ARAMAIC?

Steven W. Fitschen
President and Executive Director
National Legal Foundation
Virginia Beach, Virginia

YELLOWSTONE NATIONAL PARK burned during the summer of 1988. Fire consumed more than 1.5 million acres. Meanwhile, I sat at a table in a library 2,300 miles away, pondering it all. For eight years I had made my living as a forester. Then I enrolled at Regent University to study public policy and theology. So in May of 1989, I was torn. The Park's forests had begun a miraculous comeback, and as a forester I wanted to go see Yellowstone bounce back. But as a student I knew that the summer session would start in about a week and I needed to wrap up an independent study.

Both ideas made some sense. Watching the beginning of the Yellowstone rejuvenation would be, literally, a once-in-a-lifetime opportunity. The last time America had seen a fire this big was 1910, and before that in 1871. Yet an independent study in Aramaic was no walk in the park. If I didn't hit it hard now, the summer semester would be miserable. Weeks of all-nighters and nearly all-nighters loomed on the horizon.

As I prayed for guidance, a verse came to me: "No man, having put his hand to the plough, and looking back, is fit for the kingdom of God" (Luke 9:62). My days as a forester were in the past. The next week or so was to be dedicated to Aramaic.

I began to feel that the week was more about prayer than it was Aramaic. By the end of that week, I believed that God was leading me to invite the president of our university—the late Bob Slosser—to dinner. When I invited him, Dr. Slosser said he would be delighted to come but that it might take a while to arrange because of his busy schedule. I had no idea that "a while" would turn into a year.

But he never forgot, and a year later he and his wife showed up at our tiny townhouse. Dr. Slosser was a wonderful man of God, and he and his wife were engaging guests. We shared a pleasant evening of Christian fellowship consisting mostly of small talk. However, Dr. Slosser was used by God that night in a way that he never knew.

He asked me about my major and my interests. I explained my joint degree program in public policy and theology as well as my interest in things political and legal. He mentioned that I might be interested in the American Center for Law and Justice (ACLJ), a public interest law firm that Regent University's Chancellor Pat Robertson had recently started. The ACLJ had not existed a year earlier when God had impressed me to invite the Slossers to dinner. Dr. Slosser was just making small talk, but God was speaking through him.

I eventually became involved with the ACLJ, first as a volunteer, then a part-time student employee, then a full-time staffer after graduating from Regent, and finally as Assistant to the Executive Director.

The Lord next led me to the National Legal Foundation (NLF), another public interest law firm. The president of the firm retired two years after my arrival. Largely because of the skills I had acquired at the ACLJ, I was asked to serve as the NLF's Executive Director. It is a testimony of God's unusual way of doing things that a non-attorney was asked to run a public interest law firm and *then* go to law school and get his license.

I sometimes joke, "I went from being a forester to being a lawyer via seminary. Doesn't everybody?" The choice between Yellowstone and Aramaic was about a lot more than how to spend a week that summer. It was about the first incredible link in a chain of events that might never have happened had I not laid everything before God in prayer.

For my thoughts are not your thoughts, neither are your ways my ways, saith the LORD. For as the heavens are higher than the earth, so are my ways higher than your ways, and my thoughts than your thoughts. Isaiah 55:8, 9 KJV

THE SIXTH MEETING

"Come and hear, all ye that fear God, and I will declare what he hath done for my soul."

Psalm 66:16

Claudia DeVries Beversluis
Dean for Instruction, Calvin College

Robert L. Doty
Professor of Engish, Campbellsville University

William Tabbernee
President, Phillips Theological Seminary

David Nystrom
Professor of Theology and History, North Park University

Romaine Jesky-Smith
Professor of Education, Geneva College

Mark P. Cosgrove
Professor of Psychology, Taylor University

David P. Gushee
Graves Professor of Moral Philosophy, Union University

Ernest McNealey
President, Stillman College

N. Bradley Christie
Professor of English, Erskine College

Kathy Harrell Storm
Vice President for Student Life, Whitworth College

THINKING CHRISTIANLY

Claudia DeVries Beversluis
Dean for Instruction
Calvin College
Grand Rapids, Michigan

ALTHOUGH I WAS pretty sure I would remain a Christian in college, I struggled to know just what kind of Christian to be. There were many options, and I tried quite a few of them. One weekend I found myself sharing the four spiritual laws in the dormitory of a neighboring Christian college. Although I admired the evangelical earnestness of the group, their style didn't seem right for me.

Soon afterward I was protesting the war at an airport appearance of a famous politician. This was exciting, but at that point I wasn't sure I could support my actions with cogent arguments. I tried coffeehouse conversations, group hymn sings, spontaneous Bible studies. All these activities expressed sides of my Christian life, but none of them seemed whole. The persons involved in each group rarely connected with each other. What direction was right? The struggle that occupied a fair amount of my mental and emotional effort was about how to craft a whole, integrated Christian life.

The answer came slowly in two places, linked together by the presence of smart and caring professors. In the classroom I learned that thinking Christianly was complicated, but deep and rich and invigorating. A class on the French Revolution emphasized, as its overriding theme, the tension between "liberte" and egalite" that marked those tumultuous times. That theme illuminated current political debates in my own equally tumultuous world and marked my introduction to the power of ideas.

In social philosophy I heard the professor's vivid vision of the role of the church in enacting kingly, priestly, and prophetic functions in the world. (I still have those notes, but I don't need them because the picture is so strong in my mind.) In ethics it shook my world to learn that there could be times when we can only choose between two flawed options for action. Nothing was going to be simple.

What kept my heart full and my life whole was that I was given the privilege of worshiping in a congregation along with some of the very professors whose teaching most challenged me. I had been invited to join this congregation by several of these professors. In worship I saw some of the smartest people I have ever known, and I saw them bow their heads before God. I heard them pray. I saw them with their families. And this was especially amazing: I saw that I could bless them too through my own contributions to the congregation.

The ideas, words, and worship of my college professors helped me craft a holistic picture of Christian life in community. And when my mind was confused, my career goals were fuzzy, or God seemed very far away, I hung on to the simple fact that these smart, caring folks were worshiping God. If they could do this, then so could I.

The fear of the LORD is the beginning of wisdom, and knowledge of the Holy One is understanding. Proverbs 9:10 NIV

· ·

COMING HOME

Robert L. Doty
Professor of English
Campbellsville University
Campbellsville, Kentucky

IT IS PERHAPS TOO EASY for us who were born at the end of the Depression (1935) to think that life was a difficult struggle. But as the third in a family of five children in rural eastern Kentucky, I felt keenly the loss of my father to pneumonia when I was six. After my father died, we lived with my maternal grandmother, who also died when I was twelve.

Through all this my mother, who had few job skills, kept the family together by sheer force of will and faith. She bought a small house in a nearby village when my grandmother's estate was settled. She did this by working second shift as a cook in a village restaurant. All of her children learned to work both at home and in pick-up jobs.

During my teen years I took every sort of farm-day labor job to relieve some of the financial burden on my mother. I had a facility for learning and decided that the only way I could break this cycle was to get a good education. I went to Detroit to room at an uncle's home and enrolled in a municipal junior college in Dearborn. I studied for a year, and then was out to work for a year before returning in 1956.

I returned to Kentucky for the Christmas break of 1956–57. By this time my mother was managing a small restaurant-hotel. We were shocked to get a call at the restaurant saying that my mother's house was ablaze and that nothing could be done to save it. It was a total loss.

My mother had always been possessed of deep strength and an ability to look forward. She had a faith anchored in action and devotion rather than mere words. I was the only one of her children to enter the world of higher education. I had volunteered to stay in Kentucky, abandon my plans, and help her. She would not hear of it, and insisted that even though she could not help at all, I must go back to school. I returned to finish an associate's degree and then worked in Ford Motor Company engineering. Within a year I was drafted and served for two years in the Army, but had already decided to become a minister. I continued with my education in religion and literature and, after seminary, pursued my doctorate in literature. I am still active in the ministry.

Throughout my life I have been inspired by my mother's vision in believing a brighter future ought not be sacrificed to assuage an immediate pain or to address a temporary hardship. As she approaches 94, she still lives alone and keeps up a ministry of encouragement.

The LORD gives strength to his people; the LORD blesses his people with peace. Psalm 29:11 NIV

. . . .

TOO LATE TO VISIT

William Tabbernee
President
Phillips Theological Seminary
Tulsa, Oklahoma

FOR A SHORT TIME during my final year in seminary, I was left in charge of the student church I was serving in a suburb of Melbourne, Australia. The former senior pastor had left to take another appointment; the new senior pastor was yet to arrive. It was summertime, when parish life was not quite as hectic as normal, so it was assumed that I could be trusted to take care of the necessary tasks.

No emergencies were expected. A few weeks before the former senior minister left, he had told me about a woman who was dying of cancer, and he asked me to keep my pastoral eye on her. I had never met the woman, nor had I ever visited a cancer patient, let alone one who might die at any moment. I promised I would visit, but I was relieved when the minister informed me on the day he left that the woman in question was now in remission and that my visiting her was not quite as urgent. Nevertheless, I again promised that I would visit her when I could.

Three weeks passed by. Although partially comforted by the knowledge that my pastoral visit was not as urgent as it once appeared, I started to feel guilty that I had, in fact, not overcome my fears and gone to see and pray with the woman with cancer.

Plucking up my courage one morning, I drove to her house and knocked on the door. A man, whom I later learned was her husband, answered. I introduced myself as the student minister of the nearby church and asked, "May I see Mrs. Brown, please?"—announcing that I had come on a pastoral visit. After an uncomfortable moment of silence, the man replied softly, with tears in his eyes, "We buried her yesterday."

Recently, as I was on my way to visit an elderly friend who had been in the hospital for a couple of months, I met a ministerial colleague at the elevator who told me that he'd been up to see our mutual friend but had been told by the nurse that they needed to remake his bed. While we waited, we decided to have some coffee in the cafeteria. Before we realized it, time had slipped by as we talked about what to us, at least, were important church and seminary matters. Both of us had additional pressing appointments that afternoon, so we each decided to visit our friend another day.

I had driven about ten yards out of the hospital's parking garage when I remembered the visible pain in the eyes of the husband of the cancer patient to whom I had failed to minister more than thirty years earlier. I stopped the car, re-parked it, and went to visit my friend in the hospital after all. He died the next day.

A lesson which I have never forgotten since my student days is that procrastination has no place in an effective, caring pastoral ministry.

Be careful then how you live, not as unwise people but as wise, making the most of the time. Ephesians 5:15, 16 NRSV

THROUGH THE WISDOM OF OTHERS

David Nystrom
Professor of Theology and History
North Park University
Chicago, Illinois

I GREW UP in California and could see no reason to live anywhere else. I wanted to be a farmer. My childhood was spent in and around San Francisco, but my uncles were grain farmers in the central valley of California. By the time I was eighteen I had been driving trucks, harvesters, and tractors for years. I loved the freshening breeze of fall mornings. I loved summer evenings, the sky rose-colored, and the smell of cut grain sweet and heavy in the air. I loved riding in the pickup with my uncle. I even loved getting up early and working all day.

So I enrolled at a university with a double major in plant science and agronomy, and also considered plant pathology. I still don't know what plant pathology is, but it sounded impressive.

My first term was both exciting and unnerving. Chemistry was a real shock. Along with five hundred others, I sat in a cavernous aircraft hangar the university called a classroom and listened to my first college lecture. I had taken chemistry in high school, and figured the first two weeks would be review. I began to daydream. This was a mistake. With fifteen minutes remaining in the class period, I realized, in a rush of paralyzing fear, that the professor had already covered everything I knew about chemistry and had entered uncharted waters.

Over the next several weeks I spent many hours alone in the dark in the middle of the night, wondering how this eighteen-year-old was supposed to make decisions that would forever determine his life. Then came midterms.

I was certain that I had scored no less than a B+ in chemistry. I soon knew better. The professor said the C- I received was "a gift." Then my uncles told me that by the time I was forty their land would be converted to housing developments. My late-night sessions grew more urgent. I sought divine assistance. Here, it seemed to me, was a situation deserving of a clear sign from heaven. None came. What did come were observations from people I respected and who knew me well. They affirmed certain gifts they perceived in me.

Though I was raised in a Christian home, and while I liked and respected my pastors, I certainly never thought about becoming one. And I had never met a college professor before arriving at the university. But today I am a Professor of New Testament and a minister in Chicago.

God's will is not so much about what career or major you choose, but what quality of person you become. God speaks to us sometimes through the wisdom of others. God is a God of new beginnings, who wipes the slate clean. Although I sometimes need to relearn these lessons, they have proven trustworthy over the last twenty years.

You have made known to me the path of life; you will fill me with joy in your presence, with eternal pleasures at your right hand. Psalm 16:11 NIV

· ·

THEY HAD HIM ALL THE TIME

Romaine Jesky-Smith
Professor of Education
Geneva College
Beaver Falls, Pennsylvania

I WENT TO SCHOOL in the early 1970s and certainly should have stories of protests, rock concerts, drugs, and general rebellion. But I was a "decent kid." I respected my parents, studied hard, attended classes (most of the time), and enjoyed college life. I even attended church regularly and did not mind the Bible courses or chapel services required at my college. I must admit that I did not attend the college because it was Christian, but because it was close to my home. Without protest I participated in the regular practices of praying and studying the Bible. But initially there was no demand for any major life-changing lessons during those years. Life for me was easy, delightful, and successful.

However, as my college career progressed, I started to notice that some people, particularly many of my professors, were "different." They had a quiet confidence about their faith—a faith that accompanied them daily, moment by moment, as if it permeated their very being. I was intrigued by these people who just by the way they talked, thought about issues, and lived their lives pro claimed their faith in Christ. They caught my attention and imagination, and slowly over several semesters I began to reflect on my own faith. Whether the courses were in mathematics, the humanities, or political science, there was a difference between these people and me. I had Christ on Sundays—they had Him all the time. I knew what it meant to go through my once-a-week ritual. They knew what it meant to possess salvation.

I did not have to endure a tough experience to learn that I needed the Lord every day. No time of rebellion was required for me to recognize my need for a savior. I was changed just because people around me lived their lives with integrity and faith, reflecting what it meant to have life abundantly in Him.

Now wherever we go he uses us to tell others about the Lord and to spread the Good News like a sweet perfume. Our lives are a fragrance presented by Christ to God . . . to those who are being saved we are a life-giving perfume. 2 Corinthians 2:14-16 NLT

THE LORD OF
ALL LEARNING

Mark P. Cosgrove
Professor of Psychology
Taylor University
Upland, Indiana

IN THE FALL of my third year of graduate studies at Purdue University, I accepted Jesus Christ into my heart and life. Prior to my conversion I ago-nized over many questions about the truth claims of Christianity, and books by C. S. Lewis and Paul Little helped in my step of faith. As I continued my graduate work for the next two years, I had many wonderful opportunities to grow in my faith as well as my mind. I attended a good church, learned to share my faith, and made wonderful Christian friends. But there always seemed to be a division between the world of my academic studies and the world of my new Christian faith.

During my final summer of graduate school, as I was completing the writing on my doctoral dissertation, I had the opportunity to attend Campus Crusade staff training, which providentially was held at Purdue that year. My career plan was to become an associate staff member for Campus Crusade, and then begin teaching psychology at the college level. That summer my mind grew in the wisdom of Christian thought as I took Bible survey and theology courses from nationally known Christian teach-ers. But, simultaneously, I was trying to finish a dissertation on human color-pattern vision, the tiny details of which, by comparison, seemed so irrelevant. My busy summer was consumed by two very different, full-time jobs: Christian studies and psychological studies. It didn't take many late nights of study before I grew weary and felt like dropping my graduate work right at the finish line and giving my life over to God's work and God's truth.

One desperate night I prayed for the Lord to give me the enthusiasm and strength to finish my dissertation if that was His will. That night I began to approach my school work as God's work and God's truth, and I finished my Ph.D. race because it was for Him that I ran.

The Lord knew my path better than I did, and finishing my degree was the best thing that could have happened to my Christian life and service. That degree has made all the difference in where and how I have been able to serve the Lord. With the Ph.D. I was able to work full-time in Christian ministry, speaking on secular college campuses all over the country. I was also able to write books and articles integrating faith and learning. And I have been privileged for the last twenty-five years to teach on a Christian college campus, helping students in their attempts to integrate faith and learning. In all this the Lord has taught me that He is the Lord of all knowledge, and it is His truth that I discover and teach, and Him whom I serve, no matter what work I do.

Take my yoke upon you and learn from me. Matthew 11:29 NIV

TREACHEROUS WATERS

David P. Gushee
Graves Professor of Moral Philosophy
Union University
Jackson, Tennessee

WHEN I LEFT my home in Vienna, Virginia, to attend a state university in 1980, I was still a relatively immature Christian. I had come to Christ just two years before. While God had taught me much, I was not prepared for the challenges to my faith and values that my secular university presented.

Those challenges were everywhere. They began in the dorms, where immature teenagers were granted near-total freedom. I was confronted with officially sponsored keg parties—free beer for all—and surrounded by sexual experimentation, with overnight visitors a common occurrence.

In the classrooms, ours was a demanding university. In many ways I received an excellent education. And yet my academic experiences often posed a staggering challenge to my faith. In my first "Christian Scripture" class, the very first words out of the professor's mouth were: "Did Jesus of Nazareth really rise from the dead?" He then introduced us to one of the most extreme approaches to biblical criticism.

Especially during my sophomore year, there were a few days in which the clash between my conservative Southern Baptist Christianity and the secular paganism of my college surroundings became almost more than I could bear. My heart and my head were at war; it seemed there was no way to be both a serious Christian and an educated human being, at least as defined in the religion department.

And that was the conclusion that my best friend reached. We had attended the same high school and were thrilled when we learned that we had both been admitted to the same college and could be roommates. We had both been visible Christian leaders in our high school, and when we came to college, we were determined to bear Christian witness there. But by the middle of our sophomore year my friend had essentially abandoned the Christian faith in favor of secular philosophy.

This is not an argument for Christians to shun secular higher education. I'm sure I was where God wanted me to be. But I certainly learned that Christian students need the right kind of support in navigating those treacherous waters. I found that support in my church, in the Baptist Student Union, and in exposure to rigorous Christian reading that enabled me to *engage* the issues presented in class rather than run from them.

Above all, I discovered that there is no place a child of God can go in which God cannot be found—even the secular university. Every step along the way, God was there with me.

Where can I go from your spirit? Or where can I flee from your presence? If I ascend to heaven, you are there; if I make my bed in Sheol, you are there. If I take the wings of the morning and settle at the farthest limits of the sea, even there your hand shall lead me, and your right hand shall hold me fast. Psalm 139:7-10 NRSV

. . . .

UNEXAMINED FAITH

Ernest McNealey
President
Stillman College
Tuscaloosa, Alabama

WHATEVER ONE BELIEVES to be the Word of God and the piety of Jesus very often comes from unexamined traditions. Sets of religious practice, codes of personal conduct, and the formal order of worship are shaped by such traditions. Even the selected readings of the Bible by adherents will be guided to find harmony with the absolute beliefs already firmly in place.

My journey from home to college carried with it a set of such unexamined beliefs. As I had from elementary school and through high school, I prayed fervently about the mundane, as well as what I considered to be the significant aspects of college life. At that time, I made no distinction between God's plan for my life, what I wanted, and what I needed. I was blind to the concept that I had been given gifts that I could use.

So I prayed that the head cheerleader would find me irresistible. I prayed that I had made 100 on the chemistry exam taken a week earlier. And I prayed that every letter from home would be overflowing with cash.

To be certain, it wasn't very long before pie-in-the-sky wishful thinking in the guise of prayer became bitterly disappointing. I started to question the power of prayer and the articles of faith that I had come to know. The smorgasbord of denominations that I discovered and the new temptations that college offered accelerated this. By my sophomore year, the flame of my candle of faith barely flickered.

Late in the fall of that year, while president of my pledge line, I forgot to invite the line sweetheart to church one Sunday, as instructed by the big brothers of the fraternity. As I entered the pew absolutely horrified, prayer, my old friend, seemed the only choice. Forgiveness was the first entreaty, followed by a request for a miracle—the deliverance of the beautiful young lady that I had forgotten to invite. By the grace of God, she did go to church on this particular Sunday, the very church where I sat praying as she slid into the pew next to me. On that day, I started a new journey of faith.

Regard your servant's prayer and his plea, O LORD my God, heeding the cry and the prayer that your servant prays to you today. 1 Kings 8:28 NRSV

BELIEVER AT A CROSSROAD

N. Bradley Christie
Professor of English
Erskine College
Due West, South Carolina

MY MOTHER AND FATHER were "sufficient rope" parents: they allowed enough rope for a teenager to hang himself with, but they always slip-knotted that noose to prevent the definitive result of a hanging. So, one Friday night when I was seventeen, I knew that something was amiss when I arrived home late to find my parents awake with the light on. As I peeked in, my father said, "On Monday, you're going to call those schools and tell one of them you're coming and the other that you're not."

Here was my dilemma: At that time March 15 was a nearly universal matriculation deadline, and by then I had dutifully notified several schools that I would not be joining their next freshman class. But two remained. The end of March approached. I feared that one of these places was just where

God wanted me to be and the other was not, and that a moment's decision would spell the difference between success and disaster.

One of my remaining choices was Duke University, my father's alma mater, where I had been born during his last semester of medical school. Despite their strong ties to Duke, my parents supported all of my college choices. So they registered genuine surprise when I announced that Duke was near the top of my list.

Meanwhile, my grandfather took me to lunch at the River Club, where everything was exquisite. The message was that if I wanted to enjoy this kind of success for myself, I would be wise to choose the school with the more prestigious reputation. He wasn't pressuring me, either; it's just that, until I applied there, he had never heard of Davidson College.

I was in quite a bind. By Monday, though, I had made my choice. With some remaining hesitancy, I telephoned both admissions offices and thanked Duke profusely but told Davidson to count me in. In the following months, I would second-guess that decision many times. But in the end—indeed, every step along the way—God was faithful, even when I strayed from Him. The Lord saw to it that my college years were among the most blessed of my life.

And God had so much more in store for me. Having graduated from Davidson with some distinction and even greater joy, I applied to Duke for graduate study. Again I turned them down to pursue a Master's degree elsewhere. God blessed my time, preparing me for marriage and my first teaching job. Three years later He clearly called me to return to graduate school and complete my degree. And five years after that—thirty years after my own birth there—our first son was born in Durham, during my final year in the doctoral program . . . at Duke.

Believers at a crossroads usually do not face a good-or-bad, right-or-wrong decision about their futures. The Lord typically blesses us with an abundance of good choices—He gives us plenty of rope. As we abide in Him, He blesses richly the choices we make. And often He even allows us to choose to let Him bless us again beyond our fondest dreams.

The Lord is my chosen portion and my cup; you hold my lot. The lines have fallen for me in pleasant places; indeed, I have a beautiful inheritance. Psalm 16:5, 6 ESV

RESTLESS QUESTIONS

Kathy Harrell Storm
Vice President for Student Life
Whitworth College
Spokane, Washington

I WAS HEADING in the wrong direction, swimming upstream. Most of the other first-year students had shown up for their early days of college ready to affirm and deepen the faith that had brought them to a Christian community. They came to college with trunks full of belongings and families ready to unpack their things. I, on the other hand, arrived alone from another country with two suitcases and multiple questions. The questions were barely formed or conscious, but they were powerful, creating in me a restlessness that for many months went unnamed.

I had come to college the daughter of missionaries. My years overseas had been rich and exciting. I had hunted alligators, traveled with my father on medical ventures by canoe and single-engine aircraft, eaten rodents. I had great stories and a wonderful reservoir of unique memories. I also brought moments of changed perspective that I wasn't sure how to describe. I recalled standing on the street corner of a Latin American city thinking, "Their truths, so different than mine, are as true to them as mine are to me." I was haunted by the image of a little boy named Eriberto whose mental capacity had been forever changed by a high fever, and the words of my father that "his whole life would have been different, if only he had had a few aspirin." I brought with me the realization that, even as a child of missionaries, I was a wealthy person in a world of need.

And so the culture of my Christian college was at once warm and welcoming and at the same time unreal. I was grateful to be in a place of safety and plenty, and at the same time felt guilty and out of place. Though a lifelong Christian, I felt oddly on the fringe. A sense of the tragedy of the world made it hard for me to be interested in the preoccupations of my peer culture. Discontent with American abundance, and my own, left me feeling isolated. And it was hard to connect with worship communities full of optimism and certainty while I struggled with the meaning of culture.

It was in a religion course that I had opportunity to put words to issues I had carried with me. There a professor's honesty, a teaching assistant's support, provocative topics raised by a text, and even the haunting challenges of Bergman films encouraged candor and directness about difficult ideas. The spirit of courage that permeated the class opened a world of intellectual honesty that allowed me to face my doubts. Most important, the fearlessness of the discourse conveyed to me the robustness of God's love—the great truth that no nagging question or haunting doubt could separate me from the love of Christ.

For I am convinced that neither death nor life, neither angels nor demons, neither the present nor the future, nor any powers, neither height nor depth, nor anything else in all creation, will be able to separate us from the love of God that is in Christ Jesus our Lord. Romans 8:38, 39 NIV

· ·

THE SEVENTH MEETING

Marilyn Chandler McEntyre
Professor of English, Westmont College

Bob L. Hanley
Vice President for Student Services, Anderson College

Norman Bridges
President, Bethel College

Preston F. Harper
Professor of English, Abilene Christian University

Charlotte Thayer Wood
Professor of Nursing, Mississippi College

Lloyd J. Davis
Professor of Mathematics and Physics, Montreat College

Del Rey Loven
Professor of Visual Art, Judson College

Rex M. Rogers
President, Cornerstone University

Harry Van Dyke
Professor of History, Redeemer University College

Louis Markos
Professor of English, Houston Baptist University

GENERAL ED AND OCCASIONS OF GRACE

Marilyn Chandler McEntyre
Professor of English
Westmont College
Santa Barbara, California

COLLEGES HAVE "GENERAL EDUCATION" requirements to assure that you don't leave with a lopsided brain. If you love the humanities and approach the sciences with fear and loathing, you will at some point have to peer into a microscope and get over your phobias. Or, if the lab bench is your favorite spot on campus, you will have to venture outside, find a convenient spot on the grass, and crack open *Paradise Lost*. Christian students hear a lot about developing their God-given gifts, but perhaps less about the value of doing what you're bad at, or even bored by.

A discovery I attribute to the work of grace helped me through classes I feared would be threatening, boring, or irrelevant: everything worth knowing is potentially interesting—not just to the odd person who likes that sort of thing, but to me. I can *take* an interest. I decided to accept this admonishment in a required astronomy class.

Astronomy was not my idea of a good time. My mind boggled at distances measured in powers of ten. But in that class I began to think about awe and about the mystery of dimensions—that creation extends into largeness and smallness too large or small for our limited minds to grasp. That God is beyond dimension—inconceivably big, inconceivably small. I began to enjoy astronomy, not because I was good at it, but because it gave me occasion for reflections I might not have come to otherwise. I didn't get an "A." But I did learn something about choosing to put my heart into work I didn't love, showing me that interest is a form of love and that it can grow gradually with a little good will.

You can decide to do anything with your whole heart—not just what comes naturally or logically. Not just what seems immediately interesting. Not just what you have talent for. Everything the curriculum offers is an avenue of grace.

General education requirements also offer valuable practice in cultivating curiosity. I have come to believe that curiosity ought to be listed among the Christian virtues. A curious mind will go anywhere. Equipped with questions and the framework of faith, the curious discover that truth is larger than language, more intricate than molecular structures, more colorful than the most kaleidoscopic art form. A curious mind is open to the Spirit. Curiosity is a way of loving God. Boredom, on the other hand, is a sin. Boredom comes with listlessness, self-centeredness, flatness of affect, fatigue. It's an insult to the endlessly inventive Almighty. We are told to "choose life. . . ." Curiosity is a way of choosing life—boredom a foretaste of death. Both are decisions. The key to life-giving learning is to assume that requirements may be occasions of grace.

Whatsoever thy hand findeth to do, do it with thy might. Ecclesiastes 9:10 KJV

. . . .

APPLE PIE
AND SUNSHINE

Bob L. Hanley
Vice President for Student Services
Anderson College
Anderson, South Carolina

MY FIRST DAY at the large public university can be summed up in one word—overwhelming. Having grown up in rural upstate South Carolina, I was used to knowing everyone in my small high school and being part of a group of close friends. Suddenly everything changed. I now passed a thousand people on the sidewalk each day, not knowing a single one. I sat in classes with complete strangers and felt a deep sense of isolation and unease.

On the third day of the semester, I visited a small dining hall on the front side of campus. Sitting on a hill overlooking the university's oldest buildings, this canteen was away from the main flow of students. I walked inside, picked up a tray, and started though the food line. I had gotten only a hamburger and some fries when I paused, my mind racing back to my classes that day. I was absorbed in worry about an upcoming chemistry test and an English paper when I was startled by a laugh. I looked up to see an elderly African American lady behind the dessert counter. She laughed again and with a broad smile said, "You are really serious today. You need some apple pie to give you a boost. Add a little ice cream on top and you will really lighten your load."

I had to chuckle. As she dipped the vanilla ice cream atop the warm pie, she added, "The good Lord gives us something to smile about every day. Sometimes it's just a little hard to see it."

I nodded. "Well, what did you find to smile about today?"

She laughed again and handed me the pie. "I got to serve you and make a new friend."

As I moved down the line, she added, "And have a blessed day." I smiled, feeling my heart lighten and my spirits perk up. For the next several weeks I never failed to go to lunch there and get my apple pie with ice cream and my daily dose of sunshine from her kind words and smile. I never asked her name, but I felt like she was family.

Over those same weeks, I saw the walls of isolation slowly dissolve with the strangers in my classes. I developed relationships that for many would last a lifetime. Yet I count the kind lady who served me apple pie and made me feel welcome at the large university as my first friend in college. Through her wonderful spirit, I saw firsthand what Christ's love can do when put into service for others.

You are the light of the world. A city on a hill cannot be hidden. Neither do people light a lamp and put it under a bowl. Instead they put it on its stand, and it gives light to everyone in the house. In the same way, let your light shine before men, that they may see your good deeds and praise your Father in heaven. Matthew 5:14-16 NIV

THE TREASURE OF A GODLY HERITAGE

Norman Bridges
President
Bethel College
Mishawaka, Indiana

I GOT MARRIED in the fall of my senior year in college. My wife Janice was in the fall of her junior year. We were young, and so thought we were invincible. We carried heavy academic loads, worked odd jobs, and tutored other students. And, of course, we had the joy and stress of establishing our own home. We found a little apartment and bought used furniture.

Somewhere in that first winter together it all caught up with us. Janice's back flared up, and we thought she would have to have surgery. There wasn't enough time for all of the work and all of the study. The doctor bills were mounting, and graduation seemed far away.

One day in my discouragement, I wrote a letter to my father. It was full of self-pity and unhappiness. Didn't God care? Why were our circumstances so difficult? Why hadn't I just gone to work in the Buick factory at home instead of going off to college?

My father wrote back to me a wonderful letter, full of affirmation. He talked about God's blessing and care. He told me about hard times in his own life. He said that whatever the circumstances, he had determined he would be God's man.

I treasured that letter. It helped me get beyond my immediate difficulties and respond to all of the good things that were in my life. I quickly saw then, and have seen more clearly since, the blessing of a godly heritage. It provides us with strength during the dark periods of our lives. It helps us know that God is faithful.

Now my father is gone, and I no longer can ask for his advice and support. I have become the senior member of my family. And while I can no more solve my children's problems than my father could solve mine, I can point them to the Lord he knew and tell them that I have a personal testimony of God's faithfulness.

Following God's call has given me an exciting, fulfilling, and meaningful life. Instead of the factory, I found a career and a vocation. Our marriage of 44 years has been enriched by the shared struggles of those early times. And I have learned to trust the Lord through good times and bad, even though I do not always know or understand His purposes and plans.

But the mercy of the Lord is from everlasting to everlasting upon them that fear him, and his righteousness unto children's children. Psalm 103:17 KJV

. . . .

TO ALL THE ATHEISTS I'VE LOVED BEFORE

Preston F. Harper
Professor of English
Abilene Christian University
Abilene, Texas

BILL JOHNSON AND I were best friends. We both planned to teach at Abilene Christian University after getting our Ph.D.s at Texas Christian University. He had always been a student or a teacher. I had spent three years in the U. S. Army, so I was older than he and appreciated his relative innocence and unfaltering faith in the love and care of God. He and his wife Suzanne, who was a sincere, pure-hearted Christian and also a teacher, would make significant, lasting contributions to the church.

The Wednesday evening before Thanksgiving, Bill, Suzanne, and their baby girl set off with glad hearts for the West Texas town of Childress to be with his parents—good Christian people who always gave him and his family, especially their first grandchild, a warm welcome. They weren't far from home when the unthinkable happened. An eighteen-wheeler had jackknifed, and the trailer was blocking the road. There were no warning markers, and Bill's car crashed into it at 70 mph. Suzanne was severely injured, but she survived. Bill and the baby were killed, their bodies badly disfigured.

This was the first time a close friend had been killed, and I was deeply disturbed. Why had God permitted this tragedy? Bill had entrusted his and his family's lives into the keeping of what we all believed to be the all-loving and all-powerful God of the Bible. Questions hammered at me before and after the funeral. Is He all-loving but not all-powerful? Does He even exist?

At the time, I was taking a course in existentialism and phenomenology, and was writing a paper on *The Sun Also Rises* by Ernest Hemingway, one of my favorite authors. Despite his having been an atheistic existentialist, he was a manly man with a code that honors courage, friendship, and endurance. But he saw life as a losing battle. He believed we are trapped socially and biologically in an incoherent universe, not knowing why we're here or where we're going. The only possible victory is losing with dignity. After death there is nothing.

One evening not long after Bill's death, while driving home to take my family to midweek Bible classes, I got to thinking about Hemingway and his sad life—a life that ended in suicide. Even if there isn't a god, I thought, what I have is so much better than his that I'm going to hang onto it even if I can't answer all my questions. If there turns out to be no god and no heaven, I will have had a good life believing in them. The world is incoherent, and sometimes when your faith is weak, you have to make a pragmatic choice. Thirty years later, with a strong faith in God, I'm grateful to Hemingway and a few other atheists for helping me make that choice.

And without faith it is impossible to please God, because anyone who comes to him must believe that he exists and that he rewards those who earnestly seek him. Hebrews 11:6 NIV

A FAITHFUL FRIEND

Charlotte Thayer Wood
Professor of Nursing
Mississippi College
Clinton, Mississippi

AS A BACCALAUREATE nursing student, I breezed through the first two years of nursing pre-requisite courses at a state university. In my junior year, reality hit. I discovered that nursing school required my time, effective study habits, and personal accountability. Was I ready for this? No. My campus activities as a Panhellenic officer and sorority member required a lot of my time.

My grades and clinical performance were below the expectations of nursing faculty and friends. "You are not working up to your potential" was the tune I kept hearing. By the grace of God I passed all of my fall courses. Then the spring semester arrived with a major adult-health nursing course. I was out of my element and no longer able to "get by" on previous knowl-edge. "You are not working up to your potential," I heard again after failing the first test.

Did I want to be a nurse? How much time and energy was I willing to give to a nursing career? These were tough questions, but all my answers affirmed my desire to become a nurse; however, I could not do it by myself. God put a high-school acquaintance in my path. Jeanne was a practicing Christian actively involved in the Campus Life ministry. Since we were both nursing majors, we had taken several prerequisite classes together. God kept putting Jeanne in my life to encourage me and to remind me of the need to follow the teachings of Christ.

Jeanne offered to study with me to help me pass the adult nursing tests. She would come knocking on my door, kindly insisting that we go to the library to study. She never criticized my life, but she openly shared her involvement in campus ministries. Slowly my grades improved, and much to the surprise of the nursing faculty, I passed the course.

From that point, I determined that I needed to revamp my life. Breaking away from friends and activities was painful. "You have changed," many friends commented. Jeanne and I continued our friendship and graduated together. God continued to use Jeanne in my life as we returned to our hometown and worked together as night nurses in the ICU. Her influence helped strengthen my commitment to God and has followed me for the past 25 years of my career.

Jeanne stayed in our hometown and continued to work as a nurse, but God had different plans for my life. With a renewed commitment to the Lord, I moved to a major medical center, earned my MSN, and became active in an evangelical church. Being surrounded by Christians prepared me to be ready when God called a man from Mississippi into my life. God continued to open doors, and I began teaching at a private Baptist college.

I've now come full circle, teaching an adult health course and working with students who struggle to find their way in nursing school. I don't tell students that they aren't working up to their potential, but rather encourage them to form relationships with other students who can become their "faithful friend." God does use others in our lives in many and mysterious ways.

Perfume and incense bring joy to the heart, and the pleasantness of one's friend springs from his earnest counsel. Proverbs 27:9 NIV

. . . .

IT'S EASIER TO STEER A MOVING SHIP

Lloyd J. Davis
Professor of Mathematics
and Physics
Montreat College
Montreat, North Carolina

I GREW UP in northeast Ohio. Though I was quite active in a church of a mainline denomination, I do not recall ever coming to an understanding of the gospel. I was later to learn that some refer to that geographical area as "a hotbed of evangelical rest"! A youth conference that I attended the summer before beginning college brought me to the realization that Christianity had more substance than I had thought. Unfortunately, I was still unable to discover what was missing from my life of "faith."

I could not afford to attend either of my first two choices of university and so settled for a state university that was highly rated for both mathematics and physics. Off to Miami University I went to major in physics and to start reading the Bible for the first time. Although I did not know it then, God was *steering* me to where He wanted me.

I began a regular regimen of arising early and reading the Bible (Revelation sounded exciting!). A resident assistant down the hall found that I was interested in learning more about the Bible and invited me to join him on Sunday mornings for a Bible study sponsored by InterVarsity Christian Fellowship. The study was led by Dr. Bill Wilson, the IV advisor and a botany professor.

Dr. Wilson's teaching in the Gospel of John opened the Bible to me as never before, and I am sure the Holy Spirit was also working in me as never before. The realization that Jesus died for ME and MY sins, and that accepting that free gift was all God wanted from me in order to enter into a relationship with Him, came early in the second semester of my freshman year. By the end of the year I felt that I had grown ten feet tall spiritually! I could now see that God was *steering* me as I moved toward the goal of a college education, but He had much more in store for me than a mere education.

I continued to grow in Christ through my undergraduate years; as I approached graduation, I had to decide either to study physics in graduate school or to enter the seminary. It was tempting to just sit down and wait for God's direction, but Dr. Wilson pointed out that *it is easier to steer a moving ship*. God wanted me to move in some direction so that He could change it if He wanted to. That is a lesson about finding the will of God that I have never forgotten, and I am thankful for the opportunities I've had to share it with my students. God did *steer* me. I was accepted into Purdue University to study physics, and the only seminary from which I requested an application never responded.

I think Abraham's servant, sent to find a wife for Isaac, said it best:

I being in the way, the Lord led me. Genesis 24:27 KJV

. . . .

THE FAST TRACK
OR THE RIGHT PATH?

Del Rey Loven
Professor of Visual Art
Judson College
Elgin, Illinois

I HAD BEEN on the fast track to art world success as a painter. At age 20 I already had the B.F.A. degree, a warehouse loft art studio, a day job at an art museum, gallery representation in New York City, and my name in some prominent art magazines. But I didn't have Christ and His life-transforming Truth.

Then God mercifully brought several Christian people into my life; at age 21, I received Christ as my Lord and Savior. Almost every day thereafter I devoted time to earnest prayer for direction in my life. Could an art background be of any use to God?

Just four weeks after I received Christ, I felt strongly impressed that I should go to graduate school and become an art teacher. Immediately I applied to a prominent art college on the other side of the country, and within the month learned that I was one of only seven applicants, out of nearly two hundred, to be accepted. Also, I would receive a fellowship to cover all tuition.

When I told my Christian friends that I was going to begin graduate studies in painting, they gave me many spiritual reasons why this move was risky, and possibly not God's will. Their words made sense and raised doubts. Still I felt something calling me onward. Whatever happens, I thought, put Christ first and you'll be all right. But when would I know for sure if I was choosing the right path?

Upon arriving at that secular art college, I sought out every other Christian student, and together we formed a group and started a weekly Bible study. Eventually one professor and several students found Christ through our witness. In addition to my formal graduate studies, I devoted time to night classes at a local Bible school and became active in a wonderful church.

I continually struggled to find the balance between my commitment to putting Christ first and my responsibility to my graduate studies. During the final semester I realized that I had given a lot of time to fellowship and ministry. Had I done the right thing? The professors gave me high marks, and the degree was conferred. But no doors to teach opened for me. I was baffled. Had this been God's leading after all?

I found work as an artist for the Mayor's Office of Baltimore. There I made paintings for public buildings, and took time to share Christ with fellow artists, two of whom came to Christ. Two years later a door finally opened for me to teach full-time at a Christian liberal-arts college. The interview required a personal testimony of salvation. I told them how Christ had transformed me from a self-glorifying wretch into an artist with a message of hope. They heard how Christ had worked through me to reach family, friends, classmates, and co-workers. To my wonder, this appeared to interest them as much as my résumé and art portfolio. That interview launched a thrilling teaching career which, in twenty-five years, has brought me into the lives of over 6,000 students on three campuses!

Did I follow the right path as a new convert to Christ, risking everything to go to graduate school? Only years later could I look back and see how God was giving me not just a career path, but a faith journey. He has touched lives through me when I've put Him first. He was leading all along.

Seek ye first the kingdom of God, and his righteousness; and all these things shall be added unto you. Matthew 6:33 KJV

. . . .

REVERING HIS SAINTS AND TRUSTING HIS WORD

Rex M. Rogers
President
Cornerstone University
Grand Rapids, Michigan

ONE OF MY FONDEST MEMORIES from my college days comes from Theology 101 with Dr. Mead Armstrong. Theology was a required course and most students didn't like it. I did, but not because I was a spiritual giant. I'd been blessed with loving, dedicated Christian parents who led me to saving faith in Jesus Christ at age six and then for the next twelve years took me to every church activity one could imagine. I "did time" for nine years in a row at church camp. When it came to church experience, I'd been there, done that.

But I was bursting with questions about Creation, dinosaurs, prophecy, the Flood, TULIP, inspiration, free will, civil religion, the Trinity, nuclear weapons, infant salvation, capitalism, Christian liberty, cultural relativism, modernity, and the number of angels who could fit on a pin. You name it; in Theology 101 I asked it.

I didn't know what to call it then, but I was full of doubts. Not doubt about God's existence—the idea of God never troubled me. But I questioned Christianity and doubted that I really could be saved. My doubts were a combination of a weak faith and a rationalistic mind. I wanted to know if the Christian faith could stand the test of point-blank questions—ones that had rattled my Sunday-school teachers and ones I mistakenly thought would foil my theology professor.

Poor Dr. Armstrong was the target for all this youthful curiosity and confusion. Five days a week in that quarter-system class he patiently and thoroughly answered my questions. A seemingly unlimited font of quoted Scripture graced every answer. What I learned in Theology 101 was not another man's opinion but biblical doctrine. I can yet see him quoting Scripture and can still quote many of those verses myself.

When at last my colleagues and I had finally pressed Dr. Armstrong to the limits of his considerable Bible knowledge, he'd quote Deuteronomy 29:29, telling us to have faith in the sovereign God. This final lesson was the greatest one of all. In Theology 101 I learned to revere one of God's saints; but even more importantly, I learned to trust God and to examine the revealed Word for answers.

The secret things belong unto the LORD our God: but those things which are revealed belong unto us and to our children for ever, that we may do all the words of this law. Deuteronomy 29:29 KJV

. . . .

"LIFE IS RELIGION"

Harry Van Dyke
Professor of History
Redeemer University College
Ancaster, Ontario

IT WAS IN MY SECOND WEEK at college. I was standing at my locker when a professor walked by, then stopped. "Hi!" said Dr. H. Evan Runner. "You're from Canada, right? What brings you to our campus here in the Midwest?" His friendly face and smiling eyes encouraged me to say what was on my heart. "Well, sir, I graduated from a public high school and am tired of fighting my teachers. I want to learn a Christian approach to history."

My mood in those days was a mixture of expectation and apprehension. Was this the place where God called me? I had given up a four-year tuition scholarship at a secular university in order to attend our denominational college. Dr. Runner looked me straight in the face, gently poked his finger at my chest, and said, "Come to our club! We meet this Thursday at 8 P.M."

Of course I went. And what I learned in that club was to stay with me for the rest of my life. From childhood I had known Jesus as my personal Savior—a truth that was never in doubt. Christ was the Captain of my faith. Moreover, He was the Lord over every sphere of life and the Ruler over the kings of the earth. But how that was to tie in with my work as an aspiring academic, I had only the vaguest idea.

In the club's meetings we were challenged to pursue *integral Christian scholarship*, the kind that demands thinking with "a Christian mind," engaging in academic work while guided from the very outset by a biblical worldview. We were challenged to stop being of two minds—to stop aiming to become "excellent scholars" and in addition "Christian gentlemen." Instead, we were to pursue distinctively Christian alternatives to bodies of knowledge shaped by secular presuppositions. Our eyes were opened to the *antithesis*, to the war about which C. S. Lewis once wrote: "There is no neutral ground in the universe; every square inch, every split second is claimed by God and counterclaimed by Satan." The Bible not only proclaims the message of salvation, Dr. Runner would insist, but in doing so it also *orders our thinking*. The Word of God redirects our hearts, from which flow all the issues of life—our devotional life and our friendships, but no less our practice in disciplines like psychology, economics, and history, where we learn to define concepts and master methodologies.

Runner's articulation of the possibility of integral Christian scholarship gave me direction when I needed it most. The words my mentor often used have since become a byword: *Life is religion*. Gradually he helped me see that here was the key to unlocking the gate to a more integrated life in which I bring every thought into captivity to the obedience of Christ.

Teach me Your way, O Lord; I will walk in Your truth; unite my heart to fear Your name. Psalm 86:11 NKJV

. . . .

CRISIS IN THE DORM

Louis Markos
Professor of English
Houston Baptist University
Houston, Texas

FROM THE TIME I entered first grade, my family and I were firmly entrenched in the world of white, middle-class suburbia. Aside from having a large number of Jewish friends, my elementary and high-school years were lived out in a world quite free from diversity. At eighteen, I headed out to Hamilton, New York, to attend Colgate University, a place then barely more integrated than my high school.

As did all my fellow students, I spent my freshman year in the dorm. The experience was a positive one, and I fully planned to return to the same dorm for my sophomore year—that is, until I learned that my dorm was to be converted the following year into the Harlem Renaissance Center. The apparent goal of the Center was to promote interracial living, but what it actually meant was that, come next year, most of the black students on campus would be living in my dormitory. Having little experience with diversity, and thus overcome with unfounded apprehensions and prejudices as to what it would be like to live in a majority-black dorm, I quickly chose to move to the adjacent residential complex.

When fall returned, I was well established in my new monochrome dorm and felt fully justified in my decision to move. And then something started to happen in the Harlem Renaissance Center. A black student with a passion for the Lord and for evangelism began to pray every night that God's Spirit would move throughout the black community on campus to bring both salvation and recommitment to Christ. The Lord richly answered her prayers, and the Center was soon brimming with born-again, on-fire Christians.

Attracted by the rumors I heard of this revival, I visited the Center and spent some time worshipping and studying the Bible with some wonderfully passionate believers. It wasn't long before "some time" soon became more time, which in turn became a great amount of time. In the months that followed, I discovered that there were days and weeks when I spent more time in the Harlem Renaissance Center than I did in my own dorm.

I didn't spend all that time in the Center to try to prove I was "open-minded" or so that I could boast that I was a liberal-minded person. I was there because the Lord was there and we all were truly brothers and sisters in Christ. Skin color made absolutely no difference; our spirits were the same color.

There is neither Jew nor Greek, slave nor free, male nor female, for you are all one in Christ Jesus. Galatians 3:28 NIV

THE
EIGHTH
MEETING

Saundra J. Tracy
President, Alma College

John K. McVay
Dean, Seventh-day Adventist Theological Seminary, Andrews University

Frank Ritchel Ames
Professor of Biblical Studies, Colorado Christian University

Daniel Glenn Wiggins
Professor of Computer Science, Mississippi College

Gregory A. Boyd
Senior Pastor, Woodland Hills Church

Paul D. Mayle
Professor of History, Mount Vernon Nazarene University

Viji D. George
President, Concordia College

George A. Scranton
Professor of Theatre, Seattle Pacific University

Kevin Ingram
Vice President for Institutional Advancement, Manhattan Christian College

Margaret Weber
Dean, Graduate School of Education and Psychology, Pepperdine University

PIZZA, CATECHISM, AND A CAR NAMED ANNABELLE

Saundra J. Tracy
President
Alma College
Alma, Michigan

MY HUSBAND AND I met during our undergraduate college experience at a church-related liberal-arts college. Both of us had been active in our home churches and continued our church involvement on campus. He planned to attend seminary after college and then enter the ministry. My plans were far less clear, but the last year of college was a busy and exciting time as I finished a degree and enjoyed the starry-eyed wonder of falling in love. Pausing to ponder the big questions of faith was not part of the schedule.

At the beginning of our senior year, I realized that I would need transportation in order to do my student teaching the following spring. We also would need a car after graduation in order to manage our combined jobs and graduate school schedules. However, all of our resources were committed to tuition, room, and board. We needed some additional funds, either through increased scholarships or additional earnings above our tuition needs.

At that same time, the campus chaplain happened to mention a scholarship that went unused year after year. This scholarship was awarded to students who memorized the shorter catechism of the Presbyterian Church, a lengthy document of questions and answers about faith and reformed theology, and who wrote a scholarly paper on a related topic.

I must admit that the exercise had little appeal, but it was something my fiancé and I could do together and might result in a $200 scholarship for each of us. The combined $400 saved from tuition dollars would be enough to purchase a used car.

And so we embarked upon a fall and winter of memorizing the catechism. Our Friday night dates often revolved around a pizza and catechism questions. We delighted in trying to trip each other up with the most difficult questions. In February, we each presented ourselves to the chaplain for the test. With paper in hand and the catechism firmly in mind, we passed the questioning with flying colors. A few weeks later, we were the proud owners of Annabelle, our very used, seafoam-green Chevrolet, and $400 of scholarships had been added to our college accounts.

Annabelle is long gone, but the foundation of faith we developed as individuals and as a couple through that study of the catechism has taken us through life together. In many ways, it was the culmination of the questioning and growth that occurred in our college years. College was a time when I questioned and explored my religious convictions in many ways. But those months of study brought me back to the foundations of faith. Just like the senior project required in my major, the catechism exercise was the senior capstone experience of my college faith journey.

For the LORD gives wisdom, and from his mouth come knowledge and understanding. Proverbs 2:6 NIV

. . . .

THE FILTHY FLAT

John K. McVay
Dean
Seventh-day Adventist
Theological Seminary
Andrews University
Berrien Springs, Michigan

I REACHED DOWN to the carpet in our newly acquired lodgings and pulled up a tangled collection of long hairs. My stomach churned. How could it be? The decision to come to Sheffield, England, for graduate school had been a prayerful one. The doors had continued to open, and I had walked through them—with my wife and young son in tow.

All of that certainty now seemed to have been presumption. Our belongings, carefully shipped long before our own departure, were weeks late. We were having difficulty finding a car to buy and, worst of all, the two-room flat rented on our behalf was absolutely filthy—no place for a one-year-old child. A couple of uncomfortable nights at the YMCA and some commercial cleaning did not erase the suspicion that we had made a big mistake. And this was confirmed by the discovery that a two-room flat, a one-year-old child, and graduate research were less than a winning combination. The despair in my own heart was reflected in Pam's face and echoed, I am ashamed to say, in our prayers.

To try to pull ourselves out of despondency, we took an afternoon trip into the Peak District National Park near Sheffield. The marvelous scenery and picture-book villages eased our depression and gave birth to a silly dream. In Castleton, under the shadow of Peveril Castle, the question struck: "What would it be like to live out here?" We asked around and someone recommended that we quiz the local grocer. He responded that a neighbor of his, a barrister, was leaving for a teaching assignment in Malaysia and needed someone to rent his house for a time. We asked for his name and telephone number. The grocer refused our request, as personal information was carefully guarded in that tourist area. So we left the little store with fresh frustration. We had walked two or three blocks away when the thought came to me that I should take the grocer my business card. So we returned and I presented my card with a scrawled note and a telephone number, the only one we knew in Sheffield.

The next day we were near that telephone for all of ten minutes. During that time it rang. It was the barrister. "Could you come out this evening and examine the house?" Could we?! In short order we were ensconced in a lovely country house, "Schoolhouse," with all the comforts of home, sited in one of the most picturesque valleys in Derbyshire. Our spacious, new quarters cost about the same as the small urban flat. And at the top of a very long and winding staircase was an isolated study.

Do not worry about anything, but in everything by prayer and supplication with thanksgiving let your requests be made known to God. Philippians 4:6 NRSV

· ·

THE CARD THAT CHANGED MY CAREER

Frank Ritchel Ames
Professor of Biblical Studies
Colorado Christian University
Lakewood, Colorado

THE CARD CAME during my first year of seminary. I had completed an undergraduate degree in biblical studies and was enrolled as a divinity student in standard introductory courses, including elementary Hebrew. I was preparing for a pastoral ministry, but God intended something else and used a get-well card to redirect my steps.

The Hebrew course proved to be interesting but much more difficult than I had anticipated, and I soon discovered that I needed to devote extra time and effort to memorizing vocabulary words, reviewing paradigms, and learning the rules of grammar. I loved the language and enjoyed the course, but I had to work hard to keep up with the professor. The class met early in the morning four times per week, and students who missed two or three classes found it difficult to catch up. A number of students found it impossible and had to drop the class.

I felt a cold coming on early in the winter quarter. It quickly developed into something worse, and soon I was laid up at home taking antibiotics to fight a stubborn infection. After missing a few classes, I knew that I was behind; after missing a few more, I thought that I could never catch up. Then I received the card that changed my career. It was from my Hebrew professor. The card was brief, expressed a concern for my health, and included instructions for completing the assignments. Motivated by this simple, thoughtful gesture, and guided by the professor's instructions, I managed to complete the assignments and to catch up to the rest of the class.

Through this experience I discovered an interest and an ability that I had not recognized, and I began to devote more time to the language. The professor encouraged me to take additional courses in the field. So in the spring quarter of that first year I registered for Aramaic as well as Hebrew. Other courses in Old Testament followed, and two years later the seminary invited me to serve as a Hebrew fellow and to teach the introductory Hebrew course.

I have now taught classical Hebrew and Old Testament for more than twenty years. I had never at first imagined that I would make a career of it or that someday I would be a professor at a Christian liberal arts college. I had planned to be a pastor, but God directed me to teach, and God used a caring professor and a simple card to change my plans.

The human mind plans the way, but the LORD directs the steps. Proverbs 16:9 NRSV

· ·

PUT TO THE TEST

Daniel Glenn Wiggins
Professor of Computer Science
Mississippi College
Clinton, Mississippi

MY FIRST EXPERIENCES in college were in a large state university. Since I grew up in a small rural community of family and friends, one of those places where everyone knows everyone else, I was anxious about the many adjustments I would be facing in my first year of university life.

That first year went much better than I had expected. I met many new people with whom I developed lasting friendships. My grades were actually good, considering I prepared very little for class and spent most of my time indulging myself in something other than scholarly pursuits. To help with the cost of my education, I worked part-time in the college cafeteria. Obviously, my college life was, as it is for most students today, very busy.

As each semester passed, coursework got more demanding and my extracurricular activities increased. I was doing well in classes, but not as well as I had hoped. My expectations for myself were exceeding my capabilities. I was so stressed over my coursework and tests that I became ill before my exams.

One morning as I was trying to eat breakfast before a major French exam, I was having the usual anxiety. As a Christian, I believed that if I asked in faith, God would help me make it through an exam. However, this time God reminded me—in that still, small, quiet way He often uses to communicate with us—that "His strength was made perfect in my weakness." A verse from Philippians came to mind: *"Forgetting what is behind and straining toward what is ahead, I press on toward the goal to win the prize for which God has called me heavenward in Christ Jesus."*

I began to focus on what I knew all along. I had heard it expressed many times in this verse, in the advice of my professors, and in the wise counsel of my parents. "Prioritize your life. Put things in the proper order. Put God first, then focus on what you are here for. Study each day, do assignments promptly, and, when possible, actually work ahead. When an exam is imminent, start studying days in advance for an hour or so each day." The keys are keeping up with assignments and not losing a sense of priorities. I believed this, but I had not acted on it.

God got my attention. I began to heed that advice and put my faith into action. I started viewing tests as a reward, a challenge, a goal, something to be accomplished. My grades improved, and I found that I had plenty of time for other things. God is telling us to prioritize. He who created everything out of nothing can certainly help us order our steps throughout life.

Forgetting what is behind and straining toward what is ahead, I press on toward the goal to win the prize for which God has called me heavenward in Christ Jesus. Philippians 3:13, 14 NIV

FINDING THE GOD-FORSAKEN GOD

Gregory A. Boyd
Senior Pastor
Woodland Hills Church
St. Paul, Minnesota

FOR SEVERAL YEARS an obsession with suffering and death led me to reject a belief in God, despite my Catholic upbringing. After a profound encounter with Jesus Christ at the age of seventeen, I temporarily set this question aside. But within a year the question had returned with a vengeance.

It was not the problem of evil alone that caused me to lose my faith my first year in college. Classes in biology, philosophy, and the Bible as literature, taught from an entirely naturalistic perspective, had already been chipping away at my faith. I had also become very interested in and horrified by the reality of the Holocaust. By my second year in college, I was a re-convert to atheism.

My return to the Lord began in an astronomy lab on a cool October night. As we viewed the stars through a telescope and discussed the mind-boggling expanse of the cosmos, I thought to myself, "Someone must have created all this: There must be a God." But immediately a scene from the movie "Sophie's Choice" flashed before my mind. A mother had just arrived at Auschwitz and, as a form of amusement for a Nazi guard, was forced to choose which of her two children would be sent to the gas chambers. "But there can be no God!" my mind screamed.

As I walked back to my car, I found myself shouting aloud at the sky. "How can you sit up there and watch this nightmare?! Why can't your concern for our suffering be as great as your creation? Why can't you match your power with an equally impressive love? Why don't you experience for yourself the horror of being a little child ripped from her mother's arm?"

As I sat behind my cold steering wheel, I finished my tirade with a tormented, desperate, and tearful whisper: "Are you listening? Do you care?"

Then I recalled a verse from the Bible: "My God, my God, why have you forsaken me?" And it occurred to me: This is something God *Himself* uttered!

It was a 2,000-year-old truth that felt like a fresh new revelation. On the cross, God Himself experienced God-forsakenness! Jesus Christ bore the sin of the world, and all the punishment for that sin, because He loves. His love is as infinite as His power! This was the God for whom my heart yearned.

Though it would take several more years of wrestling through difficult intellectual issues before my Christian faith was solid, my heart could now find rest. It rested in the beauty of a Creator who experienced our nightmares on the inside in order to usher us into the eternal dream He has always had for us.

And about the ninth hour Jesus cried out with a loud voice, saying, "Eli, Eli, lama sabachthani?" that is, "My God, My God, why have You forsaken Me?" Matthew 27:46 NKJV

. . . .

SERVUS SERVORUM

Paul D. Mayle
Professor of History
Mount Vernon Nazarene University
Mount Vernon, Ohio

I HAD LEARNED early on the wisdom of paying close attention in class. Nowhere did this turn out to be more important than in "The History of Early Christianity," a course I took as an elective when I was an undergraduate at a state university.

I should have known better than to take a course offered by a professor I knew personally. He was a member of my church, attended my father's Sunday-school class, and served as a church organist. I often warmed a familiar chair in his office where I solicited and received wise advice while adjusting to the challenges of college life during my freshman year. He never complained about the amount of time I took from his busy schedule, nor did he point out the obvious fact that he was not my official advisor and was not obliged to help every bewildered freshman who darkened his doorway.

I felt I owed it to him to take one of his classes after I had completed my early semesters of study. I soon discovered something that had never come to light in any of our previous meetings. In class he had a rather unpleasant habit of singling out certain students and posing questions for which he expected proper responses. Given our mutual familiarity, this meant in practice that an inordinate share of his queries seemed to come my way. The questions typically ranged far and wide across the course readings.

One day he asked me to translate the Latin phrase *servus servorum*. I had never encountered that expression, but I had no recourse but to follow the script literally and managed to blurt out: "servant of the servants." My effort was acknowledged with an approving smile, and the class moved on.

Standing right before me, I have come to understand, was a living example of that Latin phrase. I have since forgotten what transpired in the remainder of that class, but the words stuck. And they seem to resound the loudest when I think about my relationships with others—whether with my wife, colleagues, students, or especially those with whom I share semesters at the University of Debrecen in eastern Hungary.

I strive to follow the example of my professor, who modeled what it means to be a servant of the servants. And I wish to live in such a way so as to someday hear, "Well done, good and faithful servant!"

Have this attitude in yourselves which was also in Christ Jesus, who, although He existed in the form of God, did not regard equality with God a thing to be grasped, but emptied Himself, taking the form of a bond-servant, and being made in the likeness of men. Being found in appearance as a man, He humbled Himself by becoming obedient to the point of death, even death on a cross. Philippians 2:5-8 NASB

A CHRISTIAN TO ALL PEOPLE

Viji D. George
President
Concordia College
Bronxville, New York

I REMEMBER WALKING through the campus in those early days enveloped in a fog. I was a new foreign student from India, and each day brought new surprises. Apart from the usual cultural and educational adjustments that I needed to make, the most interesting challenge was being in an environment where the majority of people were Christians.

As a Christian growing up in India, I was very used to being a part of a religious minority (fewer than two percent of Indians are Christians). Suddenly the dominant world-view in my new home was Christian. This sudden shift had both its advantages and disadvantages. First, it was comforting to be in a community of believers who shared my world-view and faith perspectives. It was a place to comfortably grow spiritually and not be hindered by what others thought or felt about my fundamental beliefs or my desire to claim Christ as the Savior.

The downside was that I also found I was losing my sense of understanding, tolerance, and compassion. Until then, I had to be able to coexist with people from other faith traditions—primarily Hindus and Muslims. But now, I found myself slowly losing that skill set. I wasn't as willing and/or able to see and treat all of God's creation as a part of His family. We as Christians are blessed, for we have heard and responded to God's call from the cross. It is not some innate goodness in us that makes us deserving to be the chosen people. It is purely a function of God's grace. Though I knew this, my world was slowly but surely being confined more and more to fellow believers. I did not make the time to do what I used to do when I was growing up in India.

It wasn't until I was ready to graduate that I began to realize that as a Christian I am called to be a living witness to all people. Therefore I must first understand and firmly believe that we are *all* created in God's image and that He desires to restore that lost image in us through Christ.

Empowered by this understanding, I was slowly able to reclaim my interest in people from all walks of life and faith traditions. Soon I began to discover the pleasure and joy that comes from trying to be a part of others' lives in a way that truly makes a difference in their daily walk.

I found that once this relational bond is in place, it is much easier to be a living witness to my faith in Christ, not only by what I say, but also by what I do.

But we all, with unveiled face, beholding as in a mirror the glory of the Lord, are being transformed into the same image from glory to glory, just as by the Spirit of the Lord. 2 Corinthians 3:18 NKJV

A PLAQUE OF GRACE

George A. Scranton
Professor of Theatre
Seattle Pacific University
Seattle, Washington

AS A HIGH-SCHOOL SENIOR, I was ill-prepared to pursue a college education without the grace of God. I grew up in an uneducated home. My father had a second-grade education, and my mother had a sixth-grade education. The only "books" I ever saw my father read were comic books and his King James Version of the Bible.

I told my high-school counselor that I wanted to go to college. "Well, George," he said, "I suggest that you get a job at the local plywood mill, find a nice girl to marry, and settle down, because *you aren't college material.*" (The emphasis is undoubtedly mine, but that is what I heard.) Based on the data which he held in his hand, he was correct—objectively. But objectivity didn't include God's grace, a series of mentors, involvement in the arts, and a little plaque.

In spite of the counsel, I attended Briercrest Bible Institute. After graduation from Bible School, I wanted to finish my Bachelor of Arts degree at Seattle Pacific College. I quickly found that I was still under-prepared for the intensity, complexity, and downright difficulty of college academics.

That first quarter, however, I was confronted by a cardboard plaque that became a constant reminder of God's grace. Every day as I left my psychology class and made my way down the stairs, I would look above the doorway at the bottom of the stairs. Someone had thumb-tacked there an insignificant little 4" x 6" plaque which simply read, "Study to show thyself approved unto God. . . ." I knew the rest of the Bible verse, but that single phrase kept echoing in my head as I went about my work that quarter. I had come to the unwelcome realization that it seemed to take me longer to do assignments than anyone else, so I had to "study" more just to survive.

The plaque became an ever-present reminder that I needed to study to show myself "approved unto God." I couldn't "waste" time as I thought my roommate (salutatorian of his high-school class) was able to do. "Study . . ." persistently resounded in my head during that first quarter when, on average, I stayed up all night twice a week to study. I barely survived that first quarter of my college career, and it took nearly four more years of "Study . . ." to complete the B.A. degree.

I continued to hear that "still small voice" repeat "Study . . ." throughout an M.A. in Biblical Literature. I heard it while pursuing a second M.A. in Theatre History and Criticism. Eventually, through the grace of God, and still hearing 2 Timothy 2:15, I completed a Ph.D. in Theology and Theatre.

From all his objective data, my high-school counselor was correct. But he could not have foreseen the grace of God working through a little plaque that continues to be a "still small voice" reminding me of what I need to do to become who God continues to call me to become.

Study to shew thyself approved unto God, a workman that needeth not to be ashamed, rightly dividing the word of truth. 2 Timothy 2:15 KJV

THE FIRE OF GOD'S LEADING

Kevin Ingram
Vice President
for Institutional Advancement
Manhattan Christian College
Manhattan, Kansas

MY RETURN HOME from my first year of college at the University of Alabama coincided with the beginning of a revival at my home church. I wasn't very spiritually focused at the time, and I attended the first night only because our church choir director asked me to share a solo I had first performed with the choir while in high school. It was the performing that got me there, but when I heard the speaker, I was hooked. Dr. Bill Lown was then president of Manhattan Christian College. Not only did his sermons capture my heart and soul, but he challenged me to use my talents for the Lord. God's gentle nudging had begun.

God worked through the tough love and grace of my parents during this time of transition from adolescent wandering to purposeful service. He taught me through their example of commitment to Christ and His church. He nurtured me during many heart-to-heart talks with my father about my future and career goals.

My minister, an alumnus of MCC, had begun planting and watering seeds many years before. He was a part of God's nudging, along with many others—the youth directors of our church, a fellow construction worker, a sister who challenged me in my faith, and all the loving people of my home church.

Little did I know that I was on my way to a life of ministry. God was using many people to lead me exactly where He wanted me to go. I just needed to start following!

A two-week trip to the Holy Lands was the time of harvest. All the seeds that had been planted in my heart were coming to fruit. While there, I made the decision to follow God's leading. The decision took me to Kansas, some 1,100 miles away from home, to attend Manhattan Christian College.

It was a difficult transition. The miles away from family made it tough, as did the climate. When we left Alabama to head to Kansas in January of 1981, it was 81 degrees. When we arrived a day later, it was 18 degrees. But God was building a fire in me that was overcoming the coldness that had slowly settled in my heart.

That fire is still burning. It has continued during ministries in Oakley, Kansas, and Great Bend, Kansas. Today it has come full circle. Following God's leading has brought me back where I started—I now serve the Lord at Manhattan Christian College.

Others, like seed sown on good soil, hear the word, accept it, and produce a crop—thirty, sixty or even a hundred times what was sown. Mark 4:20 NIV

· ·

TAKING A CHANCE

Margaret Weber
Dean
Graduate School of Education
and Psychology
Pepperdine University
Malibu, California

MY LITERATURE PROFESSOR was known to publicly ridicule students for their writing style, their personal thoughts, and especially their faith. He had made it very clear that he held little regard for Christian ideals, which presented a great dilemma when we were studying *The Scarlet Letter*.

The teacher required us to write an essay responding to this question: "If you were a judge in the case against Hester Prynne, what would have been your verdict?" I wrestled with my approach for several days. Would I face ridicule if I used a biblical perspective? How would it affect my grade?

The essay question, I felt, was a moral one. Should Hester be punished for her actions, and why was her male companion not suffering the same charges? When faced with a moral issue, I have always turned to the Bible for guidance. How could I complete this assignment without referring to the one source I knew held the truth?

As I put pen to paper and tried to take the secular approach, nothing came. Finally, I followed my heart and used the passage in John 8 about an adulterous woman who was brought before Jesus for judgment. When presented with the question of whether the woman should be stoned according to the Law of Moses, Jesus answered: "If any one of you is without sin, let him be the first to throw a stone at her." One by one, the crowd diminished until only Jesus and the woman remained. "Go now," he said to her, "and leave your life of sin."

The day soon arrived when our papers were to be handed back. Hesitantly, I entered the classroom and slipped quietly to my desk as the bell rang. In a booming voice, the professor said, "Miss Price, would you come forward and read your essay to the class?" With my heart pounding, I slowly walked to the front of the room and read the first few lines of my essay. "Speak up," the professor bellowed. I tried to find my voice and continued.

Upon completion of my reading, the professor asked how many agreed with my approach. Several hands went up. He then asked how many knew the Bible story I had referenced. Fewer hands went up. Then the tongue-lashing began. But, surprisingly, it was not aimed at me. Rather, he began a discussion about standing up for your beliefs, presenting your argument, and supporting it. He made it known that although he did not agree with my premise, I had presented a clear verdict with a well-developed thesis. He dismissed the class, telling the other students to rewrite their papers.

That day I realized that following my conscience was critical to my writing. In future assignments I did not always walk away with the "A," but I maintained the courage to share my beliefs and support my arguments within a biblical context.

Our conscience testifies that we have conducted ourselves . . . in the holiness and sincerity that are from God. We have done so not according to worldly wisdom but according to God's grace. 2 Corinthians 1:12 NIV

THE NINETH MEETING

Kenneth S. Hemphill
National Strategist, "Empowering Kingdom Growth," Southern Baptist Convention

Michele M. Willingham
Dean, School of Professional Studies, Hope International University

Foy D. Mills, Jr.
Professor of Agricultural and Environmental Sciences, Abilene Christian University

Cordell P. Schulten
Associate Professor of Interdisciplinary Studies, Missouri Baptist University

Mark A. Brister
President, Oklahoma Baptist University

Estelle Owens
Professor of History, Wayland Baptist University

Charles W. Herman
Professor of History, University of Sioux Falls

Bruce Murphy
President, Northwestern College

Donald B. DeYoung
Professor of Physics, Grace College

Ginger Ketting-Weller
Vice President for Academic Administration, Walla Walla College

HANGING UP
THE CLEATS

Kenneth S. Hemphill
National Strategist
"Empowering Kingdom Growth"
Southern Baptist Convention
Nashville, Tennessee

I ATTENDED Wake Forest University on a full athletic scholarship. The question of where I might play college athletics was never really in doubt. My father was a Baptist preacher who was proud of his roots. For a brief moment, I did consider playing for Duke University. I even called my father from the Duke campus to ask if he could pull for a son playing for Duke. He responded in no uncertain terms. For him it was a simple matter—no self-respecting Baptist would play for a Methodist school.

My football career at Wake Forest got off to an outstanding start. Our freshman team was undefeated, and I was written up in a sports magazine. I thought everything was on track for an outstanding college career. After my freshman year, Wake experienced one of its many coaching shake-ups. The coach who recruited me left, and I was shifted from defense to offense. Later, I was returned to my preferred position of linebacker, but I had missed a spring practice and had dropped down the depth charts. I did, nonetheless, make the traveling squad as a sophomore and experienced reasonable playing time.

As my college career wore on, I began to discover that college football and a pro career no longer had the same allure. God had begun to stir my heart concerning full-time Christian service. I spoke frequently at Fellowship of Christian Athletes events and began to serve as part-time youth pastor at a local church. In the meantime, Wake had hired a new head coach, and it became obvious that he was looking to the future. Playing time for upperclassmen like me would be scarce.

I was faced with one of the most difficult decisions of my young life. By this time, I had been called to full-time Christian service and had also asked Paula to be my wife. We were to be wed the summer before my senior year. We had calculated our living expenses and knew we could survive on the stipend she received through her training to be a cytotechnologist, supplemented by my part-time pay and my athletic scholarship. But now I was contemplating quitting football and giving up my athletic scholarship.

It wasn't an easy choice, but I finally decided I wouldn't return for football my senior year. We would proceed with the wedding as planned. It is true that love is blind, and it can't add too well either. Money was a problem. But these stressful circumstances gave us the opportunity to share an unusual witness and to see God provide for our needs in an unexpected way.

Because of the coaching change, several seniors had decided to hang up their cleats. Many of them were attempting to keep their scholarships even though they didn't plan to play. I never contemplated such an action. My father taught me that you don't take what you don't earn. I will never forget the look on the coach's face when I told him that I was quitting football and that I planned to give up my scholarship.

The local sports columnist heard about my story and decided to do an article about the athletes who had chosen to quit. I think I may have been the only one who voluntarily gave up the scholarship. The writer asked me about my impending marriage and how I would handle the finances without the scholarship. My response was simple, but full of faith. I told her the Lord would provide for our needs. And He did provide! Days later the university awarded me a full academic scholarship for my senior year. Another news article, announcing this event, appeared just a few days after the sports article.

What a faith experience, and a faith testimony, for an aspiring young preacher and his wife-to-be. God is faithful to provide for our needs and to honor His own name.

And my God will meet all your needs according to his glorious riches in Christ Jesus. Philippians 4:19 NIV

. . . .

SPEAKING TRUTH IN LOVE

Michele M. Willingham
Dean
School of Professional Studies
Hope International University
Fullerton, California

"WE WANT YOU to return as an RA next year, but . . . ." My two Residence Hall Directors proceeded to point out a couple of my more unpleasant personality traits. They explained, in rather painful detail, how these flaws interfered with my relationships and my effectiveness as a student leader. I was devastated. If they wanted me to continue as a Resident Assistant, surely it was because I was good at it. So why were they delving into my personal problems?

"Sure," I admitted to them. "I can be sarcastic. But it's all in fun. Well . . . yes, I can get pretty intense and uptight, and sometimes I let that get the best of me. But if people weren't so annoying all the time, I wouldn't lose my cool and bite their heads off!" How easy it was to blame my shortcomings and bad behavior on other people and things outside myself. But Shane and Phyllis were willing to "speak the truth in love," and I learned some critically important and rather amazing things about myself and about God that day and in the year that followed.

With the help of a counselor that my Christian college provided, I began to heal from the emotional pain and insecurity that I had struggled with throughout most of my teenage and young-adult life. Through the woman's care and nurture, I found relief from the psychological injuries of childhood. What a blessing it was to have some of those burdens lifted! Good relationships with others developed much more easily.

I also experienced spiritual healing as the amazing love and grace of God were demonstrated in very real and tangible ways by the Residence Hall Directors, my counselor, and other faculty and staff at my school. A relatively new Christian when I started college, I had immersed myself in classes, activities, and leadership. By this time I'd studied a great deal about God's love and grace. This lesson, however, was one best taught to me in person. It came from real people—healthy, mature Christians—demonstrating God's grace to me.

My RHDs accepted and appreciated me for who I was—gifted but flawed, capable but injured. And they encouraged me to become more. They acted in my very best interests. They honestly confronted me about what I was lacking, knowing the result would bring out more of Christ in me. Good friends to this day, I have never forgotten the gift Shane and Phyllis gave me and their willingness to invest themselves in my growth. Now I seek to honor their investment by practicing God's grace in very tangible ways in all that I do as well.

But to each one of us grace was given according to the measure of Christ's gift . . . speaking the truth in love, we are to grow up in all aspects into Him who is the head, even Christ. Ephesians 4:7, 15 NASB

· ·

COUNSEL BY
THE TRACTOR

Foy D. Mills, Jr.
Professor of Agricultural
and Environmental Sciences
Abilene Christian University
Abilene, Texas

I HAD HAD ENOUGH! As I awoke that October morning, I decided I was going home.

College had gotten off to a wonderful start. I had moved twenty-five miles from home, but it might as well have been five thousand. A first-generation college student, I had dreamed about all the things I would do at Lubbock Christian College. However, I hadn't envisioned this autumn morning.

Now it was the middle of pledge week. The previous five days had created so much internal turmoil that I shouldn't have been surprised by the emotional outburst that morning. My pledge brothers, whom I had dragged out of bed the past several mornings for our 5:30 A.M. workout, could not budge me from mine. Ignoring them, I rolled over, exhausted, and went back to sleep.

Shortly, my pledge master arrived. I angrily told him that he just didn't understand and should leave me alone. I crawled out of bed, showered, dressed, and headed for my car. I had not seen my parents in six weeks. I didn't know where Daddy would be that morning, but I knew where to find Momma.

Thirty minutes later, I arrived at the bank where my mother worked. Startled, she walked out from behind her cashier's window to greet me. My words were few. "I have had it with school, and I need to talk to Daddy. Where is he?" I bent down to hug her neck as she told me that Daddy was plowing the south quarter at my grandparents' old homestead.

I rehearsed my speech as my wheels left the farm-to-market road. A cloud of dust erupted behind me as I drove the last three miles on a dirt road. Coming to a stop, I climbed out of my car. Daddy was turning the tractor around at the far end of the field. I waited.

Dust settled as Daddy brought the tractor to a stop and climbed down to greet me. Before he could speak, a torrent of words flew from my lips as angry tears streamed down my face. When my tirade came to an end, Daddy spoke words I will never forget: "You have started a great adventure with your education. Why don't you try to stick out the semester? But, if you still feel this way at Christmas, we will work it out for you to return to the farm."

Daddy's challenge to complete the semester was a surprise coming from a man who was glad to have finished high school! Swallowing my pride, I returned to school that morning and apologized to my pledge class. And I finished the semester!

I don't know if Daddy realized the profound effect his words would have on me. But I do know this: my father knew the One who "stills the storm." I am glad he did.

The disciples went and woke him, saying, "Lord, save us! We're going to drown!" He replied, "You of little faith, why are you so afraid?" Then he got up and rebuked the winds and the waves, and it was completely calm. Matthew 8:25, 26 NIV

· ·

THE THREE LONGEST YEARS

Cordell P. Schulten
Associate Professor
of Interdisciplinary Studies
Missouri Baptist University
Saint Louis, Missouri

I WAS ON THE THRESHOLD of three of the most difficult and challenging years of my life. I had come to law school at Saint Louis University married and with three small children, yet still convinced that I was heeding God's call. Succeeding was not my first concern. Survival would be sufficient. I found assurance in the story of Daniel and his companions. Though forced by their captors to study for three years in Babylon, they were preserved by God and through His strength stood firm in faith (Daniel 1).

The first year started well. My journal entries for those early months contain scattered references to "opportunities to speak to others about the things of God," "speaking at length to a 3d year student who is a Mormon," and even accounts of Bible studies with fellow law students. But, by the middle of the spring term, the journal read "preoccupied with school work and job projects . . . so no regular personal quiet time." Though I had begun my studies as a believer seeking to practice the discipline of daily devotions, the demands of law school had steadily pushed Bible reading and prayer time out of my daily routine. I started thinking less about God and more about me.

The first year of law school had indeed "scared me to death." As I entered the second year, I was well on my way to being "worked to death." My journal attests to this, since I had completely quit writing by summer. Although I had been convinced that the Lord was leading me to law school, I was no longer looking to Him to lead me through it. I began pursuing my own interests rather than seeking the best for my family. When interviews came around for summer internships, I signed up with the big firms in the hope of landing a select position. Clerking for one of the largest firms in St. Louis that summer, I was lured all the more into aspiring to a life of affluence. Unlike my hero Daniel in Babylon, I began to dine at the king's table.

My third-year experience was true to form. I was, for the most part, "bored to death." I had a prize offer to join the firm with whom I had done my internship. They even agreed to forego the ordinary rotation through their other practice areas and allowed me to plan on moving right into litigation. I was set. What I had forgotten, though, was how I had come to succeed when at first my thought had only been of survival. I was reminded through failure. I failed to win the trial advocacy competition, and I failed to attain the final class rank for which I had been striving. Through those failures, the Lord called me back to Him and gave me a renewed sense of

His grace and of my need for constant dependence upon Him. He alone had given me the grace and knowledge to succeed through my three longest years.

To these four young men God gave knowledge and understanding of all kinds of literature and learning. Daniel 1:17 NIV

. . . .

WHOM DO YOU DESIRE?

Mark A. Brister
President
Oklahoma Baptist University
Shawnee, Oklahoma

AS A COLLEGE FRESHMAN I struggled with what to do with life. The plight heightened as I went home that first college summer. Working at a good summer job, coming home, visiting friends, and retiring at night, only to repeat the process daily, left me looking for more than mere existence. There had to be more to life than this! Reared in a Christian home, I had accepted Christ. Giving Him free reign as Lord was another matter.

That summer of 1970 was a national Vietnam season. For me it became a spiritual Jesus Movement moment. The critical juncture of decision came for me in a Sunday night worship service. My home church youth minister challenged us to be hot or cold for Christ. Quit wavering. Romans 8:5-6 beckoned: Be carnal and die or spiritual and live. Choose now.

Christ accepted me. I welcomed Him. All of life changed that night—beliefs solidified, priorities switched, behaviors changed, and positive actions resulted. Prayer, Bible study, and witnessing quickly became living, vital parts of my life.

Returning to the college campus that fall challenged me, because students who had known a freshman with few spiritual concerns saw a sophomore witness. To my joy, like-minded Jesus People emerged. We passionately shared our faith in the dorm, on campus, and throughout the community; devoured the writings of Francis Schaeffer; and sought and received Christian discipleship through Campus Crusade for Christ. Local and national mission opportunities developed.

The spiritual pilgrimage was not without difficulties. Along with life's temptations and trials, there also materialized on our denominational campus those who felt the Jesus Movement was too radical. With established religious diets, they had difficulty swallowing this new flavor of Christianity. Even our religion professors looked with bewilderment at our fervency to defend the faith at all costs. I struggled to live out the Christian faith with passion in a denominational college context reluctant to receive such a fresh witness.

Psalm 73:25 became the goal of my life: There is no one I want on earth more than Him. Across the years, God has proven His faithfulness. His living Word is true.

Whom have I in heaven but thee? And there is none upon earth that I desire beside thee. Psalm 73:25 KJV

. . . .

CALLED TO A MISSION, A PLACE, A LIFESTYLE

Estelle Owens
Professor of History
Wayland Baptist University
Plainview, Texas

AS AN ADOLESCENT growing up in the First Baptist Church of Jasper, Texas, I felt God calling me into special service, though I had no clear sense of what that service would be. I thought about medical missions, but my struggles with chemistry convinced me that God must be calling me to something else!

Even before high school graduation, God had begun leading my sister and me to Wayland Baptist College in Plainview, Texas. Since I had always loved history, I chose it as my major. Although I continued to see God's hand at work in my life, I graduated with no clear understanding of what He wanted of me in terms of a career. Although I applied for several jobs, I was never hired. As the doors to various jobs closed, the doors to graduate school kept opening; so I walked through them to Baylor and then on to Auburn.

In my second year at Auburn, I was given the opportunity to teach a class. The first day I faced the thirty eager scholars, I was petrified. But it turned out to be my Damascus Road experience. At the time, it felt as if a great light shone directly upon me, the "Hallelujah Chorus" played in the background, and a voice I knew to be God's said, "Pay attention! This is my plan for you."

At last I understood. God had called me to teach. Doors opened miraculously for me to return to my alma mater as a faculty member. God assigned me a mission to educate. I encourage students to learn from their study of our collective past and enrich their own lives to honor Him. He gave me a place in which to teach—from the main campus in Plainview, to satellite campuses as far away as Alaska, to the reaches of space via Internet courses. He gave me a lifestyle as well when the man I hoped to marry chose someone else. To accomplish what God wanted in my life, He planned for me to remain single, without children of my own, so that I could more easily mentor other people's children. Striving to remain in the center of His will for my life has meant great joy coming from immense sadness.

Thirty years have passed since that day that I first faced a group of students who were my responsibility. God has taught me over and over again that seeking His will brings contentment, even in the face of adversity. His plans are perfect.

Only fear the Lord and serve Him in truth with all your heart; for consider what great things He has done for you. 1 Samuel 12:24 NASB

. . . .

THE FIFTH-YEAR JUNIOR AND THE CALL TO TEACH

Charles W. Herman
Professor of History
University of Sioux Falls
Sioux Falls, South Dakota

CAREER COUNSELORS REPORT that college students often change majors three or four times. Although cynics may say this fact reveals how fickle young adults have become, I think it shows instead how hard it is for many students to choose a career and for Christians to discern God's "calling" in their lives. In this respect, at least, I was a typical college student.

I entered college with plans to pursue a career in ministry, probably on a mission field in some remote and exotic land. To train for such a vocation, I enrolled in a missionary preparation program, and I joined every project that had a missionary emphasis: prayer groups, mission conferences, and conversations with visiting missionaries. Although I admired the women and men who served God overseas, and I spent three years preparing to follow them, I never felt "called" to be a missionary.

I spent my fourth year beyond high school studying at a community college and preaching every Sunday in a rural church. Since I was not "called" to become a foreign missionary, I thought that working with a congregation of believers might lead me to become a pastor, but it did not have that result. Although I was enriched and rewarded when people shared their lives with me, and I generally enjoyed the work that clergy do—bringing comfort and hope to discouraged people, helping troubled people overcome obstacles with God's help, giving everyone a second chance, and affirming everyone's best effort—I did not feel "called" to become a pastor.

Still searching for a career, I transferred the following year to a Christian liberal-arts college in Illinois. While most of my friends were starting graduate programs or careers, I was only a fifth-year junior. I was starting to worry, and my decision to attend this school did not seem wise. The college was not accredited, its curriculum was modest, and the faculty was often overextended. Nevertheless, it was here that God "called" me to become a college teacher.

My history professor—we had only one!—provided a splendid example for an aspiring teacher. Scholarly, hard-working, and always attentive to his students, Dr. Vos was both a mentor and a model of what a Christian professor should be. He was also instrumental in getting me a teaching position at the school in Chicago where Salvation Army officers received their training. More than any other experience during six years of college, teaching for the Salvation Army convinced me that I wanted to become a teacher at a Christian college. Preparing lectures and helping students were equally delightful tasks; and teaching in a Christian environment allowed me to combine ministry with scholarship. Did God use a mentor and on-the-job experience to "call" me into teaching? I was sure of it, and I could not have been happier.

I will instruct you and teach you the way you should go; I will counsel you with my eye upon you. . . . Many are the torments of the wicked, but steadfast love surrounds those who trust in the LORD. Be glad in the LORD and rejoice, O righteous, and shout for joy, all you upright in heart. Psalm 32:8-11 NRSV

WHAT IS BIG ENOUGH?

Bruce Murphy
President
Northwestern College
Orange City, Iowa

IT HAPPENED DURING MY JUNIOR YEAR at Wheaton College in Dr. Batson's literature class. The assignment had been to read Katherine Anne Porter's short story, "Noon Wine," and now we were discussing it. I liked Wheaton, I liked Dr. Batson, and I liked literature, but I did not anticipate the impact this one class would have on my life.

I had been raised in a strong Christian home and as a young teen had accepted God's forgiveness in Jesus Christ and committed my life to Him. But over the next few years as I settled into the evangelical youth culture, sadly and ironically, the Gospel lost something of its uniqueness and vitality for me. Not that I consciously turned away from it. On the contrary, it became so familiar that I assumed its worth without experiencing its power. But, of course, I understood little of this at the time. In fact, I understood little of it until that day in Dr. Batson's class.

"Noon Wine" is a thoughtful character study. The major figure, Mr. Thompson, is a proud man with a strong sense of duty. He did not like Mr. Hatch, a selfish, manipulative bounty hunter. In a moment of passion when Mr. Hatch attacked another man, Mr. Thompson killed Mr. Hatch. It appeared to be a justifiable killing, but Mr. Thompson could feel no peace.

Despite the "not guilty" verdict of the local court and his own attempts to defend his actions, Mr. Thompson knew in his heart that he had hated Mr. Hatch and desired him dead. A short time after the trial, overcome with guilt, Mr. Thompson put a rifle in his mouth and pulled the trigger.

That day in class Dr. Batson carefully guided our discussion of the story; then, just when we were feeling the depth of this tragedy, she stunned us with a question: What is big enough to take away Mr. Thompson's guilt?

Literally, in a flash, the power of the Gospel became real to me again.

From time to time since that day, I have struggled with the evil and tragic pain in our world, and sometimes have forgotten the depth and power of God's love for us in Christ on the Cross. But then God leads me back to "Noon Wine" and Dr. Batson's question. How thankful I am for wise, creative teachers who love learning and our Lord.

Grace to you and peace from God our Father and the Lord Jesus Christ. . . . All of us once lived among them in the passions of our flesh . . . and we were by nature children of wrath . . . . But God, who is rich in mercy, out of the great love with which he loved us . . . made us alive together with Christ—by grace you have been saved. Ephesians 1:2; 2:3-5 NRSV

· ·

WHEN THE SYSTEM ISN'T FAIR

Donald B. DeYoung
Professor of Physics
Grace College
Winona Lake, Indiana

MY UNDERGRADUATE DAYS were spent at an engineering college where there was intense competition for good grades. Lower-tier students didn't last long in the program. The course in Materials Science, which included complex metallurgy details, was especially well known for thinning our ranks.

I well remember our midterm metallurgy exam which followed long evenings of study. Double-checking the time and location, I headed for the exam with confidence and time to spare. Entering the room, however, I was surprised to find that the test had been distributed half an hour early. The older students seemed to have known this pattern of the professor and already were at work. Those of us just arriving quietly picked up test copies from the professor and got busy. The many-page test appeared quite unusual in that neither the pages nor the questions themselves were numbered. I completed the answers in the spaces provided and confidently turned in the test.

A week later when grades were posted, I was shaken by an "F" placed next to my initials. How could this possibly happen? Hours later, gathering courage, I visited the office of the professor. He retrieved my test from his file and quickly informed me that two full pages were missing from the test. He suggested that either I had illegally taken two test pages with me from the test room, or else my test copy was not complete, in which case I should have counted the pages and reported the discrepancy at test time. With quavering voice, I replied that the test had begun early and several of us did not hear the page-counting instructions. We had no way of knowing how many pages made up the test. The professor dismissed this explanation with little comment and declared that my grade would not change. This was long before the time of student advocacy and appeals.

When the system is not fair, the reaction may either be bitterness and defeat or, in positive contrast, a resolve to succeed in spite of events. Fortunately, it was the latter in my case. I had worked hard to get a college education and was not about to give up. The remainder of the course was positive.

I learned two important lessons from the midterm experience. First, we all encounter "difficult people" in life. They provide a good opportunity for us to grow in character with patience and understanding of others. Second, having become a professor myself, I have a special regard for the fair treatment of my own students. I have forgotten much about that course in Materials Science, but the midterm test experience seems like yesterday.

Suffering produces perseverance; perseverance, character; and character, hope. Romans 5:3, 4 NIV

. . . .

FAMILY IN THE RA ROOM

Ginger Ketting-Weller
Vice President
for Academic Administration
Walla Walla College
College Place, Washington

WINTER HAD DESCENDED, cold and bleak, on the Walla Walla Valley. As a missionary kid born and raised in Southeast Asia, I was busy absorbing the cold, the clanging and pinging of the radiators in the women's dormitory, the wonder of the first snow. My wool skirt, thin tights, and flat fabric Chinese shoes did little to keep the chill out of my young bones as I trod the college pathways under gray skies and trees stripped bare of foliage. The shortening days seemed alien and depressing, bringing on hours and hours of darkness.

Not only was this to be the year of my first Christmas away from home, but three weeks before Christmas I'd also be spending a birthday alone. I came from a family in which a big fuss is made of birthdays. Everyone pitches in to make the birthday person feel like king or queen for a day. Birthdays mean cards, gifts, and a celebratory meal. So I braced myself subconsciously for a quiet birthday by myself in a strange land.

It helped to know that my birthday would fall on a Saturday that year. The day off from classes would be a treat, I would be attending church, and the season was full of awe-inspiring Christmas programming.

On Friday night I returned from a worship service at the college church and settled into my dorm room, chatting with my roommate from Taiwan, also a missionary kid.

A knock at the door announced the Resident Assistant on our hall, Desiree Josiah. Her cheery brown face and enthusiasm regularly graced our evening room checks and blessed our hall worships. Now she was looking solemn. "Ginger," she said. "The dean would like you down at the RA room right away. She didn't say why."

I couldn't think of anything to be concerned about, having been a rule-respecting student all my life. I drew my bathrobe around me, stepped into my house slippers, and made my way down the hall, down the stairs, and around the corner to the RA room. Desiree was following me, which seemed odd. As I walked through the door a warm sight greeted me. There sat the three deans for our dorm and all ten resident assistants, breaking into a rousing chorus of "Happy Birthday to You." A cake sat on the desk, candles burning cheerily.

I was overwhelmed. Alone, halfway around the world from family, and mustering my courage to face a birthday and Christmas, I'd found people who loved and cared for me. Here was God in the smiling faces and birthday cake of a Christian college. Here was family, after all.

Therefore, as we have opportunity, let us do good to all people, especially to those who belong to the family of believers. Galatians 6:10 NIV

THE
TENTH
MEETING

"Come and
hear, all
ye that
fear God,
and I will
declare
what he
hath done
for my
soul."

Psalm 66:16

Luis Palau
Founder and President, Luis Palau Evangelistic Association

Gary A. Miller
Provost and Senior Vice President, Biola University

Janice Fulbright
Head, Department of Music, Huntington College

Jon L. Dybdahl
President, Walla Walla College

Todd S. Voss
Vice President for Student Development, Indiana Wesleyan University

Joseph Jones
Dean, School of Education and Social Sciences, Messiah College

David L. Tiede
President, Luther Seminary

Donald A. Yerxa
Professor of History, Eastern Nazarene College

Peggy E. Gipson
Professor of English, Oklahoma Christian University

James D. Chase
Professor of Communication, Pacific Union College

ANY OLD BUSH WILL DO

Luis Palau
Founder and President
Luis Palau Evangelistic Association
Portland, Oregon

I HAD IT ALL TOGETHER when I attended Multnomah Biblical Seminary. I was well-educated, and fluent in English. I had worked in a bank in Argentina, and spoken on the radio and in churches. I mingled with pastors, seminary professors, and other Christian leaders.

That was the outside. On the inside, I knew I was falling apart. Everything was a show. How could God possibly use me?

Then Major Ian Thomas, founder of Torchbearer Bible Schools, spoke in chapel. "Any old bush will do," he said, "as long as God is in the bush."

It took Moses 40 years in the wilderness to realize that he was nothing, Major Thomas said. God was trying to tell Moses, "I don't need a pretty bush or an educated bush or an eloquent bush. Any old bush will do, as long as I am in the bush. If I am going to use you, I am going to use you. You won't do something for Me—I'll do something through you."

I realized in that moment I could do nothing for God. All my reading and studying and asking questions and modeling myself after others was worthless. Unless God was in the bush.

I ran back to my room in tears and fell to my knees next to my bunk. I prayed, "Lord, now I get it. I understand. I see the light at the end of the tunnel. The whole thing is 'not I, but Christ in me.'"

The reason I hated myself inside was because I wrongly loved myself outside. I asked God's forgiveness for my pride. I had thought I was really something, but God was not active in the bush. I hadn't given Him a chance.

Well, God still had a lot of burning to do, but He was finally in control of this bush. I needed to be grateful for what He put in my life—the people I met, the school I attended, the doors He opened—but I couldn't place my confidence in those opportunities. God wanted me to depend not on myself or my breaks, but on Christ alone—the indwelling, resurrected, almighty Lord Jesus.

We have everything we need with Jesus Christ literally living in us! Our inner resource is God Himself, because of our union with Jesus Christ (see Colossians 2:9-15 and Philippians 2:13). From this comes a godly sense of self-worth.

"Being confident of this, that he who began a good work in you will carry it on to completion," the apostle Paul wrote in Philippians 1:6. God can begin that work in your life today.

I have been crucified with Christ and I no longer live, but Christ lives in me. The life I live in the body, I live by faith in the Son of God, who loved me and gave himself for me. Galatians 2:20 NIV

· ·

SURPRISE IN THE MAIL

Gary A. Miller
Provost and Senior Vice President
Biola University
La Mirada, California

I WAS TREADING a precarious path, not certain where to turn. As a young sophomore at Spring Arbor College, I knew that I was at the right place. But I kept wondering how I would pay for tuition, room, and board. Track and cross-country scholarships relieved the burden only a little, and the money earned from summer jobs was quickly spent during the first week of registration. So how would I pay the remaining debt? It was due on a definite date. How would I meet it? That question haunted me for weeks as I progressed through the normal routines of classes, training, and dorm life.

I knew that God could supply my need, but I had never been faced with this type of deadline. The burden was heavy to bear, and anxiety became my constant companion. I was also struggling with the normal and customary events that bring one through childhood into adulthood. I wanted to grow up and launch out on my own, independent of my parents. But that desire demanded a level of personal responsibility that was overwhelming. I wondered, "Is this what it is like to be an adult?" The answer was clear: "Yes, it is what you wanted. Now deal with it."

I shared my need with a number of friends, and they began to pray with me for the money. My parents were unable to support my financial need, so my friends became my support group. I asked the financial aid office for help and filled out some forms. But they gave me little hope, as the request was well into the school year.

Life moved ahead, and I kept busy with track meets and class activities. I was also a member of a brass ensemble that traveled throughout the Midwest on a brief tour of colleges and churches. It seemed as if every minute my mind was absorbed with my financial need as the deadline approached. Our final concert of the tour was to take place back in the campus church on a Sunday evening. Just before the concert, I checked my mailbox to collect ten days of mail. My spirits were low, because I rarely received any good mail.

This time, things were a little different. There was a letter from the financial aid office indicating that one of my loan requests had come through (much to their surprise) and that a check was waiting for me to pick up! God had answered my prayer and taught me a valuable lesson. I learned that placing my trust fully in Him yields marvelous results!

Through the years, God's faithfulness has never been a disappointment. I have not always received checks in the mail when I thought I needed them, but His power and strength have supported me since my early lesson in college.

And my God shall supply all your need according to His riches in glory by Christ Jesus. Philippians 4:19 NKJV

SHINING LIGHT AND AWESOME PRAISE

Janice Fulbright
Head, Department of Music
Huntington College
Huntington, Indiana

IN HIS UNFATHOMABLE WISDOM, God blessed me with a strong mind, an artistic temperament, a heightened aesthetic awareness, and an often-too-assertive personality. He chose *not* to bless me with patience. School was never difficult for me, but I certainly made it difficult for my teachers with my incessant questioning. I devoted myself to the study and memorization of Scripture, but the questions kept coming and I was too impatient to wait for answers. What I failed to realize was that I was not mature enough in my faith to really discern God's Word or His purpose for my life or to calm down enough to hear the "still small voice." As diligent as I was in my Bible study, my understanding was purely academic.

All my high school teachers tried to tell me what to do with my life. Many urged me toward medical school, while others pushed literature, history, and languages. Although I loved all those disciplines, there was never a doubt in my mind that music would always be a part of my life. The only person who didn't try overtly to influence me was my beloved band director. So, being a typical teenager who resented interference, I decided to major in music, thinking all the time that I could minister while being the world's greatest band director.

I was blessed to win several music and academic scholarships that would pay my tuition at a state university, so I became the youngest-ever member of the University of Georgia Redcoat Band and spent my Saturdays in Sanford Stadium watching Hershel Walker work his way up the field to the Heisman Trophy. But, as a 14-year-old college freshman, I was too young and much too naive to handle the Saturday-night, post-game band parties. The all-nighters took a toll on my grades as well as my health, and I stopped going to church on Sunday mornings.

By the end of my freshman year, I had forgotten how to talk to God and was neck-deep in self-loathing and despair. A friend asked me to go with her to a rally at the campus Episcopal Center. The chaplain was immediately able to see into my soul and find a frightened child who loved God but had forgotten how much God loved her. She helped me learn to pray again.

As soon as my relationship with the Lord was mended, He began to reveal much to me through the music I was studying and, later, teaching. I was able to see beauty, dignity, truth, and awesome praise in every symphony, oratorio, opera, art song, or chamber work. I became more involved in theatre and opera, and I was privileged to see His power at work on the stage and in the great literature of the master playwrights. I also developed a passion for painting and sculpture and art history and the myriad ways God's love is revealed in and through the visual arts. I remember the excitement I felt when I finally realized how *all* of the arts synthesize in culture, history, and humanity to proclaim the glory of God.

The Holy Spirit has never been more real and present with me than on a day in the music library of the Cincinnati College-Conservatory of Music, where I sat studying for my doctoral comprehensives with a darkness in my heart. I had on headphones, listening to the final movement of the Brahms *Requiem*. The orchestral score was in front of me, along with my Bible and a book of Renaissance art that I loved. My senses were so alive and on fire from the music of the previous movements, and the Scripture to which they were set, that my sad heart was opened to the love and light and power of the Holy Spirit. As the magnificent recapitulation of the *Selig sind sie Toten* began, I turned a page to find Raphael's "Transfiguration of Christ." My eyes filled with tears as my heart overflowed and I grabbed for my Bible. It fell open to a verse in 2 Corinthians that I had circled long ago, forgotten, and now read every day:

For God, who commanded the light to shine out of darkness, hath shined in our hearts, to give the light of the knowledge of the glory of God in the face of Jesus Christ. 2 Corinthians 4:6 KJV

· ·

FROM CAT LAB TO PULPIT

Jon L. Dybdahl
President
Walla Walla College
College Place, Washington

I ARRIVED AT COLLEGE planning to take premed. My father is a physician, and I had grown up in a university town where the medical profession was highly respected. In a grade-school play,

I had starred as a doctor. My career path seemed clear. The only other field I had considered was law. A couple of people had suggested ministry, but in my mind that was for those who couldn't do anything else. Besides, having gone to church regularly, I knew the Bible. What could a person learn by taking ministerial training?

My freshman year was uneventful, but I learned several things. My premed science classes tended to bore me. I could do the work, but the material was uninteresting. My religion class showed me there were many things about the Bible that I didn't know. My best friend was a theology major, and he seemed to be at peace. My clear sense of what I wanted to do was eroding.

My sophomore year intensified my uneasiness. While many of my friends seemed to enjoy dissecting a feline in "cat lab," I found it tedious. At the same time, week after week I enjoyed working with the children at a church about twenty miles from college. Did I really want to be a doctor? Was that God's will for me?

At a Friday vespers service late in the fall quarter, an amazing thing happened. As the speaker shared with us, I felt an overwhelming sense that I should be preaching. I didn't hear a voice, but the experience was so strong and so different from anything I had ever felt before that I paid attention to it. That same thing happened every Friday evening for three or four weeks. I talked to my parents about changing my career path, and they were supportive. In a decisive act, I went into the registrar's office and officially changed from premed to theology. Some of my premed buddies thought I had lost my mind, yet several told me they had thought all along this was for me. Most importantly, I felt a deep peace that had been lacking. I knew I was where God wanted me and that all would be well. This experience has sustained me through hard times. When things get tough, I can look back to the amazing process of God's call in my life.

Before I formed you in the womb I knew you, and before you were born I consecrated you; I appointed you a prophet to the nations. Jeremiah 1:5 NRSV

A WAKE-UP CALL IN AN UNEXPECTED PLACE

Todd S. Voss
Vice President
for Student Development
Indiana Wesleyan University
Marion, Indiana

AFTER COMPLETING my associate's degree in pre-medicine at a local community college, I was persuaded that my medical-school odds would be better if I continued my education at a large university. I enrolled at a state university that operated a medical college, and was overwhelmed by its size. Although I was a believer, my desire to speak even privately about the Gospel to others was weak at best. I tried to be outgoing, but knew that I wasn't fitting in.

The third term of this difficult year found me in the final leg of an Organic Chemistry class with 500 students. The professor often alluded to a surprise ending to the class "that will be worth the wait," but warned that we were not yet ready. The last class of the term finally arrived, and many of us speculated about the surprise. Most agreed it was simply a ploy to keep us interested in the general topic.

The hour started with a recap of the building blocks of life: those important interconnected atoms, *again*. Then, innocently, the professor moved one carbon atom to another spot on the complex drawing. "And now, dear class, what do we have?" Someone from the rustling audience finally stood up. "Non-life?" "Correct," said the professor, "and that is true of nearly infinite configurations one can assign to these building blocks of life. This configuration is the ONLY one that supports life. Now, do you know the statistical likelihood of all of these atoms randomly aligning to create life on their own?" The room became ghostly silent.

The professor began to write a number on the overhead. When he ran out of room, he added "times 10" to the power of another massive number. It became patently clear that this building block of life was not a random event. Then he pulled out a chain from around his neck to reveal a large cross. All eyes were glued on him as he proclaimed that the only scientific explanation for this miraculous building block of life is a Creator God. He confidently explained that his work as a scientist led him to this conclusion, and then briefly described his faith journey.

As you can imagine, this lecture changed the course of many lives. I was convicted to *boldly* share the Gospel from that point on. In my senior year I started a Bible study on my floor of the residence hall, my roommate accepted Christ and was baptized, and we carpooled many students to church each Sunday. I was convinced I would be in a vocation where faith and learning could be intertwined, and God delivered.

Praise be to God for the faithful few who boldly profess His name!

After they prayed, the place where they were meeting was shaken. And they were all filled with the Holy Spirit and spoke the word of God boldly. Acts 4:31 NIV

ACADEMIC PROBATION AND THE DEAN'S LIST

Joseph Jones
Dean
School of Education
and Social Sciences
Messiah College
Grantham, Pennsylvania

I GREW UP in the South during the civil-rights era, when community meetings, churches, and schools were fraught with prayers for justice. Prayer was the key to liberation, but education was the door to equality. The two weren't always confluent topics, but I built the connection by using prayer in the effort to obtain a college education. Those prayers, I believe, hurled me into a small New England town to attend a prestigious liberal-arts college.

I had opportunities to attend Southern colleges, and even more opportunities to matriculate under an athletic scholarship, but I refused to be labeled an athlete and wanted to demonstrate the uniformity of intellect as a person of color. I moved from the South to the North, from segregation to an attempt at integration, from an intellectually safe to a cognitively challenging environment.

I felt awkward, self-conscious, and fearful that someone would suggest I was not suited for this new prodigious environment. But it was there that God guided me to humility, faith, and courage.

I was attentive to my studies, sacrificed weekend pleasures to catch up on reading, and drilled myself, weeks in advance, for exams. Even so, I became the recipient of a letter of academic probation from the dean's office. As Job said: "the very thing I feared had come upon me." Although it was not the intent of the dean to communicate my inferiority, I struggled with the shame of failure in my best efforts.

To my mind, the dean's letter would have been easier to take if I had been playing sports, partying at fraternity houses, or wasting precious time. But I was conscientious, hardworking, and serious about my assignments. The devastation of the letter drove me into the woods near the campus. In that quiet place I learned about real communion with God. I saw my pride and lack of dependence on God in intellectual matters.

In that quiet time, I distinctly felt that God wanted me to humble myself and ask both Him and others for help. Of course, I was willing to ask God to fix the situation. But I found it difficult to knock on others' doors to receive God's provision. Humbling myself before the mighty hand of God meant that I not only had to ask Him, but that I had to listen and act on what I heard from Him—and others.

In obedience to God's word I prayerfully sought help. The humility to ask, seek, and knock later grew into courage and faith to overcome my situation.

Humbling myself before God later yielded consistent dean's list grades throughout my junior and senior years.

We may be comfortable with asking, but seeking and knocking take more courage and are often more humbling. In our humility God receives the glory, our faith is strengthened, and others are afforded the opportunity to use their gifts.

Ask and it will be given to you; seek and you will find; knock and the door will be opened to you. Matthew 7:7 NIV

. . . .

THE MYTHS OF SCIENCE

David L. Tiede
President
Luther Seminary
St. Paul, Minnesota

MY LOVING GRANDMOTHER was a pastor's widow who marked me for the ministry from a very early age. Almost everyone else in the past two generations of my family had been a doctor, a nurse, or a dentist. So there I was, stuck as a pre-seminary student majoring in chemistry at St. Olaf College.

My classmates, bemused by my career plans, were headed for doctoral programs in chemistry or medical school. After a difficult organic chemistry exam, two of them caught up to me in the hall. "We think we got the call to the seminary today too!" Then they roared with laughter.

It took a lecture in inorganic chemistry from my advisor to light the lamp. Dr. Albert Finholt chaired the department and brought amazing credentials from the nuclear research of the Manhattan Project at the University of Chicago. His interpretation of the new physics shattered the literalism with which most of us had previously understood the chart of atomic elements.

What had been fixed as the letters on the wall was now subject to uncertainty, with isotopes and radicals and half-lives. The very building blocks of matter, as I had thought of the elements in their electromagnetic soup, were subject to change, even altered in their being perceived.

Don't hold Dr. Finholt responsible for my unreliable memory of what he was teaching, but to this day I hear echoes of an amazing lecture on how little we know about the structure of the atom. My high-school teachers never doubted scientific facts. Or perhaps I failed to grasp the descriptions they taught as theoretical paradigms, subject to falsification. I thought science was closing the gaps of our knowledge, persistently explaining away the wonder, the divine awe.

Now the conceptual poesis of science, its myth-making, was opened to us without apology by Dr. Finholt. The capacity of varied theories to interpret and predict both proved and limited their validity. But regarding these constructs as "the myths of science" did not demean the theories. This teacher invited us into the great adventure of human understanding, humbled by the limits of our ability to grasp or inhabit cosmic complexities, confident that durable theories are constructive adventures in human understanding. The vast spaces of subatomic and extraterrestrial galaxies swirled with indeterminacy, inviting exploration and approximation.

Maybe that was the day I decided to go to the seminary, after all—in hope and not resignation. Dr. Finholt's break with the fixed universe, the wrinkle in time, was the gift of wonder restored. "When I look at your heavens," declares the psalmist, "the work of your fingers, the moon and the stars...what are human beings that you are mindful of them, mortals that you care for them? Yet you have made them a little lower than God" (Psalm 8). On the Areopagus Paul announced that "the God who made the world and everything in it...does not live in shrines made with human hands" (Acts 17). Thus, the physical universe into which God came in the flesh was sanctified as the place where we seek God.

College faith is a quest, not a destination. It wasn't what my grandmother had in mind. But thanks be to God for great teachers who show us the way, humbly and unafraid.

When I look at your heavens, the work of your fingers, the moon and the stars that you have established; what are human beings that you are mindful of them, mortals that you care for them? Psalm 8:3, 4 NRSV

- -

THEY WERE CHRIST TO ME

Donald A. Yerxa
Professor of History
Eastern Nazarene College
Quincy, Massachusetts

SOMEONE ONCE SAID that young men's lives are essentially one continuous plagiarism. That was definitely the case for me as an undergrad thirty years ago. In unwitting anticipation of the decentered postmodern self, I lifted several personae off the shelf, with not the slightest hint of attribution.

I began my college years as a really straight-laced kid. That lasted a couple of weeks. I then tried my hand as the clown-prankster, attempting to gain popularity by outrageous antics. I was really quite good in this role, but after a year or so I tired of that and began to fancy myself a romantic skeptical intellectual, who, armed with a smattering of philosophy and poetry and a lot of underground rock music, thought really "deep thoughts." Predictably, these often ended up as criticisms of the church and my poor deluded parents who bought into its deceptions.

It seemed obvious that the church was a bloated legalistic bureaucracy that reduced Christ to a bunch of rules that were inconvenient for my life. Guilt, I concluded, was the church's main commodity. I developed an exquisite sensitivity to the slightest whiff of hypocrisy . . . except my own.

Thankfully, during my undergraduate years, I did finally make my first faltering steps on the path to a more mature faith. As with all pilgrims, traveling companions met me along the way.

One was my major history professor, who made a deep impression on me by the faithful way he lived his life. He told me that as he got older, the things that he believed were essential in Christianity had decreased to a relative few. But those that remained, he held tenaciously. I respected that.

The other companion was a brilliant and demanding philosopher, who made Christianity intellectually credible. He forced me to examine the inconsistencies in my thinking that gave me such selective indignation. Had I been reacting to a straw man of my own creation?

Neither of these fine Christian men pushed their faith on me. Rather, they posed questions, content that if I handled them with integrity, I would be pointed in the right direction.

Over the decades, I have encountered many other companions who have guided me toward Christ, but I remain tremendously grateful for the patient witness of two dedicated professors who could look past the facades of an insecure young student and see a fellow pilgrim. They were Christ to me then, providing wonderful models of the stewardship of the mind that continue to inspire me.

The Lord is merciful and gracious, slow to anger and abounding in steadfast love. Psalm 103:8 RSV

BLESSED CHOICE

Peggy E. Gipson
Professor of English
Oklahoma Christian University
Oklahoma City, Oklahoma

THE BEHAVIOR of my high-school friends was perhaps the major factor in my decision to attend a Christian college. I applied for admission to the state university that most of my classmates planned to attend, and received an early acceptance. But I soon began to doubt my choice. While my three best friends and I were having a G-rated graduation party, most of my classmates were at the nearby lake having a beer bust/orgy. I wanted to be in school with my friends, but I didn't want to be tempted to go to wild parties, and I thought that such activities were more likely to occur at a state university. I was like every other student in wanting to get away from my parents, but I didn't want to disappoint them, and I didn't want to have to choose between my friends and God.

A close friend from church was a freshman at Oklahoma Christian College (OCC) my senior year. She invited me to her house, and we talked about her college experience. All the activities were designed for students of faith. The school was small, and the students were all close. My friend showed me her yearbook and pointed out people with whom she thought I would like to become friends. One of those people was Mike Gipson, biology major and athlete extraordinary. My friend's exact words were, "You would love Mike." My exact response was, "Forget Mike." I was determined to get my degree in computer science and graduate with a four-point. I was not the least bit interested in finding a boyfriend. Besides, I had always heard such stereotypical things about athletes.

Before the end of the summer, I enrolled at OCC; but I did not forget Mike. I met him the week of freshman orientation and recognized immediately that there was nothing stereotypical about Mike. He was exactly the Christian young man I had longed to meet. We dated a year and a half before getting engaged and were married within three years. I did not get my degree in computer science, and I did not maintain a four-point, but my decision to attend OCC was the right one. I found a meaningful profession in teaching, which I love; I formed lifelong friendships with students and faculty; and I found my soul mate, my life's companion.

Mike and I have been married almost thirty-nine years. Since graduation, we have devoted our lives to Christian education, thirty-four of those at OCC, now Oklahoma Christian University (OC). We love working with students and watching them mature. When high-school students visit our campus, we appreciate what they are going through as they try to decide which college or university they should attend. We hope that their decisions will lead them to the types of things we cherish most about our OC experience, and especially that they too will find their soul mates.

And we know that all things work together for good to them that love God, to them who are the called according to his purpose. Romans 8:28 KJV

. . . .

DO CORVAIRS TALK?

James D. Chase
Professor of Communication
Pacific Union College
Angwin, California

BALAAM'S DONKEY TALKED. The serpent in the Tree talked. But do Chevy Corvairs talk?

I met one that did. Or so it seemed.

During the summer of 1967, I worked as Boys' Division Leader at Pinecrest Camp to earn a college scholarship. One day I asked our Camp Director, Charles Edwards, "May I borrow your Chevy Corvair to pick up a staff member in Placerville?"

"Why certainly, Jim," he said. "But I hope you don't mind driving a car with a little spirit."

The next morning, with a prayer for protection on my lips, I pulled out onto Highway 50. All was serene as I whizzed past tall Ponderosa pines. Passing Lover's Leap, Horsetail Falls, and Mount Ralston, I quietly expressed my gratitude to God for the gift of life.

Suddenly, the serene turned surreal. The car's horn started beeping—all by itself. Or had it? Had I accidentally bumped the sensitive horn area on the steering wheel?

A mile later, the horn beeped again. Could the sound actually be coming from another car? None was in sight. I decided to consciously keep my fingers away from the horn area of the steering wheel. Suddenly, the borrowed Corvair let out another strident "BEEEEEP!"

"This is strange," I thought to myself.

I whizzed by another mile of Ponderosa pines. No beeping. Then suddenly, unexpectedly, one more very loud, insistent "BEEEEEEEEEEP!" And with it came an incredulous thought: "I wonder . . . could it be . . . is it possible that an Invisible Intelligence is trying to get my attention?"

"God," I prayed, "this is too strange. Are You, indeed, trying to say something to me? If this horn beeps one more time . . . I don't know why—but I'll pull off to the side of the road."

Nothing happened. For the next three miles, all was quiet. I began wondering if all this was the product of an overactive imagination.

Then, as the narrow mountain road approached a totally blind curve, I was jolted by another very loud, intense burst of sound. "BEEEEEEEEEEEEEEEP!" Immediately, I swerved off the pavement onto the gravel. At that precise instant, two cars dashed from behind the blind corner, and one of them, a sports car, sped toward me in my lane. I felt the Corvair rock to the right from the compressed wind as the sports car whizzed past—missing a head-on collision with me by a fraction of a second.

Skidding to a stop, I bowed my head and most sincerely thanked God for His incredible personal care. Humbly, I rededicated my life to His service.

The angel of the Lord encampeth round about them that fear him, and delivereth them. Psalm 34:7 KJV

THE ELEVENTH MEETING

"Come and
hear, all
ye that
fear God,
and I will
declare
what he
hath done
for my
soul."

Psalm 66:16

Kenneth D. Idleman
President, Ozark Christian College

Tanya D. Woodham
Interim Vice President of Student Services, Judson College

Jonathan K. Parker
Provost, California Baptist University

C. David Dalton
Professor of History, College of the Ozarks

Ann C. McPherren
Professor of Business and Economics, Huntington College

Steve Corder
Sloan Professor of Business, Williams Baptist College

Donovan L. Graham
Professor of Education, Covenant College

Steven R. Pointer
Professor of History, Trinity International University

Cole P. Dawson
Professor of History, Warner Pacific College

Gayle D. Beebe
President, Spring Arbor University

WOUNDS FROM A FRIEND CAN BE TRUSTED

Kenneth D. Idleman
President
Ozark Christian College
Joplin, Missouri

IN THE FALL OF 1965, when I enrolled as a freshman at Lincoln Christian College, I was finishing my most recent employment with the Federal Housing Authority in Urbana, Illinois—a coveted job in our area, especially for an 18-year-old. My list of credits going back to junior high school included being an all-star baseball player, an all-state football player, a starting basketball player on a high school team that lost only six games in three years, a Sunday school teacher, a Thespian, a sports editor for the school paper, a LIFE scout, a supply preacher for small churches in the Champaign-Urbana area, a state speech contest winner, and a singer in a rock-and-roll band. (How's that for eclectic?) Did I mention that my hometown had a population of less than 1,200? Or that my high school's enrollment was around 300? A big frog in a little pond . . .

Indeed, the Christian community was fortunate to have me in their ranks. Ken Idleman had committed his life to vocational Christian leadership. The world, the flesh, and the devil were in for it now. Spiritual warfare would soon be history. God's team would win a lopsided victory with Idleman on the way.

Needless to say, I was not lacking in confidence when I stepped onto the Christian college campus. But very early on, I learned for the first time that love includes confrontation as well as compassion. One afternoon I had finished lunch and was on my way through the administration building when the director of public relations and alumni caught me in the hallway. He invited me into his office, shut the door and stunned me with his statement: "Idleman, you've got everything it takes to be a flash in the pan."

That meeting was a pivotal moment of truth. No one had ever spoken to me in such a way. From that time on, I did not take shortcuts. I did not try to charm my way through life. I praise God that a Christian college administrator had the pluck to speak painful truth into the heart of an impressionable, yet arrogant, freshman. I am indebted to this man, whom I have thanked many times, for his confrontational love which provided much-needed corrective steering for my life.

Wounds from a friend can be trusted. Proverbs 27:6 NIV

· ·

FAITH OF GREATER WORTH THAN GOLD

Tanya D. Woodham
Interim Vice President
of Student Services
Judson College
Marion, Alabama

I WAS WORKING against a deadline I feared I would not meet, so I took a step of faith and called the admissions office of Asbury Theological Seminary. God's timing was perfect. Application materials to the master's-degree counseling program arrived just in time. Three weeks later, I drove to Kentucky, interviewed, and was accepted into the program.

God called me to trust Him even more as I made plans to move to the seminary in Wilmore, Kentucky, from a small town in Alabama having a population of only about 300. An only child, I would be living more than a ten hours' drive away from my family. I was nervous, but I knew that God was directing my steps.

As I adjusted to my new life, God helped me to grow through academic classes, daily devotionals, chapel services, and many supportive people. During my second year of seminary, I met a wonderful man, Daryl, who would later ask me to marry him. It seemed as if God had hand-selected him for me. Our personalities, backgrounds, theological perspectives, and approaches to life fit together perfectly. It was an amazing answer to my prayers for a spouse.

One August day Daryl was killed in an automobile accident. All of the papers I had written in Christian Theology and Crisis Counseling seemed far removed from the pain I felt in my soul. "Why?" This question rang through my mind day and night. Something within me said, "How could I dare question my sovereign Creator?" I refused to openly question why a good God could allow such a terrible thing to happen. I suppressed my feelings, telling myself that everything would be fine.

Then one morning, as I stood at the clothesline behind my seminary apartment, the Holy Spirit began to speak. I quickly went inside to journal my thoughts and feelings in the form of a prayer. God taught me that it was okay to ask questions. It was best to be completely honest and verbal with my Lord, my Friend and my Healer. Through this journey of honesty and transparency I grew more intimate with my Father, knowing that my faith was real and my relationship with Him was authentic.

In this you greatly rejoice, though now for a little while you may have had to suffer grief in all kinds of trials. These have come so that your faith—of greater worth than gold, which perishes even though refined by fire—may be proved genuine and may result in praise, glory and honor when Jesus Christ is revealed. 1 Peter 1:6, 7 NIV

· ·

141

IF GOD IS FOR US

Jonathan K. Parker
Provost
California Baptist University
Riverside, California

DURING MY SENIOR YEAR at the University of California at Santa Cruz, a friend and I decided to offer a course on "The Theology of Francis Schaeffer." Our campus allowed some upper-division students to teach special topics courses after undergoing a rigorous application process. Schaeffer was an evangelical apologist who had influenced our thinking. We thought it was important for Christian students on our campus to know that their faith was intellectually defensible.

We prepared our proposal, with a course description and syllabus, and submitted it to the chair of the religious studies department for sponsorship. Though he presented himself as a back-woodsy sort of persona, he had received his doctoral training at a German university and had coauthored a seminal text on ecology and religion. Not Christian in his persuasion, he was so enamored with pagan rites that he once brought a live sheep to campus to show students how sacrifices were conducted. He was nonetheless impressed with our proposal and agreed to present it to the faculty committee that oversaw student-led courses.

After proposals were sent out to the committee, one professor tried to dissuade the chair from sponsoring our course. My friend and I were in the chair's office when he received the letter from this committee member, who questioned the academic integrity of the course, excoriated my friend and me for attempting to proselytize, and criticized our sponsor for even submitting the course. This last element is probably what allowed us to eventually teach the course. The chair started to rant (employing numerous expletives) about how bigoted and prejudiced the professor was and how he was going to see to it that our course was offered if it was the last thing he did at that university.

He prevailed, and we were able to offer the course. Many of the students had never heard of Francis Schaeffer, and it was their first exposure to serious intellectual inquiry from a Christian perspective. It was truly amazing to watch as several students progressed from a compartmentalized faith—limited in scope to church and family—to seeing the interrelationships between one's faith and one's philosophy, politics, and artistic expression. It was my first experience teaching at any level, and it hooked me. From that point on, I knew that my calling in life was to teach, and that someday I would be involved in university-level education.

God is sovereign and was able to use the pagan chair of a religious studies department to carry out His will. My experiences of exercising faith in an openly anti-Christian academic environment honed my commitment to the integration of the Christian faith with academic inquiry that is now so much a part of my professional life.

What, then, shall we say in response to this? If God is for us, who can be against us? He who did not spare his own Son, but gave him up for us all—how will he not also, along with him, graciously give us all things? Romans 8:31, 32 NIV

. . . .

MANNA IN THE MAIL

C. David Dalton
Professor of History
College of the Ozarks
Point Lookout, Missouri

IT WAS LATE on a Saturday afternoon in August 1982 when Noel White, our soon-to-be pastor, rang the doorbell. He had stopped by to visit my wife, Cathy, and me since we had decided to make Trinity Hills United Methodist Church (in Lexington, Kentucky) our new church home.

We had been in town for only a few weeks and hardly knew anyone. I had been accepted into the history doctoral program at the University of Kentucky, but the semester had not yet begun, and Cathy had not yet found a job. We thought it was important to make new friends and belong to a church.

But on this Saturday afternoon, Cathy and I were in trouble. The move to Lexington, the deposits, and a thousand other little expenses had eaten away at what I had hoped would be enough money to tide us over until I received my first paycheck. The cupboard was as empty as the bank account, except for a bag of pinto beans and a small box of cornbread mix.

Cathy was and is a great cook, so it wasn't long before the aroma of beans and cornbread filled the air and I forgot our financial crisis. Then the doorbell rang. We were soon engaged in conversation with Reverend White, focused on our decision to join the church and the responsibilities that came with that commitment. Suddenly, Cathy jumped up from the couch and ran into the kitchen. While we were lost in conversation, the water in the beans had cooked down and our dinner was ruined.

Our focus on God's Word and work had brought us to the brink of hunger, but we never let on that the burned beans were all that we had to eat. After Reverend White left, Cathy scraped the beans out of the pot, and we ate what little remained. That night I worried about what we would do for the remaining week until payday.

Then, in Monday's mail, like manna from heaven, was a letter from my parents, wishing us well as we got settled in—with some cash, "just in case." It was "just in time."

When we least expect it, God's blessings are bestowed upon us. I have often wondered if or how my parents knew we were in desperate need. Or were they just being normal parents? Perhaps. But the timing couldn't have been better.

Next year, my oldest son, Benjamin, will be off to college. Will I be able to sense his concerns and be there to help when he needs it most? The answer, of course, is yes, with help that comes from above. I will look for the touch of the Master's hand, and hope and pray that my son will, too.

Then Jesus declared, "I am the bread of life. He who comes to me will never go hungry, and he who believes in me will never be thirsty." John 6:35 NIV

. . . .

NO STRINGS ATTACHED

Ann C. McPherren
Professor of Business
and Economics
Huntington College
Huntington, Indiana

"WHAT'S A SYLLABUS?" "There are doctors outside of the medical profession?" Even though I was raised in a family of faith where education was highly valued, entering a Christian college presented culture shock.

It seemed like a safe place to start my academic program, but I knew that I wouldn't stay. The college didn't offer my chosen major. "Come here for a year, no strings attached," they said. So I decided to try it for a year and then transfer to a university where I could get a "real" education.

The Christian college environment seemed strange. People spoke in the language of faith/learning integration. They valued wisdom above education. Truth and service trumped knowledge and profit. How could I understand these people or adopt their values?

The first few weeks set the stage for my development. In speech class, a learned, humble, witty Christian gentleman, Dr. Carl Zurcher, addressed us as Miss or Mister. Coming from someone else, the formality might have seemed odd or inappropriate. Instead, to me it communicated a mutual respect between teacher and student. "I am an adult," I suddenly realized, "and the expectations of adulthood are here." I vowed that I would try to deliver.

I decided to use my limited creative abilities and try out for a role in the fall play production. My speech professor, now in the role of director, expected professional behavior even in the run-down little auditorium on the top floor of our old administration building. How could he care so deeply about aspiring teachers, preachers, and business people posing as actors with their plodding recitation and wooden expressions? How could he accept with gratitude the inadequate facilities and limited funds? What was he thinking at the end of the performance when he handwrote thank-you notes to each member of the cast and crew?

In religion classes I found professors discussing possible scientific explanations for biblical events. And when I traveled with biology and chemistry classes, the scientists were engaging us in the same discussions. What a joy for a young thinker to find that many Christians are called to reconcile divine revelation with our understandings of science.

These people piqued my intellectual curiosity. They opened my mind and heart. They proved that they would be a tough group to leave behind on my way to "real" education. Before long, my one year had stretched to graduation and now into more than twenty years teaching in a Christian college classroom.

My Christian college made one claim that proved utterly inaccurate—"No strings attached."

Then you will know the truth, and the truth will set you free. John 8:32 NIV

· ·

PLAYING THE SYSTEM ON THE FRINGE OF BELIEF

Steve Corder
Sloan Professor of Business
Williams Baptist College
Walnut Ridge, Arkansas

MY DREAMS of great college basketball stardom had been soundly defeated, resulting in higher levels of homesickness than I could stand. After only one semester in a small, private college staffed by faculty and others who truly cared about me, I decided to attend the state university close to home. A more abrupt change I could not have imagined.

Instead of knowing nearly everyone, I knew no one. Instead of faculty who held a strong faith in Jesus Christ and felt free to share it, I found faculty who questioned everything, did not know my name, and felt free to condemn my faith.

Yet I thought I had figured out how to work around the system. Almost by accident, I submitted an English essay that basically espoused values that were certainly marginal if not completely contrary to my beliefs. And I received an A. You can imagine the light bulb that popped on in my head. Now I knew what to do. Just write about things that are really on the fringe of my Christian beliefs. On the very next essay I did.

I suspect I thought about my instructor much like many people think about corporations—that they are not real, so normal ethical rules do not apply. I was not a student who had gone to college convinced that everything my parents said was wrong. I strongly agreed with their values. This was not my age of rebellion. I just thought I had figured out the system.

With great anticipation I waited for the paper (inspired by genius, of course) to be returned. When I got it back, I did not have an A. As I looked at the paper despondently, I realized that I had given up my integrity for no purpose, thereby missing a chance to be who I really was, not a puppet framed by the system. It was a bitter lesson, given to me by an instructor who thought I had written a bad paper. She didn't realize that, in addition, she had also given me a valuable life lesson.

The highway of the upright avoids evil; he who guards his way guards his life. Proverbs 16:17 NIV

GOD'S "REASONABLE" WAY

Donovan L. Graham
Professor of Education
Covenant College
Lookout Mountain, Georgia

HAVING BEEN CONVERTED as a graduate student in a secular university setting in the late 1960s, I was desperately trying to understand how my newfound faith should affect my studies and chosen vocation (school counseling). A minister in the church where I had come to know Christ told me that Francis Schaeffer was coming to the United States to hold a week-long L'Abri Conference at a Christian college clear across the country. Dr. Schaeffer's books were about the only thing helping me deal with the anti-Christian bias in my classes, so I was eager to attend the conference.

But I was a poor graduate assistant with a wife, two small children, and a third on the way, and thus had absolutely no money. When I told my pastor that I could not go, he responded with a completely unheard-of thought: "Well, I think we should begin to pray about that." I had no idea that one ever prayed about things so earthly as money. Taking his suggestion, however, my family and I began to pray.

The time for the conference drew near. The plane ticket would cost $204. By that time the Lord had sent me (through many different sources) a grand total of $204.25.

God's provision left me speechless! I never had conceived of God as being involved in my life in that way. But I would have to pay for the conference once I arrived, and I still had no money. Delighted but confused, I asked my pastor friend what I was to do now. His answer moves me to this day. He said, "Well, it seems to me that, given what the Lord has already done for you, the only *reasonable* thing to do is to get on the plane and go and see what He does for you when you arrive." That thought was totally off my radar screen. But how could I argue in the face of what I had seen?

When I arrived at the conference, I nervously walked through the door, wondering what I was going to say to the people who would ask for money I did not have. Picking up my registration envelope, I found a check made out to me from the college—money sent by someone (to this day I do not know who) to pay for the conference. It covered my room and board, tithe, and some books and tapes that dramatically changed my thinking. I went home with the extra twenty-five cents from the plane fare.

God's provision took me to a place that would turn my life upside down, and for more than thirty years now He has allowed me to give of what I learned at that conference to students. It seems to be His "reasonable" way of doing things.

And God will generously provide all you need. Then you will always have everything you need and plenty left over to share with others. 2 Corinthians 9:8 NLT

. . . .

BECOMING WHAT WE WERE MADE TO BE

Steven R. Pointer
Professor of History
Trinity International University
Deerfield, Illinois

IT WAS ONE OF THOSE spectacular spring days in North Carolina—trees and flowers in full bloom, the sky a radiant blue—and I was virtually oblivious to it all. Lost in my thoughts, my heart despondent, I wandered through the Duke forest and gardens. I was nearing the end of my freshman year and the growing sense of uneasiness about my present major and future vocation seemed to be cresting.

Why was I pursuing engineering, I asked myself for the umpteenth time. Oh yes, I replied, the litany now all too familiar: I had been a strong student in high school science and math, my Navy ROTC scholarship looked favorably upon such a major, and, of course, engineering students quickly adopted a condescending smugness about future job prospects in comparison to our liberal-arts peers. And yet, the smoldering doubts within me were fanning into too strong a flame to ignore. Did I really have an aptitude for design and the problem-solving skills that a good engineer would need? Even more disquieting, was my heart really into this as a calling from God? If I were truly honest with the Lord, wouldn't I have to admit that I was trying to become the engineer that my father had always dreamed of becoming, a dream first for himself and then for me?

If repentance and confession are the necessary prerequisites to forgiveness and reconciliation, then so also must honesty precede genuine change. In this case, the seeming despair of my predicament had an obvious, but until then unthinkable, solution: change my major! Only when my discomfort level had risen to an intolerable point did I "come clean" with myself and the Lord. Precisely at that moment, the answer to my dilemma was given to me. I didn't have to become an engineer to serve God or even to please my father; instead, I could do both by pursuing my real passion, the study of history. That realization, which I have always regarded as the work of God's Spirit, burst upon me as suddenly and dramatically as the shafts of the sun penetrating the trees on that glorious day. And just as suddenly I experienced the relief of a pressing burden lifted from my shoulders.

That day my life changed and I learned to accept and to enjoy the person that God had made me to be. And yes, three decades plus later, I'm still passionate about history!

We are what he has made us, created in Christ Jesus for good works, which God prepared beforehand to be our way of life. Ephesians 2:10 NRSV

ACQUIRING NEW EYES AND EARS

Cole P. Dawson
Professor of History
Warner Pacific College
Portland, Oregon

HAVING BEEN RAISED in a conservative community in the South, I brought to my Midwestern college campus a boatload of self-assured assumptions about life, people, and faith. I had lived in a segregated, hierarchical, and militaristic world. And I was quite sure that everyone else came from essentially the same place I did.

I arrived on campus three weeks before the start of my freshman year so I could attend a sociology seminar. I settled into my dorm room, roamed about the campus, and chatted amiably with some of the students. All seemed as I expected. Then came the first day of class.

We could not have been more than ten minutes into the first session before I began to realize the folly of my presuppositions. For the next three weeks, bit by bit and in a gentle manner, Professor Valorous Clear chipped away at the eighteen-year-old edifice of ignorance, naiveté, and intolerance. Through lectures and discussions he guided a serious consideration not only of the structures and systems of sociology, but, more importantly, a deep encounter with our own sociology. His version of the discipline encompassed what today many colleges teach in "faith, living, and learning" courses.

As compelling as the classroom instruction was the experience of living in close community with my two-dozen classmates. In those three weeks I learned firsthand about the magnificent riches of diversity which my childhood had hidden from me. The texture and sound of life as lived differently, combined with the vocabulary and insight of the academic work, so profoundly unbalanced my preconceived universe that for a time I despaired of my former self.

Though I would not fully realize it for months and even years, the deconstruction of my former self was accompanied by the steady encouragement of faculty and friends to renew, strengthen, and extend my faith through the use of my mind as well as my heart. In those weeks we attended an opera as well as a production of *Oklahoma!*, went to the art museum, and watched movies together. The final week culminated in a field trip to Chicago, sleeping on alternate nights at the elegant Palmer House and in the dreary YMCA. Finally, as we attended Sunday services at both a magnificent mainline cathedral and at a lively black Pentecostal church, the initiation of my developing self came full circle. I realized that the professor, the course, my classmates, and these off-campus episodes created venues for me to gain new and healthier understandings of myself in relation to others and to God.

In an authentic educational environment, I had been engaged in a profoundly spiritual experience that lives with me up to this very moment. If I hadn't previously understood the potential laid before me in those three weeks, the parting words of the professor made his intentions explicit. Instead of wishing us all the best in the coming academic semester, he sincerely blessed us with the admonition to "have a great life!"

Turning to the disciples, He said privately, "Blessed are the eyes which see the things you see, for I say to you, that many prophets and kings wished to see the things which you see, and did not see them, and to hear the things which you hear, and did not hear them." Luke 10:23, 24 NASB

· ·

CHRISTIANIZED LIBERAL ARTS

Gayle D. Beebe
President
Spring Arbor University
Spring Arbor, Michigan

TWENTY-FIVE YEARS AGO I began my own college career at a Christian liberal arts college in Oregon. I had planned to attend the University of Oregon, but a variety of circumstances took me instead to a smaller college dedicated to the liberal arts.

I had been a serious student during high school. I took all the difficult classes, loved competing in the classroom, and graduated near the top of my class. But I was not intellectually curious. My motivations for study were to get good grades, qualify for college scholarships, and stay eligible for sports. A friend once asked me what I would read over the summer. I remember replying, "You mean, besides *Sports Illustrated*?"

During the early part of my college experience I had a profound intellectual awakening that has forever changed me. Through a variety of courses, an interesting mix of inspiring professors, and especially the influence of a few key friends, I began to read everything I could get my hands on. I studied history, literature, poetry, art history, music history, communication theory, physics, astronomy, ceramics, world civilization, church history, theology, philosophy of religion—and the list goes on. I couldn't get enough of learning. I felt an overwhelming sense of excitement in the opportunity to study all of these books and ideas in intimate quarters with interesting friends. The realization of God's grandeur spread across this vast expanse of human learning riveted me to the majesty of our Creator.

Since that awakening, my life has been a living commitment to the mission and purpose of the Christian liberal arts. We know of the long and storied history of the liberal arts. And we also know of the unique and dramatic turn that was taken by the Early Church in adopting the liberal arts curriculum as its own.

To Christianize the liberal arts, to understand them through Christ, is to construct a Christian theology of learning. It elicits an exclamation like Augustine's: "I believe in order that I might understand." A full understanding of life, of our work, and of life's ultimate questions is made possible only when our learning acknowledges the enduring order and reality of God. That is probably the most important thing I learned in college. It may be the most important thing I have ever learned.

The current economic climate makes people question the relevance of the liberal arts. And Christian liberal arts will always be debated by those who may never understand. But recent studies report that 45% of all Fortune 500 CEO's attended a small liberal arts college or university. And most of those schools were originally founded with a clear Christian world view. In such places, the close influence of key faculty, the opportunity to explore key issues in an intimate setting, and the enduring influence of a community of learners continue to leave a legacy in the hearts and minds of great leaders.

My own experience forces me to testify with confidence that a lifelong involvement in the study and application of the liberal arts, all based on a solid faith in our Creator, remains the most excellent way to prepare for a meaningful life and a satisfying career.

To know wisdom and instruction, to discern the sayings of understanding, to receive instruction in wise behavior, righteousness, justice and equity; to give prudence to the naive, to the youth knowledge and discretion, a wise man will hear and increase in learning, and a man of understanding will acquire wise counsel. Proverbs 1:2-5 NASB

THE TWELFTH MEETING

"Come and hear, all ye that fear God, and I will declare what he hath done for my soul."

Psalm 66:16

H. Norman Wright
Director, Christian Marriage Enrichment

Katherine Grace Bond
Author

Orville C. Walz
President, Concordia University

A. Wendell Bowes
Professor of Old Testament, Northwest Nazarene University

Lisa M. Beardsley
Vice Chancellor for Academic Affairs, Loma Linda University

Philip R. Budd
Director, Graduate Programs in Counseling, Southern Nazarene University

Wesley Richard
Emeritus Professor of Communication, Bluffton College

H. Frederick Reisz, Jr.
President, Lutheran Theological Southern Seminary

Dedrick L. Blue
Vice President for Student Affairs, Oakwood College

Timothy J. Sanborn
Professor of Music, Grace College

OUR CHALLENGES
GOD'S BLESSINGS

H. Norman Wright
Director
Christian Marriage Enrichment
Bakersfield, California

A FRIEND ENCOURAGED ME to apply to Westmont College. Unfortunately, my grades wouldn't allow my entrance until I attended another school for a year to show I had the academic ability. So, swallowing my disappointment, I applied to the University of Southern California and was awarded a half-tuition music scholarship.

This delay in my plans (actually, God's better timing for my life) was beneficial in two ways. I had a great experience playing in three bands under quality conducting. But God also used this year to help me appreciate the next three years at Westmont. At USC, with more than 15,000 students, I was lost in the crowd—just another number in classes of three to four hundred. At Westmont, with a student body of 350, I could connect with Christian professors who cared about me. God had a purpose for me at both institutions.

During my first week at Westmont I was delighted to learn there was a "fisherman's club" on campus. Since I was a dedicated fisherman myself, I went to the first meeting to meet other anglers. Of course, I was greatly surprised when I learned the "fisherman's club" was really the group that went to the rescue mission each week to put on a gospel service for the men. Since I was already at the meeting, I decided to give this a try. I had never been involved in any ministry like this before, and I thought I could learn something. I did. Before long God began to change the way I viewed others who were different. God began a work in my heart that would continue throughout my life to mold me into the counselor that he wanted.

I discovered that God was preparing me for my life's work in numerous ways, but I didn't realize this until years later. One year I worked on the staff of the college yearbook. Six weeks before the yearbook was scheduled to go to press the editor resigned. We discovered that very little of the work had been completed. The school needed a new editor in a hurry. Without much thought I volunteered, and only then began to comprehend the momentous chore facing the staff. But I learned what happens when a group of students have the same vision, pray together, work hard, and follow through with their commitment. Through this process I was forced to write copy. This was the shove I needed by the Lord to overcome my insecurity about written expression. I began to write, and I've never stopped. God certainly does things we don't expect.

My life was changed and challenged by the daily chapel. This was a peak experience for me. I can still hear the student body singing and remember some of the speakers. One of them gave us a very specific challenge: "If you will take one chapter from the Word of God and read it out loud every day for a month, it will be yours for life." Some of us took him up on that challenge. And it was true!

In college, I learned an important lesson. When I reached out and risked doing something new, I was often surprised by what God would do in my life.

Call to me and I will answer you and show you great and mighty things . . . which you do not know. Jeremiah 33:3 AMP

RECKLESS FAITH

Katherine Grace Bond
Author
Duvall, Washington

"YOU THINK NEW TESTAMENT will be easy." Dr. Robert Wall glowered at us. "It won't be."

I disliked him immediately. How presumptuous! I worked for my grades. Certainly, I'd give a Bible class due diligence. I was determined to excel at Seattle Pacific University. But I was faced with a major distraction: Andy.

We'd met when I was 16. Now I was 19 and counting the months to our fall wedding.

"Marriage is risky business," worried folk admonished. "The divorce rate is 50 percent. Early marriage is reckless."

Reckless or not, I had found my soul mate. I longed to be with him. And after two and a half years, my virginity was wearing thin.

But these were frivolous reasons. We wanted to be reverent and deliberate. We made an academic study of marriage, taking classes, getting counseling, reading stacks of books. But deep down I wondered if God could approve something so foolish.

Each morning I argued theology with Dr. Wall. To my surprise, he responded thoughtfully. And as I learned about synoptics and exegetics, I began to respect him deeply.

"I believe," he said, "but I could be wrong. That's what faith is." He was declaring faith to be more than intellectual calisthenics, challenging me to risk.

The term paper was *What it Means to Be a Christian*. "I don't want bibliographies," said Dr. Wall. "I want you to lie on your bed and think about this question. I grade on a scale of one to ten," he went on, "and only God gets a ten."

I prickled with the injustice of this. But I had other things to worry about. Money was scarce. A fall marriage now looked impossible.

Reluctantly, we postponed the wedding by a year. It was obviously God's will.

I poured my heart into my paper. I spoke of my quest for humility, my failures. Perhaps I was *too* honest.

I had to chuckle at my score: "Ten-minus." But the comments took me straight to Dr. Wall's office.

"You don't like your grade?" he demanded.

"No, it's not that. I wanted to discuss the . . . theological implications of your notes."

I bumbled around, avoiding my real question. Finally, I turned to the section on God's will. I had used my deferred wedding as an example.

"It's what God seems to be leading us to," I wrote.

And Dr. Wall's scrawl in the margin responded, "Because it's *logical??* God is transcendent!!*"

"About this comment . . ." I attempted an aura of scholarly indifference.

Dr. Wall's face softened. "God can overcome circumstances," he said. "Perhaps you and your fiancé owe it to yourselves to rethink this decision."

My heart leapt. What a rash idea! Was he suggesting that God wanted what I wanted? Even so frivolous a thing as love?

Five months later I dropped a handmade wedding invitation on Dr. Wall's desk. "You're right," I wrote inside. "God *is* transcendent."

Praise the LORD, O my soul, and forget not all his benefits— who . . . crowns you with love and compassion, who satisfies your desires with good things so that your youth is renewed like the eagle's. Psalm 103:2-5 NIV

GOD KEEPS HIS PROMISES

Orville C. Walz
President
Concordia University
Seward, Nebraska

ON A SUNDAY MORNING in the fall of 1958, during my sophomore year at Concordia Teachers College in Seward, Nebraska, I prepared to attend the morning worship. As I checked my wallet and pockets, I realized my cash assets amounted to one dollar bill, a nickel, and three pennies. That total of $1.08 would have to last for the next two and a half weeks, when I would go home to South Dakota for Thanksgiving.

As I looked at the money, I pondered what my response would be when the offering plate came to my pew. Three possibilities came to mind: 1) give nothing this Sunday, 2) place the eight cents in the offering plate, or 3) contribute the dollar bill. I remember thinking: "Good Lord, help me!"

Walking to the church service, I made a decision. When the offering plate came to our row of worshippers, I dropped in the dollar bill. Two days later a letter arrived from home. At the end of the letter my mother added a postscript: "Just to tide you over until Thanksgiving." The envelope contained a five-dollar bill. Now it's important to remember that this was in an age long before today's presumption of immediate communication by e-mail, instant messaging, or cheap long-distance telephone rates. Mail was the standard, and it took time. My mother knew nothing of my crisis. But God obviously did, and He cared.

I had learned of tithing, but this episode at that moment of my life taught me irrevocably to believe God's promise to bless bountifully those who place Him first in their daily living. Those blessings often come in ways we could never imagine. His promise is not only a financial one. God may give to us in areas of health, work, a Christian spouse, or a loving family, and at times in areas which others might view as minute or unimportant.

After I graduated, I took a teaching position with a monthly salary of $333.33 a month, minus deductions. I began tithing, and giving more beyond tithe. My wife and I have never looked back. God has faithfully kept His promises.

Give, and it will be given to you; good measure, pressed down, shaken together, running over, will be put into your lap. For the measure you give will be the measure you get back. Luke 6:38 RSV

EVERYTHING NECESSARY TO DO HIS WILL

A. Wendell Bowes
Professor of Old Testament
Northwest Nazarene University
Nampa, Idaho

DURING MY FIRST FEW DAYS at college, all freshmen were required to take a series of IQ tests and personality tests and occupational interest tests. A few weeks later, the director of the testing program called each of us into his office and went over the results to see if the tests lined up with our occupational goals and the major we had chosen.

I remember very clearly the meeting we had that day. The director reviewed all the test scores, and then he said, "There are only two things that stand out in these tests. You like animals, and you like to work with your hands. Have you ever considered being a farmer?" I was so dumbfounded I did not know what to say. I had grown up in the city and hardly knew the back end from the front end of a cow. I came to college with what I thought was a call to ministry.

The director and I talked some more, and then he noted one score that seemed to clear up some of the confusion. That score rated the consistency of my answers. My consistency rating was only three percent. The director finally admitted that this test did not reveal much of anything about my interests because I was so inconsistent with my answers. In other words, I really didn't know what I wanted to do.

For several months I struggled emotionally with the results of those tests. Some things there did not fit the typical profile of a minister. I was very shy and did not like to get up in front of people. Also, I knew that the worst grade I had ever received was in a high school speech class. I hated that class, and yet I stuck with it because I knew I had to learn how to speak if I was going to be a minister.

During my first year at college I went to the altar several times struggling over this issue. In one service the pastor prayed with me and finally convinced me that God did not need two Billy Grahams. He wanted me just as I was, with all of my personality traits and shyness. God made me a promise that day. He said He had already given me all of the talents and skills I would need to do His will, and He would never ask me to do anything that I did not have the ability to fulfill. He has been true to His promise ever since. As God said to Jeremiah,

Before I formed you in the womb I knew you, and before you were born I consecrated you; I have appointed you a prophet to the nations. Jeremiah 1:5 NASB

· ·

REST ASSURED

Lisa M. Beardsley
Vice Chancellor for Academic Affairs
Loma Linda University
Loma Linda, California

WITH ONLY ELEVEN DAYS until finals, I felt anxious. I had been admitted to the graduate program in public health as a provisional student because I lacked some of the science prerequisites. To eliminate those deficiencies, I went to summer school to take physiology, microbiology, chemistry for nutrition, and sociology—all condensed courses geared to an emphasis in public health.

My undergraduate degree had been in theology. The humanities, theology, even Greek were easier for me than the sciences. I wondered whether I would do well enough on these finals to be accepted as a regular graduate student.

My dorm roommate came from a wealthy family and was a great student. She was also a devout Muslim. Every day she meticulously donned a head covering. Then she prayed on a mat by her bed, her forehead pressed to a carefully wrapped piece of clay dirt "from Mecca." Nothing got in the way of her devotion.

The library at Loma Linda University is closed from Friday afternoon to Sunday morning, in keeping with the institution's Seventh-day Adventist belief. So on this Friday afternoon, when our library closed, my devout Muslim roommate simply jumped into her sports car and drove over to the University of Redlands to study in that library. She spent most of Saturday there too. She had been on the Dean's List at a private college and knew that it takes discipline, focused study, and a great deal of reading to get good grades. At this crisis in our summer-school program, she believed that an extra Saturday of studying would do her good.

I admired her discipline and her devotion to her faith. At the same time, my own faith about the Sabbath prevented me from doing the same thing, but not without considerable nervousness. In fact, I felt sick. There were only one week and two weekends left before finals. What if I didn't do well on those exams? What would they say at home if I failed? Was it reasonable to think I could take a whole day away from my studies and still keep up?

Late on Friday afternoon I put away my books and got ready for the Sabbath, even though I felt I could not afford not to study. It was a critical decision—a true "college-faith" moment.

I've been putting my books and work away on Friday afternoons ever since then—for more 20 years. And what a blessing the Sabbath has been to me! Sabbaths are a wonderful time of rest, worship, fellowship, music, ministry, fresh air in nature, or an afternoon nap. I've learned that the way to be successful in the face of inevitable and unexpected demands is to have physical, social, and spiritual reserves. Balance is essential. Like a body-builder, it takes exercise *and* rest to achieve maximum results. Research has even shown that people live longer if they go to church three to four times a month (Lee, et al., 2002).

Sabbath worship and Sabbath rest are a regular part of my weekly cycle. They are the secret to how I've gotten as much done as I have, professionally and academically. Observing the Sabbath has served me well in studying for an M.P.H., a Ph.D., and an M.B.A. As the sun sets and the Sabbath is born, I have often whispered a prayer: "I've done all I can this week. Now it's in your hands, Lord. I trust that You will do the rest as I rest in You." Week after week, when I return to my academic and other burdens after the Sabbath, I find they don't seem nearly as heavy as when I laid them down on Friday evening.

My advice to students who are serious about success is simple: Six days shalt thou study, and on the Sabbath day, rest and celebrate!

Lee., J., Stacey, G., and Fraser, G. "Social support, religiosity, other psychological factors, and health." In Gary E. Fraser, *Diet, Life Expectancy, and Chronic Disease* (New York: Oxford University Press, 2003), 149-175.

If you keep your feet from breaking the Sabbath and from doing as you please on my holy day, if you call the Sabbath a delight and the Lord's holy day honorable, and if you honor it by not going your own way, and not doing as you please or speaking idle words, then you will find your joy in the Lord, and I will cause you to ride on the heights of the land and to feast on the inheritance of your father Jacob. Isaiah 58:13, 14 NIV

A FATHER OF
A DIFFERENT KIND

Philip R. Budd
Director, Graduate Programs
in Counseling
Southern Nazarene University
Bethany, Oklahoma

WILLIAM WORDSWORTH CLAIMS that he grew up "fostered alike by love and fear." That claim resonates with my experience. Perhaps the focus was more on fear than love. As fearful as God may have seemed, my father's wrath was immediate and palpable. Early in my life, I came to understand and experience the fear of not measuring up to my father's expectations.

The extension of fearing my father was pervasive. All authority figures were surrogate fathers who could punish and belittle. Unfortunately, as Ana-Maria Rizzuto illustrates in her compelling work, *The Birth of the Living God*, a child's concept of God mirrors the dominant parental figure. My father was empowered in extensive ways because of his additional role as a minister.

Upon entering Mt. Vernon Nazarene College, I tried to avoid fear by expressing it as arrogance, anger, or simply a happy-go-lucky attitude. With a 2.7 high-school GPA, I was terrified that I would fail. In spite of the masks used to protect myself, college professors were able to challenge and foster the hidden potential in me.

In my Freshman Composition class, "Doc" Seamans challenged me to think deeply and love learning. He brought out the best in me by his openness to my frequent visits to his office, even later when I was not enrolled in his classes. He taught me that I should strive to be a lifelong learner and that God wants my best. "Doc" Seamans cared deeply about me and wanted me to live up to my potential. Through him, I experienced an authority figure who sacrificed and modeled God's love.

Dr. Halverson also seemed to welcome my frequent visits to his office. I wanted his approval badly—particularly when it came to singing in chapel. In psychology, this phenomenon is called "transference": I projected onto him aspects of my father. My desire for his approval was a desire to receive my father's approval. Though Dr. Halverson did not capriciously give compliments, he affirmed me for core aspects of my life.

Dr. Garsee, who taught Introduction to Psychology, inspired my interest in psychology. His ability to integrate theological concepts with the discipline intrigued me. It was from Dr. Garsee that I discovered my fascination with understanding truth through both the hermeneutical principles of theology and the science of psychology. However, as with my other mentors, I learned the most important lessons outside the classroom. Serving as his teaching assistant my senior year offered me many opportunities to observe a person who lived out faith with integrity and honor.

Through my experiences with professors who embraced and nurtured me, I began to see God in a different light. God was no longer angry and distant, but engaging and personal. I began a journey of personal discovery that allowed me to see myself as capable and confident. I can never repay my mentors for their investment in me; but through my work as a college professor at a Christian college, I attempt to pass on to others the lessons learned from my mentors.

The LORD is compassionate and gracious, slow to anger, abounding in love. Psalm 103:8 NIV

. . . .

FIRST BE RECONCILED

Wesley Richard
Emeritus Professor
of Communication
Bluffton College
Bluffton, Ohio

AS A COLLEGE STUDENT, I continued the practice I had begun in high school of getting up early enough to spend some time reading the Bible and praying before going off to breakfast and classes. Sometimes I focused on short passages and wrote my own commentary in a journal; at other times I read extended chunks of Scripture.

During my sophomore year, most of the other men on the floor of our small dorm kept different hours than I did. In spite of their own Christian family upbringings, they seemed to regard my practice of early morning private devotions with some bemusement. In fact, one morning after concluding my time with the Lord, I discovered that one of them had reset my alarm for 4:00 A.M. and I hadn't noticed until I was dressed and ready to start my day!

It was during one of those early morning quiet times, however, that I learned a valuable lesson. The Scripture I was reading was from Matthew 5:

"So when you are offering your gift at the altar, if you remember that your brother or sister has something against you, leave your gift there before the altar and go; first be reconciled to your brother or sister, and then come and offer your gift" (Matthew 5:23, 24). When I read those words, I recalled that the previous day had ended with a serious disagreement and a harsh tone between a friend and me, and I knew I had to take steps to renew that friendship.

I found it impossible to continue my meditation and prayer. The thought of that troubled relationship nagged at me, and my prayer seemed to bounce back at me from the ceiling above my head. The sky outside my window was beginning to show signs of a new day as I pondered my best course of action. Since it was almost time for breakfast and I knew my friend would likely appear in the cafeteria early, I dressed and left my room to find him.

Just being able to talk with him reduced my anxiety. And while I don't now remember the words we exchanged or even the content of our disagreement, I still recall the sense of relief my confession and his gift of forgiveness brought to me.

In the years since that time, I have always tried to keep my relationship accounts up to date. I have discovered that unfinished business with others not only interferes with prayer, but it can interrupt sleep. Maybe that's why Paul told the Christians at Ephesus to "not let the sun go down on your anger" (Ephesians 4:26).

Reconciliation is God's gift to broken relationships.

Do not let the sun go down on your anger. Ephesians 4:26 NRSV

MAKING THE GRADE LESS THAN THE LEARNING

H. Frederick Reisz, Jr.
President
Lutheran Theological
Southern Seminary
Columbia, South Carolina

IT WAS MY SENIOR YEAR of college, and I felt that I had accomplished a lot. I was doing honors work in my English major and was looking forward to going to a seminary. The English Department faculty tried to talk me into going to graduate school rather than the seminary. They wanted their better students going to graduate schools to help their reputation. There was nothing wrong with that. But graduate work in English was not my calling.

Most of the year, I worked on an honor's thesis examining T. S. Eliot's "The Four Quartets." The poems were packed with symbolism, and I had chosen a few symbolic elements for analysis. I thought that a study of circle imagery could provide insights not widely or deeply probed in the literature. I was very excited about what I was finding, learning, and writing. I finished my intricately argued thesis and submitted it to my principal advisor. He was a teacher and a mentor for me, and I deeply respected him. We related well to one another.

Weeks went by. Finally, the professor returned my thesis. I knew that I had passed that last hurdle to graduation. I may have even felt a bit of pride; I certainly felt satisfaction and accomplishment. I opened the cover of my thesis. There, all over the first page, was a blanket of pen writing. It nearly obliterated all my writing. The next page looked much the same, as did many more to come. He had torn apart my writing! It was devastating! He gave me a "B+" on the thesis, one of my lower grades. He did acknowledge genuine insights which I had, but at that moment, everything seemed lost!

It took many weeks, months, probably years, to realize that he had respected me enough to treat what I had done seriously, take a great deal of his time with it, and make one last attempt to push me to a higher level of writing and thought.

This was serious business. It required the absolute best I could give it. It deserved my pushing myself beyond what I knew I could do. It is there that I learned respect for handling the ideas and art of others, responsibility to do not just my best but more, reverence for the gifts which God had given to me and others, and the integrity of a profession to which God called me. The professor's devastating criticism was a respectful gift and an announcement that he knew I was capable of excellence. God would desire no less!

Be transformed by the renewing of your minds. Romans 12:2 NRSV

LAUNCH OUT
INTO THE DEEP

Dedrick L. Blue
Vice President for Student Affairs
Oakwood College
Huntsville, Alabama

I DIDN'T WANT TO DO IT. It seemed foolish, if not scary, to take a year out of college and go to a foreign country to serve as a missionary. What could God be thinking? I was a city kid, "Boston born and Boston bred." Why in the world would I want to leave the comfort of college to go teach in a little village somewhere in Thailand? "Anyway," I reasoned, "would they even care to hear a black kid from America?"

For more than a year I resisted the pleadings of the Holy Spirit with the Moses excuse, "I am not eloquent. I am slow of speech and of a slow tongue," and the Jeremiah excuse, "Lord, God! Behold I cannot speak: for I am a child."

One night, as I lay in restless slumber, I had a dream. I was walking across the quiet campus when a violent thunderstorm erupted. Black clouds eclipsed the starlit night, and people ran frantically for cover. The lightning crashed and crumbled the buildings, crushing the panicked inhabitants. Screams of "Mercy, Lord!" resounded over the clash of thunder. And then, as quickly as the storm had erupted, it was over.

Waking in dread, I reached for my Bible. It fell open to Matthew 24:27: "For as the lightning cometh out of the east, and shineth even unto the west; so shall also the coming of the Son of man be." And then I heard the words echo in my soul, "Go ye therefore, and teach all nations . . . and, lo, I am with you alway, even unto the end of the world" (Matthew 28:19, 20).

It was a transformational moment—a personal, once-in-a-lifetime epiphany. God had called and I must answer. At that moment God moved me from fear to faith. The decision was sealed.

I went to Thailand, and it changed my life. That year, I touched lepers, helped deliver a baby, played with the children in the refugee camps, and introduced souls to Christ. God changed me from a Boston kid to an international evangelist, from a citizen of the United States to a representative of the Kingdom of Christ. I gained more than I gave. And I learned that God often has a greater purpose in mind, with greater blessings in store, if I will simply respond to His invitation to "launch out into the deep."

Launch out into the deep, and let down your nets for a draught. Luke 5:4 KJV

. . . .

CRISIS BY THE SIDE OF THE ROAD

Timothy J. Sanborn
Professor of Music
Grace College
Winona Lake, Indiana

MY SIX-YEAR-OLD SON leaned across the car seat and put his arm around me. "It'll be OK, Daddy."

My wife and I had moved to Bloomington, Indiana, for me to pursue further graduate work. We were there five years and had started a family during that time. Then we moved to Grand Rapids, Michigan, and lived there for five years as well, adding a second son to our collection. Still, I had not finished the work on my dissertation, and therefore had not finished my doctorate. They were immensely busy years—teaching part-time in every conceivable college in the area, and working a factory job for much-needed medical benefits. An elusive full-time contracted teaching position never came, and a looming deadline for the completion of my doctoral work cast doubts on my dreams of a teaching career.

Finally, I was released from what I perceived to be my best hope for a full-time position. The college was searching for a teacher in my field, but of a different race and gender. I felt my fate had been sealed. I needed to give up my dream and seek other career choices.

On a Friday evening in early May, my boys and I drove thirty minutes to the college to clean my office, pack my books, and go back home. We did just that. But as I left the city for the last time, all my dreams of making a difference in students' lives, all my hopes for a career, and all my aspirations for the terminal degree came crashing down around me. I had spent ten years in college and fifteen years teaching while working toward this career. Why weren't the details working out in my favor?

I pulled off the road and wept. It was at that moment that my son's little hand reached across the seat, went around my shoulder, and comforted me the way I had comforted him all his life.

My six-year-old didn't know that God had prompted him. He didn't realize, nor did I, that my losing the teaching job I had tried to earn on my own merits was God's plan. He didn't know that within one month I would be contacted by a Christian college in Texas. We would move our family to accept that position, and within eighteen months I would be finished with my doctorate. God had to pull the rug out from under me to get me to finally believe that He had a perfect plan for my life.

I've been able to share this story with many students who ask "why." God showed me that His timing, His plan, and His ways are better than my imaginations.

O LORD, you are my God; I will exalt you and praise your name, for in perfect faithfulness you have done marvelous things, things planned long ago. Isaiah 25:1 NIV

THE THIRTEENTH MEETING

"Come and
hear, all
ye that
fear God,
and I will
declare
what he
hath done
for my
soul."

Psalm 66:16

Paul A. Rader
President, Asbury College

Linda Wysong
Vice President for Student Services, Union College

Douglas C. Bennett
President, Earlham College

Joseph E. Coleson
Professor of Old Testament, Nazarene Theological Seminary

Melvin R. Wilhoit
Professor of Music, Bryan College

Ellen McNutt Millsaps
Professor of English, Carson-Newman College

David W. Whitlock
Dean, College of Business and Computer Science, Southwest Baptist University

Clark D. Campbell
Professor of Psychology, George Fox University

Kathryn Meyer Reimer
Professor of Education, Goshen College

Steve Pawluk
Vice President for Academic Administration, Southern Adventist University

FINISHING
WHAT WE START

Paul A. Rader
President
Asbury College
Wilmore, Kentucky

IN MY JUNIOR YEAR at Asbury College, I was offered an opportunity to take a year away to join a mission team for intense ministry in Japan. In the Asbury community my vision had been wonderfully widened to embrace the possibility of cross-cultural missionary service. The prospect of ministry in Japan was exciting. The world seemed larger then. The options for short-term missions were few.

While trying to make a decision as to what I should do, I spoke with Dr. Frances White Ewbank, then a professor in the English Department. She was and is wise and spiritually sensitive. She is also a master teacher with a unique capacity to open the student to the life of the mind and to engender a hunger to know beyond the curriculum and classroom. She wisely avoided too directive an approach. The choice was, of course, mine to make as I sought the mind of the Lord. "However," she advised, "God usually wants us to finish what we start. You may want to reflect on that. There may be plenty of time for you to fulfill a missions calling."

I took her advice, hunkering down to complete my preparation. It led to seminary and a graduate degree before I would embark on adventures in the "regions beyond." Gripped by a compelling sense of calling to a missionary vocation, my wife and I committed ourselves to ministry in the Salvation Army, and we eventually spent twenty-two years as missionary officers serving in Korea. God opened doors to many rewarding ministry opportunities we could never have anticipated.

I do not doubt I would have gained a great deal from a year of service abroad while a student. And I am grateful for the many opportunities students enjoy today to reach out and engage their world. But God knew well what was coming and helped me to follow through on the commitments I had made to my academic program, finishing what I had begun.

It became a life pattern. Perhaps it is why we were able to go to Korea and to stay the course of forty years of ministry and mission. In God's time we got to Asia, and to Japan on occasion, as well as to many other parts of the world, but better prepared with a settled sense of personal fulfillment and readiness.

I will instruct you and teach you in the way you should go; I will counsel you and watch over you. Psalm 32:8 NIV

THE FRIENDSHIP CIRCLE

Linda Wysong
Vice President for Student Services
Union College
Lincoln, Nebraska

IT WAS A HOT SEPTEMBER DAY when my plane landed in South Bend, Indiana, from San Francisco, California. I had graduated in June from Pacific Union College and was now beginning a master's degree at Andrews University. Because my parents lived near the campus at PUC, I had never been away from home for a long period of time. I was 22, had a college degree, and was supposed to have the world under control, yet was so homesick I cried that first night after I unpacked my suitcase. What was I doing here with all these people I didn't know? Why had I decided to leave my family and boyfriend to go to a place where winter would bring mountains of snow? I wanted to go back home!

At that time graduate students were housed in the basement of Lamson Hall, where it was quiet and they could "study" without distractions. It felt like a tomb. It didn't take long for most of us to realize that we needed each other, and soon evening visits were happening in the halls and in rooms.

Someone found out that the Seminary was hosting a grad student retreat at a nearby camp during the second week of school. We all decided to sign up for an opportunity to meet new people and learn what the graduate experience would be like.

To our delight we discovered that there were others who felt just as lost as we did in this "foreign" country of Michigan. To those of us from the West, people seemed quiet and subdued. We were excited to find a whole group of graduate students who enjoyed fun and discussions. During the closing session of the retreat, the facilitator invited us to determine what we were going to do differently after leaving the camp. Our group decided to meet on Friday nights at a teacher's home.

That was the beginning of many lasting friendships and three marriages. We met every Friday night to talk about topics of interest and to focus on service. We decided to visit a nearby church and to help the congregation where needed. We discovered there were many needs that we could help fill. In the process of filling those needs we were no longer feeling lost and alone. We had a friendship circle that drew us together and helped us through the graduate experience.

Those people are some of my most valued friends to this day. They have enriched my life through their creativity, keen minds, and loving hearts. These friends have been encouragement in the difficult times throughout life. They are a priceless gift that resulted from my graduate experience.

A friend loves at all times, and a brother is born for adversity. Proverbs 17:17 NIV

. . . .

A VOICE WITHIN

Douglas C. Bennett
President
Earlham College
Richmond, Indiana

WHILE I WAS GROWING UP, my family attended a Presbyterian Church. My sisters and I thought this was odd, because we knew that our parents—and our grandparents—were Baptists. Looking back, I realize my parents had chosen a church they admired for its care of members and its Sunday school, rather than a church that just matched their own "growing-up" denomination.

In my teens, I often was intrigued by my father's Sunday afternoon mutterings. Hours after the morning's sermon, he would be talking to himself, wrestling with points of theology. A number of Presbyterian beliefs just didn't sit well with him. Witnessing his Sunday afternoon mutterings left me skeptical about fine points of theology.

Toward the end of high school, I found myself paying greater and greater attention to the words said on Sunday morning, especially the words I was prompted to say: the hymns we sang, responsive prayers, and confessions of faith. Some of those words captured what I believed, but others were merely verbal formulas that didn't seem to voice my beliefs. It seemed to me that if I said those things, I ought to believe them; if I believed them, I ought *really* to believe them. I tried to believe them all. I grew more serious in my faith, but also more uncomfortable.

I chose to attend Haverford College for many reasons, but not because it was a Quaker College. Nevertheless, I found Quaker Meeting for worship intriguing: sometimes I didn't know what to do in the silence, but sometimes I left Meeting feeling clearer and stronger in ways I could not at all put into words.

The "fifth day" (Thursday) meeting for students was talky and often aggressively focused on contemporary events, especially the Vietnam War. These gatherings had value, but they were rarely a spiritual experience. On Sundays, I generally attended a local Presbyterian church. Other times, I went to the local Quaker Meeting. I'd leave Meeting not at all sure why I attended, but often I found the spoken messages or the silence (or both) deeply refreshing. I came to appreciate the fact that no one said any words but ones they through experience knew to be true. I was drawn to the spiritual integrity of this practice, but soon I also realized that it put a weight on me to seek truth. I could not just rely on words others had scripted.

My college years were the early years of the Vietnam War, and my classmates and I all felt the pressure to know how we would respond to the draft. Slowly I found a leading in me towards pacifism. A voice within, quiet but insistent, told me in the silence that I should have no part in the taking of life, and no part in war.

I learned something else in responding to this leading. I realized that God speaks to me in the present. And in realizing that, I came to know, too, that God will speak to each of us in the present. Revelation is not a closed book. All the words are not yet written. They are still being written as we listen to God, and some of those words are especially words for me—or for you.

Be still, and know that I am God; I will be exalted among the nations, I will be exalted in the earth. Psalm 46:10 NIV

· ·

GOD'S GIFTS FROM THE CHERRY ORCHARDS

Joseph E. Coleson
Professor of Old Testament
Nazarene Theological Seminary
Kansas City, Missouri

I GREW UP in West Michigan cherry country. I earned money for my first bicycle by picking cherries, ending the season in the orchard of John and Elnora Edlund, members of my home church.

Years later, in my first term at the seminary in Kentucky, I was in a class with Dr. Wilbur Dayton when he asked whether anyone would be interested in accompanying him in his sabbatical travels. He intended to travel through Greece and western Turkey and then visit sites in Lebanon, Jordan, Egypt, and Cyprus before going to Israel for the spring semester in Jerusalem, Israel.

I was very interested, and Professor Dayton assured me he would be glad for my company. However, the only money I had was the final installment of a scholarship I'd been awarded upon graduation from high school. In 1969, that was more than enough to cover the spring semester tuition in Jerusalem, but not enough to cover all the travel expenses getting there.

Mr. Edlund had died, but I knew Mrs. Edlund had helped a number of my friends with their schooling. Would she help me study in Jerusalem? I called her pastor, and he encouraged me to ask. So, while I was home at Thanksgiving, Pastor Rayle and I visited Mrs. Edlund in her home. She was very gracious, as always. I told her about my professor's generous offer, and asked whether she might be able to help me finance this extraordinary opportunity. Without hesitation, she reached for her checkbook on the table beside her and asked, "How much do you need?"

Looking back on the journey Mrs. Edlund's godly generosity made possible for me, I often have described it as a sixteen-hours-per-day, one-on-one tutorial with one of the finest biblical scholars I have known. Some of what Professor Dayton and I saw and experienced on that adventure has disappeared from the world today. That journey, and that first semester in Jerusalem, changed the direction of my life. I had received a call to ministry, but had no idea what form it would take. Those first six months of 1969 directed me into Old Testament studies, and I have been a professor of Old Testament and related studies for nearly thirty years now.

God could have set me on this path in a number of ways. But God did it through the loving generosity of a widow whose means came by dint of years of hard work in West Michigan cherry orchards when cherries still were king in Oceana County. Humanly speaking, I owe not only my first bicycle, but every day of my ministerial life, to Mrs. Elnora Edlund.

Trust in the LORD and do good; dwell in the land and enjoy safe pasture. Delight yourself in the LORD and he will give you the desires of your heart. Commit your way to the LORD; trust in him and he will do this: He will make your righteousness shine like the dawn, the justice of your cause like the noonday sun. Psalm 37:3-6 NIV

THE WRONG CLASS AND THE RIGHT DIRECTION

Melvin R. Wilhoit
Professor of Music
Bryan College
Dayton, Tennessee

I'M USUALLY PRETTY GOOD about details, so imagine my confusion, amazement, and embarrassment (in that order) when I found that I had signed up for the wrong college course. There I was, sitting in a class I thought was going to be Renaissance History, only to find out it was about the Reformation (same time period but substantially different content!).

As a music major with a strong interest in music history, I was hoping to gain some deeper insights into an important period in music by taking one of the history department courses focusing on that period. I was interested in cultural history, not church history. Who wants to learn about stuffy church councils or splitting theological hairs? I wanted to learn about the culture that had spawned the greatest flowering of the arts that civilization had ever known. So I rushed from class that first day and ran to check the schedule. Somehow I had signed up for the wrong class, and the one I wanted to take conflicted with my other classes. What to do?

I prayed: "Lord, I'm not sure why I ended up in this class. I have absolutely no interest in this subject, but maybe you know something I don't. Signing up for this class was an honest mistake that I can't easily change at this point. Maybe I should stay and learn what I can." And learn I did. In fact, that class gave me a love for church history that has continued throughout my life, including work related to two graduate degrees.

Often God leads us in directions we can't begin to imagine because He knows what is to come. It is encouraging to know—as I face uncertainties—that God is continually preparing me for the future. From a daily, practical standpoint, that means being faithful to the task at hand, even when it doesn't seem to be going the way I had pictured. And that goes even for seemingly irrelevant general education courses or boring old collateral courses in college. God is way ahead of us in planning and directing our lives.

"For I know the plans I have for you," says the Lord. "They are plans for good and not for disaster, to give you a future and a hope." Jeremiah 29:11 NLT

. . . .

TEACHING IN THE WRONG PLACE

Ellen McNutt Millsaps
Professor of English
Carson-Newman College
Jefferson City, Tennessee

IT WAS THE LAST SEMESTER of my senior year at Mississippi College, and I was miserable. I suddenly realized that I hated what I had prepared to do as my life's work. Student teaching in a high-school English class convinced me that I was not temperamentally equipped to handle discipline of high-spirited adolescents with diverse attitudes and motivations.

I had envisioned sharing my love of literature with students who would catch my enthusiasm. My rude awakening came quickly, however. As I announced to a class of twelfth graders that we were going to write a theme on the day's reading assignment, a bored-looking girl on the front row replied, "Oh yeah? Who's gonna make me?" I soon learned that to gain control of the class, I had to assume a Hitleresque persona. One smile from me and all control vanished.

My days became a dreaded repetition of preparing for the firing squad, enduring almost fatal blows, and collapsing in tears at the end of the day. It didn't help matters that my roommate was also student teaching and having a wonderful experience. Aptly named Joy, her bubbling recital of each day's events only exacerbated my misery. I "prayed without ceasing," asking God for answers. Had I misread God's will for my life? Were my earliest experiences of teaching dolls with a play blackboard to be my only pleasant memories of this profession?

At Joy's urging, I made an appointment with the head of the English Department, who suggested that perhaps my desire to teach was just focused on the wrong group. She advised me to consider graduate school in English. It seemed that a small door of hope was opening, so I put out the fleece. I diligently filled out applications, checking every box that offered any financial assistance. Learning that some friends were also interested in graduate studies, I applied to the same schools. As an afterthought, I also applied to the University of Tennessee.

Soon, my friends were receiving their acceptance letters, but I had heard nothing. Then a letter came from UT, offering an NDEA Fellowship (National Defense Education Act) for three years of graduate study leading to a Ph.D., the purpose of which was to encourage more women to enter higher education. Now, the dilemma began: should I wait to see if I received an offer from schools where my friends were going, or should I take this huge step into the unknown?

As time ran out, I decided to step out in faith and walk through the open door. The very next week, I received a letter from another graduate school offering me a one-year appointment—nice, but not nearly the offer that I had already accepted.

Now, looking back over a satisfying college teaching career of thirty-two years, I can clearly see God's hand leading me. I have had the privilege of teaching and interacting with countless students whose lives have touched mine and who are touching others for the Kingdom.

For now we see through a glass, darkly; but then face to face: now I know in part; but then shall I know even as also I am known. 1 Corinthians 13:12 KJV

THEY NEVER GAVE UP

David W. Whitlock
Dean
College of Business
and Computer Science
Southwest Baptist University
Bolivar, Missouri

PERSISTENT WITNESSES. They never gave up.

Several young men who were very active in our university's Baptist Student Union organization befriended me during my freshman year in college. The fact that they would do so was not in itself a remarkable event. After all, I was the grandson of a Baptist minister, and two of my great-grandfathers were also ministers—one Baptist and the other Pentecostal Holiness. But the young man they befriended was experiencing his first real taste of "freedom" and was obviously not conducting himself in the same manner as his new friends. Without a personal relationship with Christ, and uninterested in their "organized religion," I presented a real challenge.

These new friends began to invite me to church and to BSU activities, including Bible studies, campouts, and weekend retreats. It was fun, and I was drawn to them and to the message they shared and lived. However, I was also firmly entrenched in the world and continued to maintain friendships outside of these new friends' circles.

For years I lived with a heavy pull toward the things and, yes, the people of God. But I resisted, content to continue walking among two worlds, two sets of companions, two lifestyles. Yet, like the persistent widow of Christ's parable, family and friends continued to faithfully pray, witness, and love. Though it was evident at the time that their "mission" was not earnestly seeking the Lord, they did eventually see me repent and come to faith in Jesus Christ.

My friends never gave up on their mission, though I am certain there were times when they were tempted to declare defeat. But they stuck by me and poured their lives into mine at a crucial time in my life.

These young men, now older and graying (a seminary professor, an elementary school principal, and a high-school basketball coach, among others), are living examples of persistence in witnessing and friendship. They taught me the true meaning of genuine freedom and genuine friendship. Through them I learned of the One who is Master and Sovereign Lord, and yet who sticks closer than a brother.

A man who has friends must himself be friendly, but there is a friend who sticks closer than a brother. Proverbs 18:24 NKJV

. . . .

A DIFFERENT KIND OF DOCTOR

Clark D. Campbell
Professor of Psychology
George Fox University
Newberg, Oregon

I WAS CONVINCED that God had called me to become a medical doctor and perhaps serve in a mission field. I studied hard in college and did well academically in premed courses until I took my second physics exam in my junior year. Then I began to question whether I could do well enough to make it into medical school. I wondered whether I should even become a doctor.

It was a painful and lonely process. Life was organized and my direction was clear as long as I was headed toward medicine. When I began to question that career, everything leading toward it—my major in college, life after college, possible housing locations, and relationships—became unclear as well. I was not comfortable talking about this struggle with others, because it felt as if a change of direction would be a personal failure to reach a goal and do what God had called me to do.

I began looking seriously at other areas that might interest me as much as biology. Because I had enjoyed my general psychology course, I enrolled in an upper-division one. I really enjoyed that course, too, and realized that I could major in psychology and still go to medical school since I had completed the required premed courses.

The further I went in pursuing a psychology degree, the more I enjoyed it. By the fall of my senior year I had decided to pursue graduate study in psychology rather than apply to medical school. Yet I still felt as though I had disappointed God. I was ashamed that I had not achieved what He had called me to do. I was settling for His second best.

I finished my psychology degree and was accepted into a doctoral program in clinical psychology. Over time it became clear that helping others through psychological means is what God had called me to do. That was confirmed by a series of successes in classes and internships, and by a feeling of joy in what I was doing. I saw doors of opportunity opened clearly by divine intervention. In addition to clinical practice, God led me into teaching graduate and undergraduate students. I had never dreamed of a teaching career when I was an undergraduate biology major. I have also been able to teach behavioral medicine to family-medicine residents in a medical school, which is very rewarding. It is ironic that I am now teaching those who are doing what I was once convinced I was supposed to do.

When we pray, God often changes our goals and desires more than He changes circumstances or situations. God led me to fulfill a calling in life that I could not see at the time but now seems unmistakable.

**I have taught you in the way of wisdom; I have led you in right paths.
Proverbs 4:11 NKJV**

CONVERSATION IN SILENCE

Kathryn Meyer Reimer
Professor of Education
Goshen College
Goshen, Indiana

"THERE'S MORE TO LIFE than teaching, Kathy. Remember that." Dorothy had seen my surprised response to her announcement of early retirement from her middle-school English position. I was in my senior year of college, completely engulfed in long days of student teaching. I felt called to be of service in the world through teaching as I thought Dorothy, one of my role models, had been. But how could she be leaving just when she was in her prime? How could she abandon what God wanted her to do and that in which she had great skill?

Dorothy declared that she was retiring to have more time for prayer. More time for prayer?! Could her journaling, contemplation, silence, and prayer be as "useful" as her teaching had been? As one of my spiritual mentors, she could sense my doubt. She knew that I enjoy talking and could probably surmise that my stance in prayer consisted of me talking to God. She may also have seen that most of my life was geared around "doing," and my definition of "useful work" was narrow. She challenged me to try a silent retreat to learn to listen to God.

I went to Saint Gregory's Abbey near Three Rivers, Michigan. It took me more than a day to learn how to handle so much silence and to find ways to listen. With skilled guidance, an abbot helped me to see prayer as active rather than passive. The acts of prayer, contemplation, and silence became two-way conversations. I was indeed "doing" something (and working rather hard, too!). God became a conversation partner I would miss if I did not make time for silence. Prayer became a tangible act.

My life had been defined by what I was studying and what I was going to do as a teacher. But mentors showed me that there is more to life than being a skilled professional. Who I was going to be in a profession and how I was going to relate to God were as important as the profession itself. The words of Micah 6:8 became my theme song: "What does the Lord require of me? To do justice, love mercy and walk humbly with God."

Living out those words became my college quest—a quest Dorothy sent me on and one which I continue to live out in my life as a professor. I had thought that my profession was the way to live out my Christian commitment. Dorothy's words and life challenged me to realize that prayer, silence, and contemplation are as critical as any professional activities to my work as a professor.

And what does the LORD require of you? To act justly and to love mercy and to walk humbly with your God. Micah 6:8 NIV

· ·

FICTION AND BROWN FINGERNAIL POLISH

Steve Pawluk
Vice President
for Academic Administration
Southern Adventist University
Collegedale, Tennessee

SHE GAVE ME A PASSING GRADE. I didn't deserve it. It was one of those grace grades that professors give to some students.

The professor was Barbara Youngblood. It was 1972. I was a freshman at Pacific Union College and enrolled in a required English course.

Professor Youngblood seemed pleasant enough, but she wore brown fingernail polish. And she assigned literature for us to read. "Fiction," I called it. I was surprised that PUC would hire professors like that.

Because I declined to complete the assigned readings, Professor Youngblood invited me to come to her office. Two times. During these visits she patiently attempted to reason with me. She talked with me about the usefulness of understanding the human condition. She explained the advantages of perceiving life through the eyes of other people. She encouraged me to broaden my horizons. I would have none of it. For every reason that she proposed, I gave her quotations from our faith tradition that I thought settled the matter. When she tried to explain the context of those quotations to me, I refused to listen.

So Professor Youngblood provided me with alternative assignments. One was based on *The Pilgrim's Progress*. And I was pleased that I had been a faithful witness, just like the prophet Daniel. I wondered if campus administration was aware of Professor Youngblood's curriculum, and her fingernail polish.

Professor Youngblood couldn't teach me much literature that quarter. But her genuine Christian patience and kindness, packaged in the same person who explored literature and wore fingernail polish, created a level of cognitive dissonance that led me to learn some important things.

Twenty years later I wrote Professor Youngblood a letter of apology. I was a new professor at Walla Walla College and was struggling to educate some earnest students in my classes who were very much like I had been, refusing to explore and examine their world for fear of becoming defiled by information. (It was, by the way, a fear not shared by the prophet Daniel.)

In my letter, I thanked Professor Youngblood for modeling God's patience. I assured her that I had, finally, realized the value of understanding multiple perspectives. She had shown me that a teachable spirit is much more sanctified than a rigidly closed mind. I didn't mention her fingernail polish in my letter. (If she reads this story, it will be the first time she will hear about it from me.) I have observed, since 1972, that faithful believers come dressed in a beautiful variety of ways, and that they view the world through a wonderful diversity of lenses. And I've come to understand that God has the time for each of us to learn and mature spiritually at different rates.

Oh, there is so much more I want to tell you, but you can't bear it now. When the Spirit of truth comes, he will guide you into all truth. John 16:12, 13 NLT

THE FOURTEENTH MEETING

"Come and hear, all ye that fear God, and I will declare what he hath done for my soul."

Psalm 66:16

Alan S. Cureton
President, Northwestern College

Rosanne Osborne
Hixson Professor of English, Louisiana College

David Horton
Professor of Music, Lee University

Michael E. Williams
Dean, College of Humanities and Social Sciences, Dallas Baptist University

Robert R. Mathisen
Professor of History, Western Baptist College

Michael Vander Weele
Professor of English, Trinity Christian College

Evaline Echols
Professor of Business Education, Lee University

Timothy C. Homan
Professor of Chemistry, Grove City College

Ralph E. Enlow, Jr.
Provost, Columbia International University

Kevin W. Mannoia
Director of Spiritual Care for Graduate and Adult Programs, Azusa Pacific University

STUMPED IN FOOTBALL

Alan S. Cureton
President
Northwestern College
St. Paul, Minnesota

THE QUESTION STUNNED ME.

"How can you play football and be a Christian?"

Fall two-a-day practices were underway. It was my second day on campus. As a freshman I was adjusting to several new experiences: being over 600 miles away from home, making new friends, living with three roommates, adjusting to a small rural community, enduring intense August heat and Kansas wind. But I wasn't expecting my faith to be challenged at a Christian college! The question caught me completely off guard and left me speechless.

Coming to a Christian college meant I would be in safe and secure surroundings where a feeling of "church camp" would permeate the campus ethos. My anticipation was grounded in the perception that all students attending a Christian college would be Christians, like me, full of faith and enthusiasm. After all, I thought, didn't every Christian college student desire to grow in faith?

I quickly found out this simply was not true. My teammate was serious. He was staring at me, waiting for an answer. I could tell by the look on his face that it was an honest inquiry. By the way he asked the question, I could tell he believed the two were incompatible. Because he wanted to play football, he apparently felt it wasn't possible to be a Christian. Why did he think that?

"Well?" he roared. I just looked at him, never responding or answering his question. He walked away, shaking his head.

Immediately, an overwhelming feeling of loss swept over me. My lack of response was disappointing and troubling to him, of course, but even more so to me. Here was a sophomore asking me, a new student, how I could integrate what I believe into what I do.

Little did I realize at the time that his challenging question would become a transition point in my faith journey. My teammate was asking me how faith in Christ permeates *everything* I believe and do. Are we able to integrate and shape our worldview through the authority of Scripture and through an active and personal faith in Christ? How does faith in God impact every atom of our being?

Searching the Scriptures, I found passages in James that spoke to the importance of deeds reflecting the Christian's faith walk. "Who is wise and understanding among you? Let him show it by his good life, by deeds done in the humility that comes from wisdom .... But the wisdom that comes from heaven is first of all pure; then peace-loving, considerate, submissive, full of mercy and good fruit, impartial and sincere" (James 3:13, 17).

I read over and over the words of Christ in Mark 12:30: "Love the Lord your God with all your heart and with all your soul and with all your mind and with all your strength."

The challenge is not to compartmentalize faith, but to yield to God's Spirit in all areas of life. It is easy to hold on to various segments of life and thus compartmentalize our faith, such as behaving one way on Sunday and differently on Friday night. But a "complete walk" with Him requires that we integrate our faith with who we are, what we believe, and how we act every moment we live.

Who is wise and understanding among you? Let him show it by his good life, by deeds done in the humility that comes from wisdom. . . . But the wisdom that comes from heaven is first of all pure; then peace-loving, considerate, submissive, full of mercy and good fruit, impartial and sincere. James 3:13, 17 NIV

· ·

FROM DISGRACE
TO WISDOM

Rosanne Osborne
Hixson Professor of English
Louisiana College
Pineville, Louisiana

MY SOPHOMORE YEAR I was delighted to learn that I had been appointed a summer missionary to Mexico by our state Baptist Student Union. Having spent the previous summer working at a Baptist encampment in New Mexico, I was mesmerized by the enchantment of the Southwest.

The work would consist of ten weeks of Vacation Bible School in the state of Chihuahua, and all of the work would be in Spanish. The state director of student work talked with my Spanish instructor about whether my language skills were up to the task. Now the instructor was a very fine Christian man of faith. He assured the director that he would give me extra help in the months before summer, that the Lord would provide, and that I would be completely prepared.

My desire to travel and to live in Mexico clouded my vision of the reality that I was only an average one-year language student. In my naiveté, I believed that when I crossed the border, I would miraculously have the gift of Spanish proficiency. My pride kept me from assessing my situation clearly.

My partner for the summer was a Mexican-American from Texas, and we met in El Paso and flew together to Chihuahua, the capital city. We conversed in English, but when our supervisor met us, English was a language of the past. The conversation, the billboards, the street names, the restaurant menu—these were beyond my limitations.

I sat in my silent vacuum during dinner, hating my lack of faith and feeling that I was a complete failure. The supervisor was astounded that I had been audacious enough to believe that I could be of any assistance to the mission, but, not knowing what else to do, he put me on a train to Jimenes the next day.

The first week revealed me for the fake that I was. Try as I might to teach the small primary children entrusted to me, I left them staring in wonder, trying desperately to figure out what was being communicated by the halting speech and unintelligible accent. I was also forced to face another reality. The space I was taking up in the small three-room home, and the food I was eating, were the gracious sacrifice of the pastor of the church.

At the end of that week, I knew that the only honorable thing for me to do was to return to the States and cease to be a burden. My supervisor agreed. In the first hours of my return, relief replaced embarrassment. And then I had to face my failure.

The experience indelibly marked my consciousness of the meaning of Christian responsibility. Not only are we given a heart with which to respond to the mandate of discipleship, but also we are given a mind to perceive the exactness of our skills and talents. We cannot be swayed by ego, by the counsel of others, or by our own desires. We are called to wisdom as well as to service.

When pride comes, then comes disgrace, but with humility comes wisdom. Proverbs 11:2 NIV

· ·

KNOWING THE TRUTH

David Horton
Professor of Music
Lee University
Cleveland, Tennessee

SURELY NO ONE would dare say what we had just heard. Granted, this was a state university, but we were in the deep South in the heart of the Bible Belt. We sat in stunned silence. After a time, one young lady raised her hand to challenge his statement. The professor used the full force of his position and training to badger her until she fell silent. No one else dared speak.

He said he was a Christian, yet he never talked of his faith—only his doubts. He had come to the University of Southern Mississippi from a prestigious Ivy-League university, apparently with the mission to disabuse all of us ignorant, Bible-believing Southerners of the certainty of our faith. He was not satisfied to be an agnostic—he was an evangelistic agnostic. He had baited us all semester, and he was moving in for the kill.

He said, "No truly educated person believes the Bible is really true." I did not have the knowledge to argue the point. Like many of my colleagues, I was the first of my family to attend a secular university. My father, a well-known Pentecostal preacher, was widely read and had the most impressive vocabulary of anyone I knew. He imparted his love of language and learning to me. But he was self-educated. Not having been around many people with advanced college degrees, I could only wonder about what my professor had said.

The following June I had the opportunity to meet a remarkable man, Dr. Bill Swan. His credentials were impressive—a Ph.D. in physics, Director of Microwave Research at the Dow Chemical Company, and assistant rector of an Episcopal church. He was coming to speak at a church where I had a summer job assisting with music.

Dr. Swan walked to the pulpit and bowed his head. I could not tell you one word he said; yet I knew that when he prayed, he was talking directly to God—and God was listening! It was as if God put aside everything else and said, "Yes, Bill, what do you want?" His prayer was a conversation with God. He was a man of science, a man of faith, and a "truly educated" man. He accepted the Bible as the Word of God.

I now knew that my professor had misled our class. He had taken advantage of our lack of knowledge. He knew, or should have known, that there are multitudes of consummately educated people who believe the Bible is true.

As Christian scholars, we must give due diligence to discovering the truth. Not everything that is spoken or written by someone who purports to be an authority is true. Every idea put before us must be examined with care. Truth can bear up under the most careful scrutiny. You will discover for yourself that the Word of God can withstand every challenge.

But examine everything carefully; hold fast to that which is good. 1 Thessalonians 5:21 NASB

· ·

DAD'S INTRODUCTION

Michael E. Williams
Dean
College of Humanities
and Social Sciences
Dallas Baptist University
Dallas, Texas

"HI, MY NAME IS Charlie Williams, and this is my son, Mike." As a shy, rail-thin, 18-year-old college freshman, I cringed as my father introduced himself to the first stranger he met in the dormitory hallway after helping me to move my things into my room. As a newcomer, I hoped to blend quietly into the scenery and gradually acclimate myself to the surroundings of the campus of Troy State University. My father's outgoing nature, however, was not going to allow me to be a wallflower of any sort. Not only did he introduce us, but he also proceeded to find out more about this older sophomore named Gary.

As it turned out, Gary was a student returning to the university after a yearlong absence, and he was just as congenial as my father was. Gary's younger brother, Randall, was a freshman rooming with yet another freshman, Rickey, only a few doors down from me. It was through this simple introduction that I met Randall and Rickey, who within a few days would welcome me into their crowded dorm room, Alumni Hall 312B, as a third roommate. With Randall and Rickey I would forge lifelong friendships and develop a Christian brotherhood.

Over the next four years, Randall, Rickey, and I truly became as close as brothers. We laughed and cried together. We lamented romantic woes and sweated over tough exams together. We struggled with career decisions and debated the difficult questions of life. We made late-night runs to McDonald's, took road trips at odd times, played pranks, and grew up. We also matured in our Christian faith in the midst of a campus that was sometimes more "secular" than I was prepared for as a rather naive, sheltered young man. Randall, Rickey, and other Christian friends, including Brenda, who five years later became Randall's wife, became my "community" on campus.

Even now, more than twenty-five years later, Randall, Rickey, and Brenda remain among my closest friends and are people I know I can call upon at any time of the day or night. Our friendship became so recognizable as we became campus leaders that the TSU annual did a feature on us in 1981. Out of crowded 312B came a youth minister (Rickey), a minister of music and Christian university professor of music (Randall), and a pastor and Christian university administrator and history professor (myself).

When my father introduced me to a stranger in the fall of 1978, I never could have imagined how life-changing this one encounter would become and how important this budding community of friends would be for my development as a Christian and as a person. From them I learned the importance of having a Christian community and the accountability of such a brotherhood.

A friend loves at all times, and a brother is born for adversity. Proverbs 17:17 NASB

WHEN THE UNEXPECTED HAPPENS

Robert R. Mathisen
Professor of History
Western Baptist College
Salem, Oregon

HAVING CONCLUDED my undergraduate work in the spring of 1968, I set off to graduate school that fall to begin a new phase in my student life. The decision to pursue a graduate degree in history had nudged aside the options of going to seminary or law school.

My goal was to earn a master's degree as quickly as possible and then make myself available to the scores of Christian colleges that would be begging for my services. How naive I was. A few deans replied politely to my job inquiry, suggesting that I get back to them after I had the doctorate in hand; most did not answer.

Life became increasingly complicated the next two years. With full-time graduate study, Sundays given to interim preaching at a small church ninety miles away, and the arrival of our first child, my wife and I were looking forward to life after graduate school. It was a good time in our lives as we trusted God for our future.

Upon completion of doctoral coursework and some of the comprehensive exams, I signed on with a Christian college for my first full-time teaching position. My dissertation topic had been approved, so teaching and researching made the weeks go by quickly. The teaching was everything I had hoped for, and steady progress was being made on the dissertation.

Little did I know what I would be facing. As each chapter of my dissertation was approved by my committee chair, I was confident all would end well. Finally, the time came for scheduling the oral defense of the dissertation.

The morning of the defense I delivered the required copies of the dissertation to the graduate school. I was actually looking forward to the appointed hour. After two hours of examination by the committee, the verdict was in: NOT APPROVED—but with conditions for possible future approval. I was shocked, as was my committee chair, when the department chair cited the deficiencies of my work. The conditions for future approval were couched in terms that convinced me over the next several weeks that the dissertation never would be approved.

Was I a "failure"? Perhaps. Several months later I commenced work on another doctoral program at a different university, and was able to transfer some credits already completed. The second dissertation, which was approved three years after the first was rejected, launched me in an entirely different direction in my classroom teaching, for which I have no regrets.

Am I glad for the pain I experienced with the first dissertation? No. Am I grateful to the Lord for granting me the perseverance to complete successfully the second try? Yes, indeed. I may never know this side of heaven why it happened that way. But then it will not matter.

But we also glory in tribulations, knowing that tribulation produces perseverance; and perseverance, character; and character, hope. Romans 5:3, 4 NKJV

. . . .

MARX, MAHALIA, AND THE SHOWING PROFESSOR

Michael Vander Weele
Professor of English
Trinity Christian College
Palos Heights, Illinois

IN OCTOBER OF 1969 I almost dropped out of school. It wasn't that I hadn't liked college up to then. In fact, the first day of school had felt as if I were breathing a new air: no bells, no tunnel hallways, no sharing or rigging of lockers. Instead, there were benches to sit on between classes, and trees to lean up against, and Frisbees spiraling through the air.

But then came a book in philosophy called *In the Twilight of Western Thought*. It took me seven hours to read the first thirteen pages. By the time I made it to the end of a paragraph, I had no idea where the paragraph had begun. I had to start over again, and again. This got bad enough that a friend of mine—now a doctor *and* lawyer—and I talked seriously about dropping out of school. Thankfully, a sophomore or junior student—now an inner-city community developer—overheard us as we walked away from the classroom building, stopped us, and asked us to give philosophy another chance. It had made a difference in his life, he said. *In his life!*

So we gave it another chance. And it made a difference in our lives, too. Our professor—did we have any idea then that he was only 37?—was a scholar named Calvin Seerveld. He regularly sported a tan corduroy jacket and green tie, stood at the board with chalk in his left hand and his left foot always on tiptoe, and seemed to carry an armful of books wherever he went. He regularly played above our heads, and then did everything humanly possible to get us there.

One day the various sections of Philosophy 101 met together in the chapel. We were going to hear a presentation by a Marxist, a graduate student in philosophy who had answered Seerveld's ad in a U of C (University of Chicago) student newspaper for a practicing Marxist, preferably an atheist. Up to this point, we had learned that everyone began with a worldview based on a few presuppositions; but now we were to hear the real thing.

After the presentation, we stuttered out our questions, which were sometimes reshaped, sometimes added to, by Seerveld. But long afterward we remembered meeting a Marxist, not only Marxism.

Another day Seerveld told us about a recent interview he had conducted with Mahalia Jackson. She was quite old by then, too old evidently to come to campus, but he had gone into Chicago to visit with her. "Never underestimate the power of the African-American church," she had told him. He learned, I think from her, that the human voice was still more important than the sweetest instrumental note. His voice was that for us, too. We thought he was telling us about the importance of a Christian world and life view. Later we knew he was showing us.

For God was pleased to have all his fullness dwell in him, and through him to reconcile to himself all things, whether things on earth or things in heaven, by making peace through his blood, shed on the cross. Colossians 1:19, 20 NIV

. . . .

CLARITY VS. TRUST

Evaline Echols
Professor of Business Education
Lee University
Cleveland, Tennessee

A YOUNG CHRISTIAN seeking direction in life spent three months at Mother Teresa's mission in Calcutta. He asked that she would pray that he have clarity. She refused. "Clarity is the last thing you are clinging to and must let go of," she said. "I have never had clarity; what I have always had is trust. So I will pray that you trust God."

The lack of clarity often opens a gateway into a trust that is not dependent on circumstances—trust that is built on a stronger faith than what is seen.

For twenty-seven years I served as administrative assistant to the president of Lee University. During those years I attended classes at night and finally completed a bachelor of science degree in business from Lee and a master of education in business from the University of Tennessee. But my long-term goal was to teach full time in the business department at Lee.

After a series of adversities within a three-year period—an automobile accident that crippled me for nine months, the death of my parents, and the dissolution of my marriage of 25 years—I felt that the rug of security had been snatched from underneath me, destroying my comfort zone. I needed to trust!

One morning in my devotions, God spoke to me through Deuteronomy 32:11, 12: "Like an eagle that stirs up its nest, that hovers over its young, He spread His wings and caught them, He carried them on His pinions. The Lord alone guided him."

That fall I made the plunge into teaching. When I told my major professor at the University of Tennessee of my new position, she said, "If you are going to teach, you must get your doctorate. Since I am transferring to Louisiana State University, why don't you live with me this summer and take some courses to test the waters?"

That summer was so successful, I returned the next five summers and one full year when Lee granted me a sabbatical. God used my major professor to advise me, just as He used Mother Teresa when the young man sought her advice. My professor motivated me to step into a new career, a territory of trust without the clarity and support of family, friends, and familiar surroundings. Yet it was the "Lord alone" who guided me.

When waves of disappointment and loneliness raged around me, almost consuming me at times, I was forced to develop my unused "wings of trust." Isaiah 40:31 became my emotional raft—something to cling to during the storms. Seventeen years later I can advise students who come to me during times of adversity not to seek clarity, but to try their new wings of trust.

Yet those who wait for the LORD will gain new strength; they will mount up with wings like eagles, they will run and not get tired, they will walk and not become weary. Isaiah 40:31 NASB

HONEST QUESTIONS COMPELLING ANSWERS

Timothy C. Homan
Professor of Chemistry
Grove City College
Grove City, Pennsylvania

I WAS BLESSED to have been raised in a loving Christian home. My family was actively involved in churches and other organizations that emphasized the dos and don'ts (mostly don'ts) of being a Christian. Christians go to church, memorize Bible verses, and witness. Christians don't smoke, drink, dance, play cards, go to movies, or associate with people who do such things. It was a very straightforward formula for living the Christian life.

However, I struggled with a deep insecurity about my own salvation and lacked any assurance that I was saved in spite of living by the formula. I asked Jesus to save me a hundred times, but never had a firm conviction that I belonged to Him and that my faith was authentic. I found it very difficult to share my faith with others, because my simple code did not answer many of my deepest questions. On those rare occasions when I did express my doubts to a leader, I left disappointed and discouraged by the shallow, canned answers I received.

I attended a Christian college that affirmed many of the same views as the churches I grew up in. As a result, I continued to wrestle with my faith and became more distant from God. After graduation, God began to confront me in a very powerful way. A pastor introduced me to the works of Francis Schaeffer. Never had I encountered someone who so thoughtfully analyzed our culture from such a consistently Christian perspective. I read several of his works which addressed many of my deep questions of meaning, purpose, and significance honestly and biblically.

Upon entering a Ph.D. program in chemistry at the University of Colorado, I was immediately struck by the radically different lifestyles of many of the students and faculty. Because they were steeped in relativistic thought, all those issues (don'ts) that I had been taught as so important to my Christian witness were completely unimportant to them. If anything, my colleagues considered my Christian faith to be a curiosity. Their only objection was my belief in transcendent truth, because it asserted moral absolutes.

During my first year I met the InterVarsity campus minister, Andy DeJong, who challenged me to dialogue with my colleagues and to think Christianly, recognizing that "all truth is God's truth." If during our discussions I retreated to pat answers from my past, he immediately played the devil's advocate. He pressed me to see the inadequacy of those answers and then led me to see the richness, fullness, and compelling nature of thoughtful biblical responses. Through Andy's influence God brought me to a much deeper faith in Him. My spiritual insecurity faded, and I had a growing sense that I truly did have good news to share. It radically affected the way I viewed every area of my life. I became good friends with several fellow graduate students and had the joy of sharing Christ with them through some very candid and mutually respectful conversations.

For it is by grace you have been saved, through faith—and this not from yourselves, it is the gift of God. Ephesians 2:8 NIV

GOD'S BIG INTERRUPTION

Ralph E. Enlow, Jr.
Provost
Columbia International University
Columbia, South Carolina

AS THE DAYS OF MY SENIOR YEAR in college marched inexorably toward commencement, I struggled to discern God's leading for embarking upon my career. Since childhood, I had repeatedly sensed and answered affirmatively a call to surrender myself to the Lord for "the ministry." But deciding what role of ministry that calling entailed and which immediate possibilities I should pursue proved perplexing, to say the least.

Through my student ministry experiences as a junior and senior, I started to recognize that God had gifted and motivated me to teach. I began to explore opportunities for teaching Bible and coaching in a Christian school setting. As I investigated possibilities, my conviction intensified. God's will for me was coming into focus—or so I thought.

Just days after graduation, on a final student ministry tour, our musical ensemble performed a concert at Fort Belvoir, Virginia. Just before the performance, the host chaplain entered our prayer room and began to distribute mail that had been forwarded to us along the tour route. Handing an official-looking letter to me, the chaplain smiled ruefully. "Ralph, I hate to be the bearer of bad news, but I know what this letter represents. You are about to be drafted."

The chaplain was right. I became one of the last of the Vietnam-era draftees. By early fall I found myself in a military uniform, with a military haircut (definitely not in style in the early '70s), undergoing intensive physical and military training in a spiritually hostile environment. At the time, I struggled to see the connection between my ministry calling and what I viewed as an unplanned and unwelcome interruption. Now I know better.

Although I had sought God's direction for my life sincerely, systematically, and sensibly, God providentially overruled the plans I was so confident He had revealed. I served for three years in the Army's elite 82nd Airborne Division. My military experience was crucial to my personal spiritual development. It helped me discover and develop some latent natural and spiritual gifts that are now central to my calling as a Christian higher-education leader today. I learned that, while I have a responsibility to actively seek and discern God's will, my heavenly Father sometimes graciously and wisely supersedes what I think are His plans—always for my good and His glory.

In his heart a man plans his course, but the Lord determines his steps. Proverbs 16:9 NIV

· ·

A COLLEGE OF CONVENIENCE AND COMMUNITY

Kevin W. Mannoia
Director of Spiritual Care
for Graduate and Adult Programs
Azusa Pacific University
Azusa, California

I HAD DECIDED to enter a well-known university in Washington, D.C., major in political science, work for the State Department, and eventually become a U.S. ambassador. Having grown up overseas, I enjoyed the idea of being a world citizen and making a difference.

In my last year of high school, however, I agreed to go on a mission trip to Brazil. It cost a lot, but I felt it was worth the leadership experience. When it came time to put out money for college, I realized I had blown my wad on the mission trip. But it proved a blessing. I was forced to change my college plans: I attended the school in the town where my father was pastoring, and lived at home.

Roberts Wesleyan College, a small, Christian college in Rochester, did not represent the kinds of ambitions I had. It didn't have the majors or the connections I needed. But, hit with the need to be practical, I enrolled and purposed to transfer in a year.

It wasn't the curriculum or the academics that began to find their way into my life. It was the people -the students and the faculty. It was the sense of community. Though it was a Christian school, it was not obsessive or oppressive. It wasn't as though we stood around talking about God all the time (though, in the best sense, that is not a bad idea). Our faith was the ever-present foundation that was simply part of everything. Relationships formed. Connections developed. My interests were shaped, perhaps in ways I even then didn't perceive. Suddenly, a year had passed and I hadn't made plans to transfer to that well-known university in Washington, D.C. I had enrolled at that Christian college out of necessity and convenience. I decided to stay because of community.

During the summer after my freshman year, I traveled with the Ambassador Quartet that represented the college at churches and other gatherings. It was at a youth camp that I realized what I needed to do. I had to make another change in plans.

When I had enrolled in college the year before, I had declared a major in sociology simply because it sounded innocuous and safe. But that summer, as I traveled, sang, fellowshipped, and engaged in the work of the church, I realized that I could not envision a future for myself outside the focus of active Christian ministry. That was where I belonged.

When the summer ended, I simply went to the registrar and changed my major. There were no bells, no voices, no epiphanies. Looking back from a more mature perspective, I am amazed at how arbitrary—perhaps even shallow and impulsive—my choice may have been. Yet, by God's grace, and His hand in my circumstances, I began a journey that I would not exchange for anything.

Fortunately, my college community and family didn't fret; they allowed me to embrace the moment. Although some of the faculty tried to encourage me to tilt more to the academics, I remained staunchly committed to what I felt was a "healthy balance" between academic pursuits and a ministry focus. The only defense I then knew how to offer was that I *enjoyed* the experiences I had during that defining summer. Fortunately, their patience and understanding were probably the best response they could have given me. They seemed to trust that God would effect His will. And they were more concerned about my character than whether I achieved stellar grades or had an impressive transcript. That taught me. Their calm faith in God's providence fueled my own trust that God would work through those experiences to shape me.

As I return to that campus now as a board member, I remember the place and moment when, for the first time, I verbally articulated my desire and plan to be a leader in the church. Little did I know of the path God had laid out for me. My original, well-laid plans and ambitions were not His. But learning to embrace experiences as a gift from God and the value of deep character has taken me on a far greater journey than I could ever have imagined.

Your attitude should be the same as that of Christ Jesus: Who, being in very nature God, did not consider equality with God something to be grasped, but made himself nothing, taking the very nature of a servant, being made in human likeness. And being found in appearance as a man, he humbled himself and became obedient to death—even death on a cross! Therefore God exalted him to the highest place and gave him the name that is above every name, that at the name of Jesus every knee should bow, in heaven and on earth and under the earth, and every tongue confess that Jesus Christ is Lord, to the glory of God the Father. Philippians 2:5-11 NIV

THE FIFTEENTH MEETING

Merlin F. Ager
Dean, School of Social Sciences and Professional Studies, Cedarville University

Gail P. Greene
Professor of Mathematics, Indiana Wesleyan University

Harry Farra
Emeritus Professor of Communication, Geneva College

Peter W. Teague
President, Lancaster Bible College

J. David Gillespie
Vice President for Academic Affairs, Presbyterian College

Becky Huechteman
Professor of Education, Evangel University

Jacob A. O. Preus
President, Concordia University

M. Dwaine Greene
Provost and Vice President for Academic Affairs, Campbell University

E. Donald Lorance
Professor of Chemistry, Vanguard University of Southern California

Darrell L. Bock
Research Professor of New Testament Studies, Dallas Theological Seminary

BEYOND ANSWERS

Merlin F. Ager
Dean
School of Social Sciences
and Professional Studies
Cedarville University
Cedarville, Ohio

I WAS RAISED in a humble, blue-collar family. My godly parents—a stay-at-home mother and hard-working father—kept their two sons spiritually sheltered, separated from the worst elements of prevailing culture. They took us to church faithfully.

My primary exposure to the "world" took place in public school, although that exposure was relatively limited by today's standards. Although I had friends who were not believers, my close friends were churchgoers and lived similar, sheltered lives.

I moved on to a small Christian college and majored in education with a minor in Bible. I looked ahead to seminary and a career in Christian ministry.

In an attempt to validate my Bible education, I entered graduate school at a state university with a major in guidance and counseling. The new campus, of course, had a much more liberal atmosphere than my college, especially intellectually. I hadn't had this kind of agnostic challenge before, and I began to ask myself the usual philosophic questions: "Was there really a God?" "Were my beliefs simply a result of my upbringing?" "Was my belief system the only valid one, or was it just one of many equally valid options?" The "goodness-of-man" assumptions of prevailing counseling theory and the epistemological challenge of empiricism all raised questions and doubts about my Christian faith.

One day on campus I was delighted to see an advertisement for a public debate on the topic of "Christianity vs. Atheism." I eagerly attended, expecting to get some empirical support for my belief system, and hoping for angles on the "design-requires-a-designer" argument.

Much to my surprise, the representative of Christianity did not use the expected logic of "Christian evidences" to support his point. Instead, he gave a poignant testimony of his personal experience with Christ. Leaving aside theological language, he described his spiritual condition as "wanting" and told how he had discovered that the forgiveness offered by Christ met the need in the "laboratory of his life."

The atheistic opponent admitted he had no answer to such an existential explanation. The debate ended with crowds around the Christian asking for elaboration.

I walked away with a new, mature courage. I realized that I did not really need all the so-called answers, because many of them, on this side of eternity, are beyond the reach of our limited minds. Rather, I could—with child-like faith—proceed confidently in the search for truth because I know where the beginning of wisdom really is.

Whoever humbles himself as this little child is the greatest in the kingdom of heaven. Matthew 18:4 NKJV

· ·

THE BLANKING MOMENT

Gail P. Greene
Professor of Mathematics
Indiana Wesleyan University
Marion, Indiana

IT WAS ALMOST 11:30 at night and much too early to quit studying for my Calculus III test. But I had been studying so intensely for several hours that my mind suddenly went blank. It was as if a mountain had risen up and said, "Stop! You can't go any further!" I panicked—and then went to bed.

My crisis was the direct result of not knowing how, when, and what to study. It also was a result of neglecting my mathematics homework. During the first two years of college as a mathematics major, I had spent most of my study time on general education courses, especially the ones that required considerable reading. I had done my mathematics homework in a sporadic, careless manner, hoping that the increasingly difficult areas would somehow work out in the end. My grades were slipping, and no one knew that I was scared, embarrassed, and beginning to think that mathematics should not be my major.

At approximately 4 A.M. I awoke to pray and finish studying for the calculus test. I felt refreshed. Spatial insights seemed to come more easily. The test was not a disaster. I earned a high "B," one of the highest grades in the class. I resolved to do better in the future.

In retrospect, I have seen this incident as an important turning point for my life. Mathematics later became the vehicle for rewarding work and for continued graduate study and research. I have been privileged to be a high-school teacher, biostatistical consultant, clinical data evaluator, epidemiologist researcher on skin cancer, industrial hygienist for a chemical plant, director of institutional research and of assessment, and college professor of mathematics.

God's hand was upon me at that "blanking moment" when I knew there was nothing I could do but go forward and face the consequences, trusting Him to make a way in spite of my failures. I did not know then that one of the greatest indicators of completion of a college degree is perseverance. That is what I tell my students today: do mathematics six days a week and be consistent—there's no gain without academic pain. This discipline is well worth the rough road of sacrifice, hard work, and intellectual challenge. It is rewarding in the end when it is begun with submission to God's will for your life.

There hath no temptation taken you but such as is common to man: but God is faithful, who will not suffer you to be tempted above that ye are able; but will with the temptation also make a way to escape, that ye may be able to bear it. 1 Corinthians 10:13 KJV

THE BREAD AND THE BROOK

Harry Farra
Emeritus Professor
of Communication
Geneva College
Beaver Falls, Pennsylvania

"HERE'S A HUNDRED DOLLARS. That's all I can give you. I wish it was more," my mother said. That was a few days before I left our California home to catch a ride off to college in Minnesota with a friend of mine.

My father had drowned when I was in elementary school, so my mother, brother, sister, and I had very little money through the years. When I told my mother in my senior year of high school that I wanted to go to college, she was stunned.

Now here I was, on my way to Northwestern College in Minneapolis, Minnesota, thousands of miles away.

Though I left home with a great show of confidence, underneath lay deep fear. Did I have enough resources to last even one year? I had a scholarship for tuition and $600 from working that summer. My mother's gift of $100 was tucked away in my wallet, too. Beyond that, I was in God's hand, and I sensed His promise.

I was going to a Christian college. Evangelist Billy Graham had been president of Northwestern College just a few years before I arrived. His spiritual fervor was still stamped on the institution. So, things began in a great way.

Over the weeks and months, however, my situation started to unravel. My finances dwindled. I could afford only two small meals a day on my dining-hall card. I could find no part-time job to keep me ahead, and, with a Minnesota winter revving up, I had no winter coat.

Slowly, above this scenario, God began to work His quiet but sure way. By the end of that school year, I could look back and see God's remarkable work. Someone from the church I attended in Minnesota gave me a winter coat. Several times when my money ran out, I went to my mailbox and found that some anonymous person had placed an envelope in my box with seven or ten or twelve dollars in the envelope. I lost weight, but I had gone to college on the heavy side. I went home after that first year, a slim, trim man. And, I met a young woman at college who later became my wife. From all this, I knew experientially that God was a keeper of promises.

In the Old Testament, Elijah often ran into trouble. One time, God told him to flee an area and go into hiding. God also made a promise to provide for his needs: "And it will be that you shall drink from the brook, and I have commanded the ravens to feed you there."

It is one thing to make a promise, and another thing to keep that promise. The writer of 1 Kings adds this commentary about God's faithfulness to Elijah: "The ravens brought him bread and meat in the morning, and bread and meat in the evening; and he drank from the brook."

Elijah discovered the One who is both Bread and Brook. And so did I.

"And it will be that you shall drink from the brook, and I have commanded the ravens to feed you there." . . . The ravens brought him bread and meat in the morning, and bread and meat in the evening; and he drank from the brook. 1 Kings 17:4, 6 NKJV

. . . .

THIRSTY FOR SATISFACTION

Peter W. Teague
President
Lancaster Bible College
Lancaster, Pennsylvania

OF ALL THE SKILLS I gleaned from my college experience, getting along with my roommates was by far the most important. I was required to submit a "roommate form" before I left home for my future alma mater. That comprehensive document appeared to suggest that the college was going to exhaust every effort in trying to match me with someone, well, just like me.

The dormitories, for that is what we called them in those ancient days of higher education, stood three stories high with outside stairways. Four young men were to share a small study area, separated from a sleep area by a two-foot-wide space generously referred to as a closet. In a space no larger than the living room of a modest home, four eighteen-year-old males were expected to live in peace and harmony . . . without committing murder.

By the time I checked into my room, Mike had already staked his claim for the bottom bunk bed closest to the window. "Wait until you meet Ed," was his greeting as we passed each other for the first time in our doorway. Mike had already spread his bags over two-thirds of our room's floor space.

Ed, from the east coast, rumbled in with a stereo system and stacks of Beatles records. Dick hailed from the Midwest, and rolled in last to discover what was left of our room. Because Dick and I were approximately the same height and weight, we reasoned that we should share a bunk bed. As we settled into our new lifestyle, I found myself asking, "Why did they have us fill out that form? These people are not like me."

We were all sizes and shapes, from various places across the country, and with different socioeconomic backgrounds. After I got past the initial, "What were they thinking?" I quietly told myself, "If I can survive this, I can survive anything."

Remarkably, we didn't kill each other that first year. What I did learn, as a scared boy one thousand miles away from home, was that people are not merely machines that behave, or computers that process, or organisms that feel. Rather, we are human beings who long deeply for satisfaction. The four of us, despite our visible differences and idiosyncrasies, were thirsty for the water of a loving relationship and meaningful impact.

In reality, every human being longs for this water, which only God can supply. Everything else is like a high-calorie, nutritionally void soft drink. It tastes good going down, but ultimately doesn't quench the thirst. It is God alone who gives us a satisfaction to respond in gratitude to Him and to demonstrate real concern for others. That is the lesson I started to learn my freshman year with Mike, Dick, and Ed. I wouldn't trade that year in the dormitory and all the experiences that came with it.

Jesus answered, "Everyone who drinks this water will be thirsty again, but whoever drinks the water I give him will never thirst. Indeed, the water I give him will become in him a spring of water welling up to eternal life." John 4:13, 14 NIV

THE PROFESSOR AND THE PROPERTARIAN

J. David Gillespie
Vice President for Academic Affairs
Presbyterian College
Clinton, South Carolina

TAKEN OUT OF CONTEXT, the words my professor uttered that day may not seem profound. But they changed my life. "Mr. Gillespie," Professor Richard Hoffman said, "sometimes human rights are more important than property rights."

It was 1964, and Hoffman's political science class at a Baptist college in North Carolina was discussing the Civil Rights Act of 1964—an act which, among other things, denied providers of public accommodations the right to discriminate on the basis of race.

Born in the South, I grew up in a black-majority county, yet never before college did I sit in a classroom with a person of color. My parents were not racists. Once when I was six, my father and I entered a streetcar in New Orleans, and I immediately noticed that all African-American patrons were sitting in the rear. That was the day I learned about Jim Crow. I asked my father whether blacks were Americans. He replied that they had a kind of second-class citizenship. I inquired if that was how things should be. "No," he replied. "It is terrible; it is just how things are." But my father died when I was eight, and I grew up accepting many of the racial prejudices of Southern whites during the civil-rights movement.

I did not consider myself a racist that day in class. I was a constitutionalist, a propertarian with ideas descended from Locke. I had read Ayn Rand.

Hoffman's words came in reply to my expression of outrage that now a restaurant or hotel owner had no choice but to serve anyone who could pay. He cited evidence that in many parts of the South black families simply did not travel because until this act there were no decent accommodations available to them.

I went back to my room. I thought of an older brother who had joined the movement for civil rights. I thought of Dick Hoffman's remark to me in class. He had spoken to me so calmly and kindly. There in my room, I prayed. I knew I would never be the same person after that day.

Like Hoffman, I went on to become a political scientist, a professor, and eventually a chief academic officer. Some of the students I have taught over the last 28 years have been gracious in what they have told me about the power of a professor to transform lives. Hoffman died in the mid-1990s. I regret very much that I never let him know how important his homily in class that day was for me. It transformed my values. It contributed markedly to whatever success I may have had as a teacher. It made me a better Christian.

Let justice run down like water, and righteousness like a mighty stream. Amos 5:24 NKJV

CALLED TO BE A SERVANT

Becky Huechteman
Professor of Education
Evangel University
Springfield, Missouri

AS A CHILD, I enjoyed playing school, especially if I could be the teacher. My pedagogical skills were sharpened on my dolls, my stuffed animals, and even some of my school friends who needed a helping hand with homework. It seems that even though I traversed through a period of planning to be a nurse, I returned to my first love . . . teaching.

My father was a pastor of an Assemblies of God church in a Midwest town. My mother was very active as a pastor's wife and stay-at-home mom. The mindset of most constituents at that time was that Christians who were "called" by God were serving as pastors or missionaries in a foreign country. A female could be called to the role of wife to a pastor or missionary. However, I did not feel "called" and sometimes suffered a bit of guilt for my true feelings regarding this subject. Because of my desire to help others and to serve God with my whole heart, I became a leader of our youth group and a children's Sunday-school teacher. While teaching children, I was learning about God and what it meant to be a Christian leader. I somehow knew that as God directed my paths, teaching would be a vital element of my journey. My parents encouraged me to enroll at Evangel College, a fairly new college sponsored by our denomination, to pursue a career in teaching.

While a student at Evangel, I was required to take several Bible courses, including one dealing with Christian leadership. During one class discussion about God's purposes for our lives, I sensed an overwhelming freedom from all of the misgivings and questions that I had about God's call in my life. Throughout the following months, I was able to internalize the concept that we are all called to a career of service to God. Geography and titles are not important. I was going to be a servant of God reaching out to the children of America . . . those who struggled to learn, those who suffered abuse, and those who possessed untapped gifts of creativity and intelligence. I was even called to teach the seemingly unteachable and to love the unloved.

God's master plan for my life included finding my husband, also a teacher, while attending Evangel. After several years of teaching elementary-school children and a few more years at home with my two sons, I returned to Evangel to serve as a professor of education. As a teacher educator, I have been given a new challenge: to prepare my students to become the teachers of tomorrow. I have no doubt that God has led these vibrant young people to me, just as He directed me to them.

In all your ways acknowledge Him, and He shall direct your paths. Proverbs 3:6 NKJV

· ·

GOD IN THE NORMAL AND ORDINARY

Jacob A. O. Preus
President
Concordia University
Irvine, California

I THOUGHT LITTLE about it at the time. It all seemed so normal, so matter-of-fact. It's only now, nearly thirty years later, that I've gained the perspective necessary to understand what was happening.

During my first year of graduate school God gave me what I have come to see as the second greatest gift in the world. The greatest gift, of course, is the Gift of God's own Son, Jesus Christ. But, after that, the greatest gift God gave to me was Sherry.

We were high-school sweethearts. I was sixteen, she just fifteen years old, when we began to date. We went together for more than five years. I don't think I had a profound understanding of the importance of the love that was maturing between us back then and how much it would come to mean to me. I just sort of fell into what I thought of as a natural pattern.

After I graduated from college, I went to graduate school at the University of Missouri—Columbia in Latin American studies. I remember talking to Sherry over the telephone and saying, "Why don't we just get married during semester break?" We had talked about marriage for several years. And so we got married. There was no romantic "popping of the question." We had a very short engagement. I don't think I really understood what I was getting myself into and what married life involved. It just all seemed so normal.

And over the years, God has led me to see what a great thing He did for me and with me through what appeared to be such a matter-of-fact event. He completed me. He shaved off my rough edges (most of them—that's an ongoing project!). He set me in a family and gave me a life in which I have never known loneliness. He provided me with a soul mate who has given me joy beyond my wildest dreams. He provided us with three wonderful children who have helped expand our joy beyond ourselves. As I look back from this vantage point today, I am amazed at how unaware I was of the miracle God was working back then.

And that's the point. It is through the mundane and the apparently natural and unremarkable events of our daily lives that sometimes God works the greatest miracles. Through a relationship that evolved by a more-or-less natural process as we grew up and worked and studied our way through college, God gave me the second greatest gift in the world. God works His good not only through the dramatic and extraordinary, but also through the normal and the ordinary. Thank God!

God sets the lonely in families. Psalm 68:6 NIV

· ·

A TASKMASTER CALLS FOR THE BEST

M. Dwaine Greene
Provost and Vice President
for Academic Affairs
Campbell University
Buies Creek, North Carolina

I ENTERED COLLEGE in the fall of 1975 as an athlete primarily intent upon success on the baseball diamond. I had little interest in matters academic. Even so, the defining memory of my first months in college was not from the diamond, but of an elderly professor who could barely pick up his feet as he shuffled down the hall, held upright by a back brace. He would prove to be the single most demanding undergraduate professor I would encounter.

As an 18-year-old freshman, I found myself in the grasp of this Greek grammar professor by the name of Dr. Cronje Earp. Approaching the end of his career, he was an unrelenting taskmaster about whom my emotions only slowly matured from fear and disbelief into admiration and love.

Major test days in his course were extraordinarily intense. Typically, students would arrive early to cram last-minute details. As Dr. Earp entered the room, he would view a class full of studying, sweating, and praying students. Characteristically, Dr. Earp would burst forth with his famous dictum, "Don't expect God to do for you what He gives you the ability to do for yourself."

Later I learned that such advice is well rooted in Judeo-Christian tradition. But at that point in my life, as a freshman trying to adjust to college-level expectations, it seemed the harshest dose of medicine I could receive. Yet I soon learned that Dr. Earp was without question a fine Christian man. And he was one who lived by the principles that God does not bless poor effort, and that to give less than our best is an insult to God as well as ourselves.

Those principles were to prove invaluable to me not only for further years as an undergraduate, but also for subsequent graduate and professional endeavors. In his life and words Dr. Earp had been demonstrating the indissoluble Christian paradigm of believing and doing, of faith and works.

For as the body without the spirit is dead, so faith without works is dead also. James 2:26 NKJV

. . . .

THE GOD OF CHEMISTRY

E. Donald Lorance
Professor of Chemistry
Vanguard University
of Southern California
Costa Mesa, California

HAVING GROWN UP in the home of a conserva-tive evangelical minister, I was taught essentially from birth about the deity of God and about His Son, Jesus Christ. I was taught about His great love for us and accepted Christ as my Savior while still a child. Through high school I was active in my church and never seriously questioned my beliefs.

Matriculation at a large state university brought questions that I was ill-prepared to answer. Secular humanism was bad enough, but also I was becoming a scientist. There seemed to be little room in the modern scientif-ic community for my old-fashioned Christian beliefs. Many of my professors viewed Christianity as just another myth. There seemed to be no room in the study of chemistry for God.

I struggled to find relevance between what I studied during the week and what I heard in church on Sunday. As a result, I began to compartmen-talize my beliefs. I believed in all that I was learning about chemistry, and I also believed in God and that He loved me enough to send His Son to die for my sins.

This approach seemed workable, so I entered graduate school still attending church on Sunday and being a secular scientist during the week. The jump to graduate studies was difficult and the workload heavy. But one event allowed me to discover by direct observation that there was no real dichotomy in my life and that my belief in God was relevant to everything I did in chemistry.

I was scheduled for a very important midterm examination in my major field. This exam had only four questions. I was as prepared for the exam as it was possible for me to be, and I approached it with confidence. When I read the questions, I realized that I had indeed prepared well for the exam. I answered the first question without difficulty and went to question two. It covered an area which I had studied carefully and extensively, but as I read it, no answer came. I went completely blank.

I knew that my grade would be poor if I could not answer the question. I put down my pen and closed my eyes. On Sundays I was taught that God loved me and was concerned about all aspects of my life. Maybe that even included chemistry. I silently reminded God that I really had studied, and if He got involved in mundane things like chemistry exams, I could really use some help. I picked up my pen, reread the question, and proceeded to score 24 of the 25 possible points. I also did well on the rest of the exam.

I discovered that God knew a lot more about chemistry than I was ever likely to learn. God's love was not limited to my soul and my eternal future. He even loved me during the week in my chemistry classes.

For I know whom I have believed and I am convinced that He is able to guard what I have entrusted to Him until that day. 2 Timothy 1:12 NASB

THE SOUL
OF FELLOWSHIP

Darrell L. Bock
Research Professor
of New Testament Studies
Dallas Theological Seminary
Dallas, Texas

PERHAPS THE BEST COUNSEL I got about college faith came when I was advised to join a student fellowship group. The moment I hit campus I joined one. I eventually joined a second such group as I tried to find my way in a secular school with more than 40,000 students.

The Young Life group on my campus led me to minister in a local high school for two years. This experience allowed my college friends and me to see God work in the lives of other people. It encouraged us to serve others, making our faith come alive in actual practice. Some of my best friends in college came from this group. Ministering together stretched our faith.

In my sophomore year I also helped host a Bible study for college kids in our apartment. The group began with six attending. By our senior year we had more than 60 students attending each week. We spent about 90 minutes singing, praying, studying the Bible, and encouraging each other. Our goal was to challenge ourselves with some serious study and reflection on God's Word. Students brought their friends, and we had the privilege of seeing some come to the Lord as a result.

I also committed to attending a discussion-oriented Bible study while I was in college that had nothing to do with any campus group. It was led by more mature and experienced Christians. In this older group I could ask honest, important questions of those who had more experience in life than I. College life inevitably raised many questions in my mind and forced many new choices. This group became a good sounding board to discuss those important life issues. I had a trust relationship with people at least ten years my senior. Thus, I could avoid the common mistake of simply pooling my own ignorance with that of my student friends regarding college life and college faith.

In this group, we often spent as much time after the study talking as during the study time itself. This was rich and valuable fellowship and discipleship that proved helpful in making my Christianity connect with the real world of life.

This experience with older believers also drove me to be involved in a local church and participate in a Sunday-school class where I could get to know others of different ages. This church did not organize classes by age, so I was able to develop friendships focused on mutual growth. This is the heart and soul of real fellowship. It keeps faith alive and vibrant by causing us to look to the Lord together.

Let us hold fast the confession of our hope without wavering, for He who promised is faithful; and let us consider how to stimulate one another to love and good deeds, not forsaking our own assembling together, as is the habit of some, but encouraging one another; and all the more as you see the day drawing near. Hebrews 10:23-25 NASB

INDEX OF AUTHORS

INDEX OF INSTITUTIONS

INDEX OF INSTITUTIONS

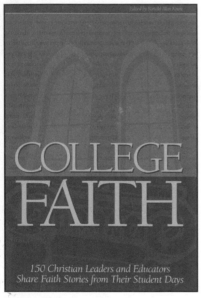